Reliable Fundraising in Unreliable Times

This material augments the information in this book, taking you more deeply into fundamental fundraising concepts or providing you with more details on specific fundraising strategies.

The Chardon Press Series

Fundamental social change happens when people come together to organize, advocate, and create solutions to injustice. Chardon Press recognizes that communities working for social justice need tools to create and sustain healthy organizations. In an effort to support these organizations, Chardon Press produces materials on fundraising, community organizing, and organizational development. These resources are specifically designed to meet the needs of grassroots nonprofits—organizations that face the unique challenge of promoting change with limited staff, funding, and other resources. We at Chardon Press have adopted traditional techniques to the circumstances of grassroots nonprofits. Chardon Press and Jossey-Bass hope these works help people committed to social justice to build mission-driven organizations that are strong, financially secure, and effective.

Kim Klein, Series Editor

Additional Titles from Chardon Press

Working Across Generations: Defining the Future of Nonprofit Leadership, Frances Kunreuther, Helen Kim, Robby Rodriguez

Change Philanthropy: Candid Stories of Foundations Maximizing Results Through Social Justice, Alicia Epstein Korten

Fundraising for Social Change, Fifth Edition, Kim Klein

The Accidental Fundraiser: A Step-by-Step Guide to Raising Money for Your Cause, Stephanie Roth, Mimi Ho

Tools for Radical Democracy: How to Organize for Power in Your Community, Joan Minieri, Paul Gatsos

Inspired Philanthropy: Your Step-by-Step Guide to Creating a Giving Plan, 3rd *Edition*, Tracy Gary and Nancy Adess

Grassroots Grants: An Activist's Guide to Grantseeking, 2nd *Edition*, Andy Robinson

Stir It Up: Lessons in Community Organizing and Advocacy, Rinku Sen

The Nonprofit Membership Toolkit, Ellis M.M. Robinson

Level Best: How Small and Grassroots Nonprofits Can Tackle Evaluation and Talk Results, Marcia Festen, Marianne Philbin

Fundraising in Times of Crisis, Kim Klein

Selling Social Change (Without Selling Out): Earned Income Strategies for Nonprofits, Andy Robinson

Raise More Money: The Best of the Grassroots Fundraising Journal, Kim Klein, Stephanie Roth, Editors

Reliable Fundraising in Unreliable Times

What Good Causes Need to Know to Survive and Thrive

Kim Klein

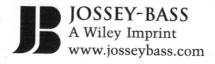

JOSSEY-BASS
A Wiley Imprint
www.josseybass.com

Published by Jossey-Bass
A Wiley Imprint
989 Market Street, San Francisco, CA 94103-1741—www.josseybass.com

Readers should be aware that Internet Web sites offered as citations and/or sources for further information may have changed or disappeared between the time this was written and when it is read.

Jossey-Bass books and products are available through most bookstores. To contact Jossey-Bass directly call our Customer Care Department within the U.S. at 800-956-7739, outside the U.S. at 317-572-3986, or fax 317-572-4002.

Jossey-Bass also publishes its books in a variety of electronic formats. Some content that appears in print may not be available in electronic books.

Library of Congress Cataloging-in-Publication Data

Klein, Kim.
    Reliable fundraising in unreliable times : what good causes need to know to survive and thrive / Kim Klein.
        p. cm.
    Includes bibliographical references and index.
    ISBN 978-0-470-47950-6 (cloth/website)
        1. Fund raising. 2. Nonprofit organizations. I. Title.
    HV41.2.K54 2009
    658.15'224—dc22
                                                                    2009021527

Printed in the United States of America

FIRST EDITION
HB Printing 10 9 8 7 6 5 4 3 2 1

Contents

For my mother and father, who taught me generosity, honesty, and the importance of always considering the common good.

Preface

In 1999, I wrote a book called *Fundraising for the Long Haul.* It was a companion to my book, *Fundraising for Social Change,* and in it I looked at the particular challenges faced by an established organization working for social change. The book discussed what happens to your fundraising when you have been around for a few years and the excitement of being new has worn off but the work is more needed than ever. What do you do when you have a founder who built the organization who now is past her or his own ability to run it but won't leave? Or when you have strayed from your mission in order to attract funding? Or when you have neglected your individual donors and now you need them? I also looked at how to plan for the future and the role of endowments and reserve funds.

Soon after the book came out, much of its relevance was pre-empted by the economic crash that started in 2000, the attacks of September 11, 2001, and the subsequent wars in Iraq and Afghanistan and the war on dissent at home. Many nonprofits working for social change were dying on the economic vine. Government-funded programs, already heavily slashed, were losing even further funding, nonprofits were being asked to do more and more with less and less, and the USA PATRIOT Act and other protective or reactionary legislation was testing our willingness to speak out against government policies that were not only hurting immigrants, poor people, and many others of our constituents, but also hurting the ability of nonprofits to do our work.

Further, the sector was rocked with scandals, from embezzlements to self-dealing, so that just when we needed public confidence in nonprofit groups the most, we had it the least. In response to that situation, in 2004 I wrote *Fundraising in Times of Crisis,* which was selected as a runner-up for the prestigious Terry McAdam Book

Award for outstanding contributions to the advancement of non-profit management in 2005. As the economy recovered, nonprofits came out of their crises but did not recover from their problems, which continue to dog us to this day.

As I reflected on both those books, I realized they needed to be combined, with two other elements added: how to create and maintain a strong but flexible fundraising program that can ride the waves of whatever is happening, and how fundraising needs to be part of the broader solutions to the endemic problems of our sector.

The organizations for which this book is written have budgets in the $250,000 to $2,500,000 range. They are probably not just starting out; rather, they have at least two or three years of experience. They have two or more staff (who can be volunteers), need a bookkeeper to keep their accounts straight, and struggle with whether and how to offer pension plans or child-care to longtime staff. They have some regular individual donors, although not enough of them, and many of them have some foundations that like and fund their work. They are respected by other organizations, and they work in coalitions on some issues. Although they work on a variety of issues and use a variety of methods to achieve their goals, they are committed to social change: to identifying the root causes of social problems and working to solve them.

These organizations are very important, yet fragile, and they are under more—and sometimes different—threats today than similar organizations were a decade ago when I wrote *Fundraising for the Long Haul* and even more recently when I wrote *Fundraising in Times of Crisis*. Although much of the advice in those books is still useful, a great deal has changed. The technology that informs a lot of fundraising today was nascent at that time, and the generational shifts among those working in nonprofits, so prominent now, were still barely visible on the horizon. *Fundraising in Times of Crisis* worked from the premise that the wars would be short-lived and the financial crisis would end. We still hope that both wars will end, but we know we will be paying the cost of war for at least a generation, and we now know that the economy will probably always follow more of a roller-coaster path of highs and lows, for which we need to plan.

What You Will Find

The purpose of this book is twofold. First, it details what is true about fundraising *all* the time—no matter the political or economic landscape—and provides the steps an organization needs to take to create a disciplined, systematic fundraising program that is both flexible and durable and that will survive most of what comes its way. Things that are always true are more important during hard times. For example, if you are personally in need of money or ill in the middle of the night, knowing which friends would give you a loan or drive you to the hospital on a moment's notice is crucial. Similarly, for nonprofits, planning for when times might be rougher than they are now—especially if you can foresee your funding sources shrinking—is a wise step to take.

Second, this book addresses today's economic reality. Although the general economy is not in good shape, the United States is not actually in a financial *crisis* at this time. A crisis begins and ends. A hurricane, for example, creates a crisis: it does terrible damage, but it passes through, and people clean up and rebuild. A fire ravages, but it is put out, damage is assessed, and people go on as best they can. A crisis leaves scars, to be sure, and some people—and some organizations—don't survive. A crisis is a big deal. But the economic turmoil we are in now has no end in sight. We cannot hunker down and wait for it to pass over. Although the country as a whole has to take huge steps to deal with the financial situation that now exists, it will be many years before the pendulum swings the other way again. In the nonprofit world, we have to build fundraising programs that thrive on this kind of roller coaster and that take advantage of the opportunities inherent in big change. This book addresses that roller coaster and tells you how to see and make the most of those opportunities.

But because some organizations really are in crisis, this book will also give you a blueprint of what to do if yours is in deep trouble because of the economy, scandal, mismanagement, or (fill in the blank). Parts One and Two are devoted to helping organizations stay strong. Part Three is devoted to helping good organizations that are going through a hard time—in fact, facing a crisis—to get through it so they can then use the information in Parts One and Two.

Part Four looks at challenges that bedevil nonprofits no matter what is going on in the external landscape—how boards can fulfill their fundraising responsibilities without feeling overly burdened, how organizations can adapt to changes in generational leadership, how to practice good time management habits, how the context for fundraising will continue to change, and the opportunities that are presented by turmoil.

The economy is going to go up and down and down and up and up and up and down. You need to give up hope that things are going to get better and instead think, "This is as good as it gets. This is it—a great time to raise money." There is no better time than now for the work of your organization and no more opportune moment for big ideas and bold initiatives, as well as straight-up community service.

Although the book will be helpful to many types of organizations—new and not-so-new, struggling or foreseeing future difficulties—it is aimed at the audience I have always primarily worked with and spoken to: organizations that place social justice at the forefront of all they do.

About the Stories in This Book

Dozens of different groups are mentioned in this book. People who know me or my work well may be able to recognize some of them. I do not identify any of them by name because many of the groups are described in terms of a problem they were having, and I didn't want to violate confidentiality or embarrass them. On the other hand, all organizations have problems; problems are nothing to be ashamed of, they are simply information about what needs to be done next. Therefore I have also not identified groups that I use here as positive examples, because next month they will have some problems, too.

In many instances I have changed a number of details about a group so that it cannot be identified. In a few cases, I have created a composite of two or three groups that had the same issues.

I am grateful to all the groups discussed here as well as to the hundreds not discussed for sharing with me their struggles in raising money to create social change. I rely mostly on memory and my personal journals of the time, using both to be as accurate as possible. However, being human, I have undoubtedly made some mistakes; any errors or omissions are mine as well.

Reliable Fundraising in Unreliable Times

Part One

Get Ready: Reality Will Change

I have been in fundraising in one capacity or another for almost thirty-five years. In that time I have seen tremendous variations in the U.S. economy: I have seen interest rates top 18 percent (1979–80) and watched the stock market lose 30 percent of its value in one day (October 1987) and change directions seventy-five times in one day (October 2008). I have watched housing prices rise, crash, rise again, crash again. I have been in some parts of the country where unemployment was 1/10 of 1 percent and a few months later might be 10 percent, and I've been in other places where unemployment was so chronic that the number of unemployed people in the statistics went down only because their unemployment benefits ran out and they stopped registering that they were looking for work. The "dot-com bubble" of the '90s is the "dot gone" of this new century; start-ups soared, then ended up bankrupt. But what strikes me now, having lived through all that, is how we tend to think that whatever economic climate we are in right now is here to stay. When the market crashed in 1987, some pundits said it would never recover. President Reagan, in one of the few statements he ever made that I agreed with, said it was a "correction" and the market would recover very quickly. He was right. But he didn't stay right: by 1990 the economy had shifted again. Nothing in the economy is permanent, and we who are in fundraising must constantly adapt to whatever constitutes the current economic reality. That reality, reviewed over a few decades, does show a certain pattern, and that pattern is cyclical, but over time the cycles have gotten shorter, with much higher highs at the high points and lower lows at the low points. Moreover, the increasingly global nature of economic interactions—from financial institutions to commodity goods—lends speed and even more unpredictability to these cycles.

Good fundraising programs must adapt to these ever-shifting realities, starting with understanding that donor and funder reactions to what is happening in the economy are not always going to be most helpful to nonprofits. Take foundations, for example. Foundations are required by law to spend 5 percent of their assets every year (that 5 percent may include their own operating costs for such things as staff, research, trustee compensation, and publications as well as funds granted). The law sees this as the minimum payout, but most foundations equate it with the maximum payout. Most foundations use a three-year average to determine their grantmaking, thus evening out the ups and downs of the market. Their grantmaking grows and shrinks as their assets grow or shrink. But in good times, when assets may grow even 10 percent in a year, foundations could afford to increase their payout to 6 percent or even 7 percent, giving away much more money. Yet it is the rare foundation that would decide to use a time of growth to pay out more than 5 percent of their assets—because, they explain, they need to have the money available in hard times. But in hard times, they cut their spending and keep to the same 5 percent. A more logical approach would be for foundations either to pay out more than 5 percent in high-earning years, which would give them the capacity to truly address pressing social problems, or to pay out more than 5 percent in low-earning years, to keep their actual grantmaking dollars the same. Unfortunately, most foundations do not use either of these approaches. So just when organizations are suffering from a downturn and need foundations the most, foundation funds are least available.

Corporations provide another example. From years of marketing research they know that customers prefer to buy from corporations that give money to nonprofits over those that don't, and that, in fact, in choosing between two brands of a similar item, a customer will choose the one with a charitable reputation over the other one. Some, although not all, studies show that this is a higher motivation than price difference or perceived quality (unless price and quality are at a large variance). So you might think that in good times, when corporate profits are higher, corporate giving would go up to attract customers who are spending. But it doesn't. Corporate giving shows little variation from year to year, remaining at about 5 percent of all private sector giving.

As I will discuss throughout this part of the book, foundations and corporations account for very little of overall private sector giving. In fact, in all the years that the fundraising profession has studied the various income streams for nonprofits, we have observed that in the private sector—made up of foundations, corporations, and individuals—in general, individuals give about 85 percent of all the money donated (75 percent from living individuals and 10 percent through bequests), foundations about 10 percent, and corporations about 5 percent.

So the other reality that most healthy organizations adapt to is that their private sector funding needs to come mostly from individuals, and it is most effectively raised using grassroots fundraising strategies. Individual giving does not vary nearly as much as foundation and corporate giving, but individuals are affected by world events and by economic realities, and we have to take those into account as we raise money from them. Wealthy individuals, whose gifts may have come from highly appreciated assets such as stocks, tend to cut back when the market falls. Retired people, or people living on the income from investments, also cut back when that income falls. People who become unemployed obviously also cut back on their giving. In all these cases, though, it is rare for anyone who is a giver to stop giving altogether, which shows the power of giving. In fact, in some recessions giving will go up as people see the need to work for the common good.

People who are employed, remain employed, and have very little reason to think they will become unemployed, also change their giving habits during economic downturns. Some cut back, fearing unemployment; some give more for a wide variety of reasons; and most are more thoughtful about their giving. Some donors start giving directly to friends or family who have lost jobs or who have huge medical bills and no insurance, and they cut back on giving to organizations they have supported. Sometimes they give more to fewer charities during economic hard times, and they ask more questions about the effectiveness of organizations they do support.

I believe this global economic meltdown will not end any time soon, and that it provides an opportunity; in fact, it requires nonprofits concerned with social justice to step back and really look at our whole sector, our whole way of fundraising and running our organizations. Every economic and political assumption is up for grabs right now. With Obama's presidency, we see that our country can make profound changes, and we need to continue the momentum and the desire for change that can be seen all over the world to actually think through what those changes should be and to make them. Fundraising must change along with everything else.

This part of the book looks at the endemic problems that nonprofit social change groups have in doing fundraising, no matter what the economic climate. Much that is being blamed on the economy has actually been true and problematic in all the different economic times we have lived through for the past three years. These include difficulties asking for money, a clear understanding of the role of taxes in funding nonprofits, and ways in which nonprofits undermine themselves by trying to do more and more with less and less. The part concludes by looking at what must change in order for nonprofits to be able to raise the money they need to do their work.

Chapter One

How Nonprofits Think (or Don't) About Money

To fully understand the funding tribulations that community-based organizations are facing in the first decades of the twenty-first century requires that we examine two endemic flaws, related to the sources of funding, that ripple through the nonprofit sector.

The first flaw is that although nonprofits know they need money to operate, they don't want to face the realities of how that money needs to be raised, so they wind up looking for money in the wrong places.

The second flaw is the lack of understanding and comprehension in the sector, as well as in the public at large, about the role of taxes in providing funding to nonprofits. As a result, the sector fails to demand that the government provide appropriate funding for services that should be the government's responsibility.

First Major Flaw: Nonprofits and Wishful Thinking

Most nonprofits tend to engage in a form of wishful thinking about how they can raise the funds to do their work. Having heard of large gifts made by foundations, corporations, and some wealthy people to some groups, they chase after these sources of funding, usually in vain. To understand why it is largely futile to seek such funding, we need to see these sources in the context of all the funding that goes to the nonprofit sector.

There are three sources of money for all nonprofits: the government (public sector); foundations, corporations, and individuals (collectively known as the private sector); and earned income, such as from fees and products. Of these, government funding from its various branches (federal, state, and local) makes up about one-third of all the funding to nonprofits; private sector funding accounts for about one-fifth; and the rest—about half— comes from earned income. For most small secular nonprofits, however, as well as for almost all religious organizations, most of their money comes from the private sector, even though many of these organizations also have a revenue stream from rental of space, sale of products, or fees, which can range from contributing a tiny portion of their budget to providing a significant percentage of income.

Private Sector Giving

People new to nonprofits often think that foundations and corporations give away most money. This mistaken impression comes from the fact that, when they do give, foundations and cor- porations often give sums in the thousands of dollars, and they often publicize their giving widely. In fact, however, as noted in the preface, the majority of the money given from the private sec- tor comes from individuals (both living and through bequests). Only about 10 percent of all giving to nonprofits comes from foundations and only about 5 percent is from corporations. (The exact percentages vary 2 or 3 percentage points from year to year. For exact numbers in any given year, see the report called *Giving USA*, issued by the Center on Philanthropy at the University of Indiana.)

Further, of the money given by individuals, the majority of gifts come from households with incomes of less than $90,000— which happens to be 80 percent of U.S. households. Certainly, some households among the other 20 percent of the population, and particularly among the 6 percent of the population that earns 33 percent of all income earned in the United States, are very gen- erous. But the most generous people are still those in the income ranges that contain the most people: middle-class, working-class, and poor. This compilation of statistics points to one important conclusion: the majority of nonprofit organizations can start a successful and profitable individual donor program to raise most of the funds they need to do their work without wealthy donors. As the program builds, the organization will attract more and more donors, some of whom will be able to make very large gifts.

The myth that most money comes from foundations and corporations keeps many organizations from doing the work they need to do to get their funding from the most likely source: people in their communities. They may believe their constituents are too poor to give, or that foundation funding is easier to raise than "a lot of little gifts," which is how they interpret an individual donor base. Many believe that individuals give primarily to their religious institution and will not support secular causes. In fact, although about one-third of all money given away does go to religious organizations, that's because about one-third of nonprofits are churches, synagogues, mosques, or temples. In other words, faith-based organizations raise only their market share. Further, and perhaps as important, people who give to religious groups are more likely to give to secular organizations than are people who have no religious affiliation.

Because organizations believe that most charitable dollars come from foundations, corporations, or wealthy people, or even from government, those that are big enough will tend to hire "development" staff who are charged with bringing in the money. Rather than understanding and supporting the fact that the job of a development director is to coordinate the fundraising efforts of the entire organization, groups will split their development staff off from the rest of the group, often even excluding them from program staff meetings, even though people who discuss the group's program with donors and funders need to be as articulate as anyone else about it. Even development people who are included in meetings or planning sessions are often brought in to provide information rather than to offer their opinions.

In some organizations, development directors are paid on a different scale than other staff, leading to misunderstanding and resentment. For example, in many organizations the development director is paid the same amount as the executive director—or more—even though the development director and program director are equal on the management chart. Sometimes development directors are given a bonus at the end of the year when no other staff is rewarded this way. Sometimes they are paid on commission—a practice highly frowned on in the field, for a number of reasons. (See premium content for the article, "Why Good Fundraisers Are Never Paid on Commission.")

Though having development staff is a good idea (one I recommend), their job is made difficult by being measured only by how much money they bring in, even though they may have little control over all the other variables that affect fundraising— such as the timeliness and appeal of program activities—and in spite of the fact that there are many other equally important measurements of development success, including the number of donors acquired, quality of materials, thoroughness of research, and adequacy of records. Especially if they are to write proposals to get grant funding, development directors may be spending a lot of time and organizational resources trying to raise money from a source where either the money is limited or its availability is of limited duration. On the other hand, if they are charged with building a base of individual donors with no or little help from board or staff, their efforts will be equally frustrating. A lone development person does not have enough hours in the day to do all that must be done to maintain and expand a donor base.

Reluctance to Talk about Money

The second part of the wishful thinking flaw is that the fact that ordinary people give away money collides with many people's deep-seated reluctance to ask for money. I have rarely had someone disagree with the premise that, over the long term, raising money from a broad base of individual donors would provide an organization with the freedom to stay mission driven, the stability to make long-term plans, and the capacity to grow in good times and bad. But I rarely find an organization that truly acts on that knowledge, in large part because talking about money remains taboo in our culture. The consequence of that taboo is that some people find asking for money demeaning and others are afraid that if someone actually responds to their request by giving the organization money, then they will owe that donor a personal debt. Perhaps that person will ask them for a donation in turn, and they fear they can't afford to give to every cause their friends are involved in.

People bring a lot of mixed meanings to money. For example, if we say of someone, "He does very well" or "She earns buckets of money," we don't mean simply that this person has a good deal of money at their disposal; we also tend to mean that by dint of this person's success—however it was come by—he or she enjoys a higher social status than someone who doesn't have very much money. The many sayings about money sometimes contradict each other: "It is more blessed to give than to receive" contrasts with "A penny saved is a penny earned." The values of thrift, frugality, and prudence live alongside those of generosity, liberality, and open-handedness. One person may think of himself as careful while his colleagues may find him stingy. "Money doesn't buy happiness" is often followed by the rejoinder, "If you think that, you don't know where to shop." Or "The Golden Rule means that the person with the gold, rules" contrasts with "You can't take it with you."

All of these shorthand ways of thinking about money that, with all their contradictions and discomfort, have permeated our culture mean that many organizations find that their fundraising efforts are hampered by the reluctance of their volunteers and board members to ask for donations. Board members who are in every other way wholly committed to an organization have told me that they would rather rip their own fingernails off than ask for money.

Over the past thirty years, there has been a lot of effort in both the fundraising and finance worlds to begin to break down the taboos around talking about—and asking for—money, but it is very difficult to expunge them from the cultural psyche. To be sure, progress has been made. We can see this generationally: in a room full of board members or volunteers, the younger people will have a shorter list of inhibitions about money than the older people, regardless of race, class, or gender. But we have a long way to go, and the fundraising profession needs to help lead the way—not just in breaking down current taboos, but also in creating an attitude toward money that emphasizes using it for the common good, and in seeing money as a tool for creating the society we want.

The Politics of the Money Taboo

The taboos we feel around talking about and asking for money aren't just random cultural baggage. They serve a very important cultural agenda. Their main purpose is to maintain the dominance of a small group of people who have a great deal of power in a capitalist system. For example, if I can't ask for money, I will be shy about asking for a raise. If I can't ask someone at my workplace what they earn, or if it is "not done" to reveal my salary to my coworkers, I will not learn that I am paid more because I am white, or less because I am a woman. Children show us that our inability to ask for money is strictly learned behavior. Children have no trouble asking for money, nor do they take offense when the answer is no. Just as for other things they want, they believe in asking frequently—they think it is part of what they have to do to get what they want. As they get older, they learn that to fit in to this society, they must stop being so straightforward about money. However, those of us who question "fitting in" must also question this money taboo. In fact, if we won't deal with money, learn how it works, and be willing to ask for it, we who work for social change wind up collaborating with the very system our work is designed to change.

Seeing our inability to ask for money in a more political context helps us overcome our anxiety.

Reluctance to Ask Affects Our Dealings with People Who Give

Our reluctance to ask for money for our work not only hinders getting friends or colleagues to give but also inhibits us in how we deal with current donors. Our embarrassment about asking carries over into talking with or writing to people about their giving. This reluctance, coupled with segregating development directors from the larger program work (and, meaningfully, not integrating development into the program work), contributes to the disorganization many nonprofits experience in their fundraising. The sending of donor communications such as thank-you notes, newsletters, renewal letters, and annual reports are seen as functions separate from running the organization, so they go out late or not at all. Nothing is personalized, and a donor has no reason to think that the organization even notices his or her gift.

Let's take an example. A board member invites a friend to join an organization. The friend joins and receives a thank-you note from a staff person; in subsequent years the friend gets a form renewal letter. The board member does not want to embarrass his friend by sending a renewal letter and putting pressure on the friend to give again. However, from the friend's viewpoint, the board member does not seem to care one way or the other about whether he renews. In fact, the board member doesn't even seem to care that he gave in the first place, as the thank-you note wasn't from him!

Here's another example: an organization writes a compelling direct mail appeal and hundreds of people respond. However, all the subsequent appeals to these new donors say the same thing as the first appeal. They carry no acknowledgment of the first gift and no sense of building a relationship with the donors. Or an organization offers a quarterly newsletter as a benefit for giving, but the newsletter comes out only once a year. Or an organization has a sign-up box on their website where a donor can get the group's e-newsletter; dozens of people sign up, but the e-newsletter never materializes.

What has happened in all these examples? Most likely, the executive director or development staff is overwhelmed with work, while there is an underwhelming involvement of volunteers in fundraising, caused in large part by their deep anxiety about asking for money. As a result, the organization has a chronically high turnover in donors, with many giving once and not again, and with the organization soliciting them over and over and then having to replace them with new donors who will be treated and alienated the same way. Much money—and time—is lost in this scattershot approach to fundraising.

Second Major Flaw: Not Understanding the Role of Our Tax Dollars in Funding Nonprofits

The second flaw among nonprofits when it comes to sources of funding takes the form of a philosophical dispute, or impasse, in coming to an understanding about the role of taxes. Since the Reagan presidency, and particularly during economic downturns, federal, state, and local governments have cut funding, especially from public services, with little consequence.

The public simply does not demand that public schools, public libraries, public pools, public hospitals, or public parks be funded by the public through taxes.

Mirroring the public at large, people in nonprofits fall all along the spectrum in what they believe is appropriate for the government to fund—from those who believe that all social services, arts, and culture should be entirely tax supported; that our country should have universal health care, universal education, and a guaranteed annual income; to those who favor government funding for some of these elements but not all; to those who believe government should mostly stay out of private lives. Those at the "less government support" end of the spectrum tend to think that with lower taxes, people will give away more money and the lack of government funding will be mitigated by private donations.

Many people, whether they be for or against using taxes to fund social benefits, experience government as inefficient. Those who believe that taxes should pay for social services are also often critical of government waste and bureaucracy. Those who believe that the government should pay for as little as possible often support a strong military, which uses the lion's share of today's tax dollars, and those who believe in using taxes more widely may also resist paying for war. When issues of public policy—such as gun control, reproductive rights, charter schools, prisons, or environmental protection—are discussed, the lines will cross and recross a number of times.

Those in the nonprofit sector are as divided as people throughout the nation on these issues, and those in nonprofits whose work encompasses public policy and tax issues debate each other and provide the research and information for the debates carried on by politicians and commentators.

Most taxpayers often see the issue in very practical, if narrow terms—they would usually rather pay lower taxes. Although they will support federal tax cuts, they will also vote for bonds to improve the schools, or to pay for parks and wilderness areas, or for bike paths. These actions show that they understand the role of taxes in their local communities, even if they do not see the benefit of a large federal government. Because our tax structure is regressive—

a higher percentage of income is paid in taxes, including sales tax, by those in the middle class—it is hard to make the case that people should pay more taxes.

At the same time, it is clear that private funding cannot replace government funding for services that affect large swaths of the population. There just isn't enough private funding to ensure a decent level of education, health, and other services to the entire population. What is required, then, is nonpartisan education about the role of taxes, including a discussion of the way taxes are levied and the types of taxes we pay. For example, in states with no state income tax but high sales tax, efforts to institute an income tax usually fail, even though it can be shown that poor and working-class people will have more money by paying state income tax if concurrently the sales tax is lowered. In another example, Americans will generally favor lowering the capital gains tax even though many people will never be faced with paying capital gains tax and would be better off if capital gains were taxed at the same (higher) rate as income tax.

Estate tax (insidiously and incorrectly renamed the "death tax" by conservatives) is the most obvious of the problems in the tax debate. Estate tax is a redistributive tax that keeps us from becoming an aristocracy by trying to prevent a small group of extremely wealthy individuals from passing on large sums of money to their heirs. There can be no such thing as even a rough social equality when some people are born with no financial assets at all and some are born with millions of dollars. Health, education, self-confidence, and opportunity are related to the environment in which you grew up, and that is influenced by what parents inherited and are able to pass on in turn to their children.

Only 2 percent of estates are large enough to warrant paying estate tax, yet many Americans, who probably sincerely believe in equality, will vote to abolish the tax altogether—an indication of the skillful way conservatives have corralled public thinking on the issue. On the opposite side, some nonprofits whose mission is to educate people about the economy and taxes have often been effective in changing minds in this debate. For example, United for a Fair Economy enlisted a number of very wealthy people—such as Bill Gates, Sr., and Warren Buffett—to speak in favor of maintaining the estate tax. Hearing very wealthy people talk about the importance of the estate tax is both inspiring and convincing; in the long run, we can hope that such education will ensure that we keep the estate tax and, in fact, broaden it to include more estates.

The discussion about estate taxes is not simply academic. The revenue from taxes pays for some of the essential work done by nonprofits, and when there isn't enough tax-funded support, all nonprofits turn to the private sector for support, where there is not enough money. Further, nonprofits are bolstered by the tax benefits wealthy people receive from making donations from income, capital, or estate. For that reason, the tax debate should be of concern for fundraisers and for the nonprofit sector as a whole, yet historically, except for organizations specifically working on tax reform, the nonprofit sector has tended to stay out of the debate.

Unlike many Western democracies, we in the United States do not have a national consensus on the role of taxes. It is unlikely we ever will without a much more informed debate on this issue, and a lot more public education. If we don't want nonprofits to be at the mercy of each successive government administration in terms of the availability of government funding for any particular issue, we must begin this education now in all our organizations.

Educating Your Constituency

Your fundraising program cannot be separated from the macro issues I have discussed here; in fact, an exciting challenge is to integrate fundraising into all your other program work and also use your nonprofit (whatever you do) to help educate your constituency about all the larger issues I have raised here. Start with yourself, your staff, and your board. Work with other organizations to hold town halls and teach-ins. We are a country capable of enormous and swift change, and nonprofits are capable of providing leadership for this change. We simply need to recognize the need—and begin.

Chapter Two

The True Cost of Doing Business

The macro issues about the funding of nonprofit work outlined in Chapter One are compounded by a number of smaller but still significant issues that also affect the fundraising context for non-profits. Foremost among these issues is a question that relates to a number of the other issues; namely, how much money should nonprofits spend on the tasks of administration and fundraising? Unfortunately, the public expectation of what such a figure or percentage should be is unrealistically low, given the realities of the costs of doing business. The issues I am describing here have been true for decades. In this decade, however, they add to and exacerbate the more recent economic problems already plaguing the sector. Nonprofits must change their fundraising programs in some fundamental ways, described in this book, in order to be strong enough and flexible enough to survive the many funding storms that swirl around them.

Overhead Costs

Many organizations report that the first question a potential donor asks of them is, "What percent of my donation goes to overhead?" The problem with this question is that there is no simple or right answer. Nor do donors have much idea what answer to hope for, other than a very low number. A favorite pastime of many newspapers is to "expose" how much money a nonprofit uses for administration. Headlines like "Questions Arise on the Accounting at United Way" or "Nonprofit Compensation Up" or

"A New Charity Watchdog Rises" give the impression that many nonprofits do not use money wisely. As a result, a constant obsession for many nonprofits is to try to disguise the amount of their administrative overhead. Organizations often ask questions such as "If our fundraising appeal has an educational element, can we put some of the cost of the appeal under program costs?" or "Do we have to show rent as an overhead cost or can we divide it among all our projects?"

The real question is not how to bury overhead costs but how to reclaim administration and overhead as a legitimate cost of doing business. Take two groups (true stories, slightly disguised):

Organization A organizes in three counties on issues related to water. They have three full-time community organizers, one of whom also serves as the director, and one office manager, who valiantly attempts to keep up with everything that is not directly related to organizing. The organizers do not have time to write reports to foundation funders documenting their work, so this task falls on the office manager. She works long hours piecing together the information needed for various reports and keeping track of when proposals are due. Several times she has managed to meet a deadline and save a source of funding, even though proposal writing is not her job. The organization also has an ever-decreasing number of individual donors who are rarely contacted, and then only when the organization wants more money. The office manager writes them thank-you notes, but the website is seriously out of date and there hasn't been a newsletter in several years. The director writes a letter to those donors once a year and is surprised by how small the response is. The office manager suggests that the executive director hire a development director to take over fundraising, but the director does not want another administrative hire because it will increase the percentage the organization spends on overhead. In frustration and exhaustion, the office manager quits, and the board votes not to replace her. "Cut overhead" says the board chair. It is only in her absence that everyone realizes all that she did and that must be done to keep an organization running smoothly. Fortunately the lesson, although an expensive one, is learned in time for Organization A to save itself.

Organization B has an executive director who loves "program work." He does not like fundraising or doing supervision. He has two other staff who are largely left to their own devices to figure out their work. One has figured out that he can steal upward of $2,000 a month by forging reimbursements, embezzling petty cash, and charging office supplies to the organization's account, then reselling them to other people for cash. The treasurer of the board discovers an inordinate amount of money being spent on office supplies and tells the director to "cut overhead." The ongoing stealing is not discovered until the audit, six months and $15,000 later. An audit is an administrative cost, and suddenly everyone realizes that a certain amount of administration is required in order to know that money is being handled properly.

Of course, some nonprofits do waste money on overhead costs, such as unnecessary travel to conferences or convenings, or uncontrolled reimbursements. The vast majority, however, do not. Mr. or Ms. Generous Donor does not have an accurate way to figure out which overhead costs may be justified and which are excessive, and the donor is being told by various nonprofit watchdogs that finding out how much a nonprofit spends on "administration" or "overhead" is a key element in deciding whether a group is worthy of support. The less an organization spends on such items, the thinking goes, the better the organization. That such thinking is at best simplistic and at worst dangerous can be easily demonstrated. We hear of wealthy donors contributing thousands and sometimes millions to their favorite causes. They are quoted as saying, "This is not going to go for administration. This is only going to go for programs." But the question that comes to my mind is, "Well, how is your stock that is going to fund this gift going to be sold? Who will send you the records you need for your taxes? Who will report to you on how your gift is being used? Without any administration, there will be no accounting for your gift." Donors who are promised that "all of your gift will go to programs" need to realize that, when this is true, it is because 100 percent of someone else's gift is going to administration.

Simply looking at percentages or amounts spent on salaries and other overhead compared to other costs tells donors nothing. The nonprofit sector as a whole needs to educate the public about what questions will really get donors the information they need. Once donors understand that it takes money to put on the programs they are so interested in supporting, nonprofits will be able to come out of the closet about the issue of administrative costs. (See premium content for the article "Outing Overhead.")

Fundraising Costs

In addition to the issue of overhead costs, fundraising costs raise a similar set of issues. "How much should a group spend on fundraising?" is a common question, but knowing that percentage will not tell you very much. There are many deeper questions and variables that must be taken into account. For example, a brand new neighborhood association with no staff will spend more, proportionately, on fundraising than a hundred-year-old institution with a sizeable endowment. A direct mail program costs much more than a planned giving one, but an organization cannot start its fundraising with a planned giving program. Rarely will a donor's first gift be a bequest! Direct mail and online fundraising will attract the donors who will eventually become planned givers. A special event may raise a lot of money or raise no money and still be very successful, depending on what the organization wants to accomplish. Given these types of variables, for fundraisers, the issue of "how much it costs" to raise funds for their organization is a constant headache.

Disguising the Cost of Doing Business

Another cost-related issue is this perennial problem: for most social change nonprofits, the true cost of doing business is simply unknown because of the assumption and the practice of most staff working overtime, without compensation or time off. In every nonprofit organization, there is some work that must be done on evenings and weekends. People who want a straight 9-to-5 job will probably not find a happy home in a nonprofit. But when a person has to work three evenings each week or every weekend in addition to working full days, something is wrong. Amazingly, some community organizing job descriptions call for a regular sixty-hour work week! The problem is, a job that takes sixty hours a week to do is not one job—it is a job and a half. To pay one person for that amount of work disguises the true cost of the function that person fulfills. When that person leaves, another person may not be willing or able to work that hard. She or he will then be blamed for not getting enough work done. Related to the expectation of using personal time to get the job done is the problem of talented staff leaving an organization because they want to have a family. They do not see a way to both do their job and have a child (or even to simply do their job and have a personal life, too). This situation falls particularly hard on women, and it has been the subject of a number of workshops at community organizing conferences during the past twenty years.

Another way nonprofits disguise the cost of doing business is to "save" money by paying for few or no benefits. More than 30 percent of nonprofits do not offer health insurance to their employees, and many more offer plans that have very high co-payments. Only a tiny handful of organizations will include dental or vision care coverage. Most nonprofits do not have pension plans or provide childcare (either in-house or by reimbursing for care).

As a result of all these deficiencies, there is high turnover in nonprofits, and the cost of the turnover—advertising for the job, interviewing and hiring, training new hires—is far greater than the cost to pay people decently to work a humane work week with adequate benefits, and thus to retain them.

Fundraising, Not Cost Cutting, Is the Solution to Funding Problems

Whenever there is a funding problem, the tendency of most people in nonprofits is to think about how to cut corners rather than to look at the larger picture: how to raise more money. Although lack of fundraising, or the failure of a fundraising plan, may be seen as the problem, instituting more fundraising is rarely seen as the solution. On the other hand, simply putting more work on the development staff is not the answer either. The attitude of the board and executive director—which should be "How can I help with fundraising? What should I do? Let's create a plan together"—is far too often "Get more proposals out" or "How are you doing on identifying major donors?" For people in development, this attitude translates into a job with high responsibility and little authority. The development person is responsible for raising the money needed to run the organization, but has no say in correcting the problems that may lead donors or funders not to give.

Nonprofit organizations that prosper in the years ahead will be the ones that understand the true cost of doing business and that respond to the discovery that expenses exceed income by redoubling fundraising efforts by the whole organization. These organizations will also be clear about what they can and cannot do and will not take on more than they can reasonably accomplish. These organizations will spend time educating the public—particularly their own donors—how to know that donations are being well used, so that donors are assured that money is being properly stewarded and organizations are freed to spend the money required to administer the organization properly.

Chapter Three

The Future Must Be
Different from the Past

At first glance, the title of this chapter seems to state the obvious. But I mean it in an urgent way. As I have tried to indicate in the previous two chapters, we cannot continue to build the nonprofit sector in the way we have been and hope to have real, long-term success. In this chapter I discuss the fact that we who work in nonprofit social change need to forge a different path in order to reshape our present and build a very different future.

The nonprofit sector in the United States has mushroomed over the past twenty years. It is now immense. There are 1.5 million organizations incorporated under the Internal Revenue Service 501c law, which includes twenty-eight different designations, with varying degrees of tax exemption. The most common (and the ones this book is directed to) are the 501(c)3; the c6, which covers service clubs; and the c4, which applies to groups that can lobby using non-tax-deductible donations. The total income of the sector is about $1 trillion per year; if it were a single industry, it would be our nation's largest. The nonprofit sector employs 10 percent of the workforce and is, in general, an enormous economic driver.

I am proud to say that I have worked in the nonprofit sector all my adult life. I believe nonprofits make the world a better place, but our sheer size has sometimes caused us to forget why we—and particularly social change nonprofits—exist. We have to come back to the fundamental purpose of social change nonprofits and how they are different from businesses, government, or even a lot of other nonprofits. Nonprofits that infuse social justice values into all they do build a world in which justice, peace, and equality are paramount. To remember why we exist is to have a vision of that world—a very specific idea of what we want for all our work. An example of such a vision is in Exhibit 3.1.

Exhibit 3.1: A World Vision for the Year 2045

Too many of us in the nonprofit sector have lost the ability to articulate a vision beyond generalities and platitudes. I have a vision of the world I would like to live in, and I share it here as an example of what I am talking about. According to the actuarial tables, I can reasonably expect to live to be ninety-two, which is a little less than four decades from now. As you read about the world I want to see when I am ninety-two, keep in mind that many of the things I want for the United States already exist in many other countries of the world.

In my desired world, all of the following will be universal, which means available at no extra charge beyond taxes to anyone who needs them: health care; elementary, secondary, and college education; public transportation, parks, swimming pools, libraries, and legal services; arts and culture and community centers. All facilities will be completely accessible to people with disabilities. All of these social elements will be paid for not only by a progressive tax structure, in which people earning the most money pay the most in taxes, but also by a major cut in military spending.

By the time I am ninety-two, clean air and clean water will be the norm. Corporations will include in the cost of manufacturing goods both any pollution that is a by-product of production and the cost of disposing of the product at the end of its life. As a consequence, corporations will use their technological know-how to create clean industries, and recycling and reuse will be the norm. Pollution of air or water will be extremely unusual and punished with high fines. We will no longer need fossil fuels, which is good since they will no longer be available. We will have dodged the major bullet of global warming, and the Earth will be healing. We will have long since abandoned the patriarchal notion that people are superior to animals and animals to plants; instead, we will understand ourselves to be part of a larger ecosystem, stewards of the Earth. This understanding will inform all environmental public policy.

By the time the next four decades have passed, the United States will have an income floor and an income ceiling. First, in one of the very few ideas of President

Nixon that I agree with, we will provide a guaranteed annual income to all adults that will ensure that no one lives in poverty. Second, there will be an income ceiling—a maximum that, though varying from business to business, will never be more than twenty times the wage of the lowest-paid person in the business. This will be the most dramatic change, as today CEOs of large corporations earn, on average, 491 times as much as their lowest-paid workers. (The idea of a maximum wage being held to twenty times that of the lowest-paid worker comes from management guru Peter Drucker, who got the idea from the banker J. P. Morgan.)

Our military forces will be much smaller, although in just forty years we will still be in the process of demilitarizing our country. However, as today our military is larger than that of the next nine most-militarized nations put together, in forty years we could have shrunk a great deal and still be number one in military might. This enormous decrease would represent a dramatic shift in policy, saving about $750 billion a year in today's dollars. So if you wonder where the money will come from for all social components that will be universally freely available, know that a good portion will come from the trillions of dollars we will save while still having the world's largest military. (My long-term goal is that we have no military infrastructure beyond the national guard, who will mainly be deployed in the event of natural disasters.)

I am a realist, and I know our country will still have problems when I am ninety-two. We will still be dealing with racism and sexism, but there will be huge government programs to deconstruct these and other forms of oppression. Prizes will be given for the best ideas and plans that eliminate racism in education or sexism in the media.

There are many other components to this society. Changes in structure will both follow and lead changes in attitude. People will take a much greater part in the democratic structures available for governing themselves; the nation as a whole will try to do what is best for each person and will value each person as an individual. Every individual will consider what she or he does in terms of what is good for the whole.

Possibly, above all, the society of my old age will also be one that is characterized by a high degree of respectful debate, in which ideas are put forward and discussed, modified and put forward again, with no one having the final word. This tone has already been set by President Obama, and his legacy will continue. People will be eager to engage in respectful and forward-moving dialogue.

Four decades from now, we will still have many thorny issues to sort out: for example, who, if anyone, should go to prison? Should voting be mandatory? There may still be domestic violence, sex trafficking, drug addiction, and child abuse.

➤

There will still be people in need of service and advocacy, but in this society, there will be far fewer nonprofits because there will be much less need.

I am not describing a utopian society. It is simply a description of a possible society, possible in the course of the next forty years. To achieve such a vision requires big goals. Dorothy Day, founder of the Catholic Worker Movement in 1933, said, "We must always aim for the impossible: if we lower our goal, we also diminish our effort."

In the nonprofit world, our goal must be that every organization that addresses a social problem plans for how it will put itself out of business, or at least how it will seriously scale down. We will ramp up in order to eventually close. We will ask, how much money and what other resources will it take to address, for example, institutional racism? Or our affordable housing shortage? Or air pollution? A major change from the way we run nonprofits now is that we will start by aiming for what we want to see and not just what we can get funded to do.

To be able to articulate this large vision, and to set appropriate goals to meet it, will require deconstructing the charity model entirely. At its extreme, charity is a one-way street: I, a good person working for a good organization, help you, a sad sack. You do not help me, because I do not need help. In the nonprofit model today, organization after organization provides services, training, tutoring, leadership development, even organizing—all for free, because the constituency is described by the agency as needing this help. But no one wants to be on the receiving end of charity, and often the gratitude of the constituent is mixed with resentment that they have to ask for this help in the first place. Without a vision of how to address the root causes of social problems and to involve everyone in working toward these solutions, we simply perpetuate a system that is broken and dehumanizing.

Along with deconstructing the charity model, we have to stop fetishizing professionalism. The notion of being of service has been replaced with the idea of being a professional. Collectively, we have replaced building a movement for change with building a highly professionalized nonprofit sector. Many young people have told me that they want to be a nonprofit professional, and asked me what career track they should follow, what degree they should get, and what kind of organization they should work for. These are all legitimate questions, but they skip over the first questions, which are "What do I most believe in?" and "How can I best help to realize a common vision of a much different world?" When we stop asking the first questions, the answers to the rest of the questions become corrupt.

Collectively, we also have to challenge the gap between rich and poor, which grows wider every year. As I indicated in Chapter One and as is implied in my vision of the world I want to see in 2045, we have to look at tax policy as a way to narrow and eventually eliminate that destructive gap. According to Forbes, which does an annual survey of America's billionaires, prior to 1986 the number of American billionaires averaged around thirteen. In the whole world, there were perhaps twenty billionaires before 1986. Then the Reagan administration in 1986 implemented tax legislation that favored the top 1 percent of American taxpayers. In one year, from 1986 to 1987, the number of U.S. billionaires almost quadrupled, to forty-nine! More and more tax cuts and tax shifts followed, so that now, according to Forbes, there are about 446 billionaires in the United States alone and 1,062 billionaires in the world (source: http://www.forbes.com/2008/03/05/richest-people-billionaires-billionaires08).

The explosion in billionaires worldwide cannot be blamed solely on Reagan, or even on the United States. Globally there has been a movement away from progressive taxation and a related movement toward privatization. It is beyond the scope of this chapter to explain how all this happened; in the Resources section there are several helpful books for readers interested in better understanding the factors contributing to massive inequality. The fastest-growing class in the world, these super-wealthy people own $3 trillion in wealth. In fact, the combined wealth of the world's 1,062 billionaires is about 30 percent more than the combined income of the four billion people worldwide who live on less than $2 a day. That's right: one thousand people have more money than four billion people.

This huge gap in wealth contributes to some of the poorest conditions for people on Earth. As we can see, the money exists to solve almost every problem in the world. It is a question of how it is distributed and the policies needed to distribute it more equitably. It is also important to keep in mind that some of the most competitive economies in the world have redistribution of wealth built into the way they govern themselves. For example, the World Economic Forum named the world's most competitive economies for 2007; the first three were Switzerland, Finland, and Sweden—all countries that levy what Americans would consider very high taxes on their wealthiest citizens. However, among the many variables that caused these countries to be so competitive were the fact that they support universal education and universal health care, that they are willing to have budget surpluses, and that they have a transparent and trusted government along with a respected private sector.

Going back to our vision of a better world, we know that making the changes we want to make will take massive infusions of money. Some of this money will come from a more equitable tax structure; some of it will be raised from individuals in order to lead the charge for the bigger changes that must take place. In the process of mobilizing people to give money, we will be more successful with our fundraising and our vision of the world if we also help people realize that we really can make our world very different from the way it is now. The nonprofit sector must lead that visioning process, or we will gradually fade into insignificance, with neither vision nor money.

In this time of great economic and political upheaval, every assumption is up for grabs. Old certainties are no longer certain; old ways of doing business no longer work. This time presents an opportunity not just to strengthen your own fundraising program and to make your own organization stronger and healthier, but also to place your organization among those that are working to bring about serious and lasting progressive change in the world we live in.

Part Two

Keeping Your Nonprofit Strong and Healthy

I argued in Part One that the entire nonprofit sector has serious flaws that must be corrected, and that this correction begins with creating, and then being driven by, a vision of what our society should be—today, tomorrow, and far into the future. We don't just create a vision, then put it in a drawer and go back to work. We construct our way of working in a different way—and to do that, we must carve out time to think through what changes we want to make and how to make them. We may even (gasp!) have to take time off from our day-to-day work and work with other nonprofits across issues, across town, and across other barriers that have kept us apart.

In this section, I also ask you to step back, take a deep breath, and reconstruct your fundraising program. Those of us who live in California work a lot with metaphors related to earthquakes; a common one is the concept of making a building "earthquake-proof." Seismic upgrades are expensive, and unlike other expensive changes you might make to a house, such as remodeling your kitchen, you don't see the result of that work unless an earthquake hits. Similarly, we have to make our organizations "economy-proof" so that no matter what is happening with the economy, we are able to keep raising money. We change our strategies and our goals based in part on these external realities, but we don't live in a state of anxiety and fear about what is going to happen to our groups.

The metaphor goes further. Sometimes people think a building that has been seismically upgraded isn't going to move at all in an earthquake. On the contrary; surprisingly, the upgrade works—the building is far less likely to fall off its foundation and be destroyed—because the building is able to sway and move slightly and absorb the shocks of the quake. A completely rigid building will not survive an earthquake. Similarly for nonprofits, the goals of good fundraising are (1) knowing what to change in your fundraising practices and how to do so as conditions change, (2) knowing what doesn't ever change about successful fundraising, and (3) being able to stay flexible and forward-moving.

To get there, you need to reexamine your whole fundraising setup, from the basement to the attic. This part of the book starts with what is always true about fundraising—the basic principles that are never going to change, no matter what happens in the world. It then moves on to helping your organization understand the philosophy of grassroots fundraising, and why an organization needs a philosophy of fundraising. The next chapter gets more specific, with suggestions for creating a healthy work environment, followed by a chapter on how to be a healthy worker in that environment. These chapters focus on what you need to do and how you need to do it in order to succeed and lead your organization's fundraising in these times.

With those fundamentals in place, I then show how you can analyze your current fundraising efforts and, using that evaluation, choose and use strategies with more accuracy and efficiency. I then take you through very specific elements of fundraising: segmenting your donor lists, building a team of volunteers, understanding why personal asking is imperative and how to do it, and learning to identify possible gaps in your fundraising strategies that may be costing you money. I conclude with some suggestions for building financial security.

The overworked development director will be tempted to go right to the chapter on segmenting donor lists or building a team. You are, of course, welcome to do that. But I fervently suggest that you actually read this part from start to finish so that you can make the changes you need to make from each chapter in a systematic fashion. A proper office environment will enable you to do better segmenting. If you are happy in your job, you will be more effective with volunteers. If you are grounded in a philosophy of grassroots fundraising, you will find it easier to ask for money in person. The section ends with a quiz to help you set priorities about what you are going to work on.

If you don't retrofit your house, each little quake causes more cracks, which lead to leaks, which lead to wood rotting around windows and doors. Next come termites or sometimes even mice and rats who chew through this rotting wood to get under your house and build their nests. As any of you who work in prevention know, prevention isn't easy to measure, and it sometimes seems like a theoretical undertaking. But even though in a really serious earthquake some buildings will fall and be unsalvageable, the adage "an ounce of prevention is worth a pound of cure" can protect even some shaky buildings from that fate. The same is true of organizations in financial upheaval. Your organization does important work and needs to survive the rocking of the economy, but managing survival is not simply a matter of luck—it involves examining all our old assumptions, actively planning and evaluating everything we do, and intensively working with other people who also share the organization's vision, mission, and goals.

Chapter Four

What Is (Probably) Always True About Fundraising

In Part One, we looked at problems and flaws in the sector that have been true for some time, and we discussed how they might be corrected. In this chapter, I want to look at what *doesn't* need correcting that has also been true for some time, or perhaps always has been. Building your fundraising program on this foundation will get you through all kinds of times.

If you gather a group of people with a lot of fundraising experience (whether paid or volunteer) and ask them what things are always true about fundraising, I guarantee that no matter where you are, no matter what your cause or your population demographic, the following ten things will be on the list:

1. *In every country where fundraising and philanthropy have been studied, the majority of people give away money.* Here in the United States, seven out of ten adults give away money. In Canada, eight out of ten give away money. England, Australia, South Africa, South Korea, Mexico, Brazil, Finland, Japan—the list goes on, but the commonality is that giving is an important value to people (see the Charities Aid Foundation briefing paper "International Comparisons of Charitable Giving, 2006" and "The Rise of the Nonprofit Sector" by Lester Salomon, *Foreign Affairs Journal,* July 1994). In the United States and Canada, more people give away money than vote or go to any house of worship or volunteer.

2. *The majority of donations come from income, and most people remain employed.* Even if unemployment reaches 10 percent, and even in communities where unemployment is 20 or 25 percent, most people remain employed, and they will continue to give.

3. *People are going to give away their money.* In hard economic times, some people cut back on their giving, but others (who remain employed and whose personal finances have not changed very much) give more, and most people continue to give the same amount. Those who have to cut back their giving because their financial situation has worsened often start volunteering. The need to give, to be engaged, to be part of a community, seems inherent in being human. People who are invited to be part of community, at any level, in one way or another, feel more part of the human family.

4. *People give when they are asked; the corollary is that they tend not to give when they are not asked.* These are not simply different ways of saying the same thing. In studies and in the anecdotal observation of fundraisers, when we ask people why they made their last charitable donation, 80 percent of them will say, "Someone asked me." And when we ask people who say they do not give money away why they don't, 80 percent of them will say, "I was never asked." Our observation of people who don't give is that they feel *not* invited. Most of the people who don't give away money also don't vote and don't volunteer and are not engaged in their communities. Similarly, when we ask volunteers, "How did you come to be involved in this organization?" many will say they started out giving money and later were invited to become more active.

5. *Fundraising works best when the person doing the fundraising makes her or his own gift first.* All organizations should have at least as many donors as there are board members and management staff. When an organization has no individual donors, it is in trouble not just financially but also because of a fundamental failure to invite those people closest to the group to express their commitment in a tangible and simple way.

6. *After making their own gift, the people doing the fundraising have one job: to respectfully invite other people to give.* The people who are invited to give (whether personally, by mail, by a "donate now"

button on a website, or at an event) either accept the invitation, decline it, or take a rain check. The person doing the fundraising should not take any response personally. If someone chooses to give, the fundraiser is pleased but does not take credit. The fundraiser should not say to herself, "I got the gift." Nor, if the prospect declines to give, should the fundraiser think, "I must have messed up." Too often, fundraising is made into an adversarial situation, as evidenced by fundraisers using language such as, "I hit her up," "I twisted his arm," "I sat on them until they coughed it up," or "I squeezed it out of them." Less violent but equally problematic are ideas such as "I buttered him up," "I flattered her to death," "I gave him this song and dance about how much we needed the money." Don't just use appropriate language with the prospects—use appropriate images and metaphors in your own head. If asking for money makes you anxious, stop thinking about yourself. Think about the cause and the prospect. Stop thinking of your prospects as adversaries; instead, try putting yourself in their place and think how you would like to be approached.

7. *Most people, when invited to give money to an organization, say no.* We have to ask far more people than the number of gifts we need. Fortunately, there is a body of knowledge that allows us to predict what percentage of response we will get, depending on what strategy we use. (See also Chapter Eight for a breakdown of strategies and percentages of response.)

8. *People continue to give when they feel appreciated and kept informed about what the organization is doing.* Organizations that promptly send personal thank-you notes generally have higher donor retention than those who thank with a form letter or thank weeks and months after the gift was made, and they have much higher retention than those who don't thank at all. On the other hand, many people tell me that half of the organizations they give to don't thank them. When the economy is doing well, people will continue to give small amounts to organizations that they believe in, whether or not they are thanked. But in hard times, donors begin to cut back on the number of organizations they give to, and they remain loyal to organizations that have shown them some attention. A simple thank-you is not enough, however. Organizations

also need to have a newsletter and a good website, and they need to give the impression through their written materials that they care about their donors all the time and not just when they need money.

9. *The greatest number of donations come from working- and middle-class households with incomes of less than $90,000.* Fortunately, that characterizes most people. Further, middle-class, working-class, and poor people tend to give more money as a percentage of their income than do wealthier people (for more on giving by income bracket, see *Patterns of Household Charitable Giving by Income Group, 2005,* published by the University of Indiana Center on Philanthropy).

10. *Good fundraising focuses on the donor, not the donation.* The purpose of fundraising is to build relationships. Donors are not ATMs; someone who gives money for several years and then stops because of a changed financial situation still should be treated as a donor. We are sometimes reluctant to talk with donors who we know have lost their jobs or whose assets have taken a tumble. We claim we don't want to embarrass them or add to their stress, but it is really our own embarrassment we are worried about. People want to know that you like and value them with or without their money. In hard times, you need to practice what you are going to say to people who have lost their jobs or have watched their retirement funds evaporate. As anyone knows who has worked with cancer patients or in hospice, people need to be invited to talk about their situation, in case they want to do so. And even if they don't want to talk about it, they generally appreciate your interest. When people who are having financial problems get back on their feet financially, they're likely to resume giving.

You can see that fundraising is possible under even the most extreme circumstances, as anyone who has ever raised money in communities characterized by high degrees of poverty can tell you. But you can also see that fundraising is a process—we don't just swoop in, get the money, and skedaddle out. The chapters in this section expand on these premises.

Chapter Five

Creating a Fundraising Philosophy

In the previous chapter, we looked at what has been and probably will continue to be true about fundraising. In this chapter we explore what should be the foundation of what is true about the fundraising your organization engages in—its fundraising philosophy.

Most organizations have a fundraising philosophy of sorts, which might be stated as follows: "Get the money. Use legal and ethical methods, and don't take money from really gross places. On the other hand, don't ask too many questions about the sources of the money because in the end they all will turn up something we don't agree with." Although it might stand you in good stead most of the time, this is a fundraising philosophy by default.

Our entire sector has gotten into trouble because we failed to answer a simple question: "How should we be supported?" In other words: "Ideally, what kinds of income streams will best help us accomplish our goals and objectives and will do the most to fulfill our mission?" As I noted in Part One, we don't answer this question sector-wide, and we tend not to answer the question even for our own organization.

This chapter discusses the philosophy of grassroots fundraising and what an organization really needs to believe to be successful with the kind of fundraising discussed in this book.

The reason most organizations don't have a conversation about their sources of support is clear: if we don't have money, we can't do our work, and we don't have time to stop raising money long enough to step back and think about how our work might be enhanced by how we raise our money. But that vicious cycle is what got us where we are today: with not enough money and not enough time, and further away from accomplishing our goals and objectives than we need to be.

The philosophical issues involved in fundraising arise when we consider the various sources of funds available to us: foundations, corporations, government, and individuals. Foundation fund-raising involves researching foundations and writing proposals to obtain grants. Corporate fundraising means figuring out how our nonprofit—what we do, who we serve, who we have contact with— might help a corporation so that they would want to partner with us and give us some money. Government fundraising means learn-ing what funds provided by taxes could be applied to our projects and programs. And grassroots fundraising means raising funds from your community. Although fundraising is a pretty straight-forward concept—we need money, and to get it, we have to raise it—each choice we make about pursuing a source of funds or a combination of sources says something about our beliefs.

Let's focus here for a moment on grassroots fundraising, as that is the main focus of this book. People often misunderstand the term *grassroots fundraising* as being about getting a lot of little gifts or just being some politically correct thing to do. In practice, however, the term *grassroots* is used to denote any kind of effort that derives most of its power and reason for being from a com-munity and from common, ordinary people. Grassroots political movements are characterized by organizing in specific communi-ties or among specific types of people, such as factory workers or students, and helping these groups to advocate for the changes they want to see. Any kind of grassroots effort denotes the com-mon people as constituting a fundamental political and economic group. Grassroots fundraising follows the same principles. Grass-roots fundraising means that an organization uses a range of strategies to invite as many people as possible to give donations of widely varying amounts. Given that strategy, grassroots fundrais-ing also, beneficially, means that a lot of people are involved in raising the money needed.

A grassroots organization is independent: no one source of money is of ultimate importance to that group. If a person or a corporation says, "We don't like what you are doing and we don't want to fund you anymore," the nonprofit can say, "We are sorry to hear that and we will miss you." The nonprofit will not say, "Oh, no, don't leave! We will change what we are doing to please you!" Similarly, no new program or organizing idea is evaluated against the question, "Can we get it funded?" It is evaluated as to whether it promotes the mission or not.

A grassroots organization is also independent of any one person: it has leaders, but no one leader is so important that if that person left or died, the organization would not be able to continue. Leadership is shared, skills are taught to all members of the organization so that each person in the organization has her or his job but also has skills to do other jobs, and a goal of the organization is to share information and skills among as many people as possible as well as to invite as many people as possible to give money. Grassroots fundraising welcomes and encourages small donations and large donations.

All the ways you raise money to do your work reflect your values, whether you have articulated those values or not. So, for example, if there is government funding available for the work you do, in taking such funding you are expressing the value that the work you do should be supported by taxes. In most countries, social services that aim at keeping people out of poverty are provided by government funding. If you get most or all of your money from corporations, on the other hand, the implicit value is that the work you do can be done in partnership with for-profit companies and that your agenda as a nonprofit can exist in harmony with the agendas of corporations. In many countries, a lot of arts and culture, as well as research and higher education, is supported by corporate giving. If, however, you feel that the work you do should be supported by the people who most benefit from it, and that you want to have the maximum amount of independence in what you choose to do and how you choose to do it, then you will want to have your money come from as many people and places as you can manage. That is grassroots fundraising. Grassroots fundraising does not preclude an organization from also receiving corporate, foundation, or government support, but it means the organization is not mainly dependent on any one source.

You can begin to create your own fundraising philosophy by using Exercise 5.1.

EXERCISE 5.1: CREATING YOUR
OWN FUNDRAISING PHILOSOPHY

Your organization needs to create a fundraising philosophy of its own. You may use much of what you read here, but take the time to go through the following exercise to make sure everyone in the organization is on the same page.

This exercise can be done alone, but it is more effective and more fun if done with a combination of board and staff and possibly some key volunteers.

Have everyone sit quietly for a moment and imagine something that right now seems unimaginable—that we can foretell the future, and that your organization can raise money however it wants. Whatever type of fundraising you put your hand to will be successful. Under these conditions, where would you want your money to come from? Write down your thoughts, along with your hesitations and your questions.

Now take thirty minutes or so for the group to discuss what each of you came up with. Some people will be tempted to say, "Five rich people who live far away and just send in their money." Yes, that is a fantasy, and we can all enjoy a laugh at that. But you have to raise the question, "If that happened, would that be the most mission-fulfilling way we can raise funds?"

You may want to look at some other questions to expand your thinking:

- How are organizations like yours—or services like those your organization provides—supported in other developed social democracies, such as Denmark, Norway, or Canada?

- What sources of funds would give the general public the most confidence in what you do?

- What role should taxes play in your work?

- What mix of fundraising sources gives you the strongest future?

- See if you can pull out a few key elements that all of you agree on. These will form the basis of your philosophy. Don't make this too complicated. The following examples of two organizations—one that had a fundraising philosophy and one that did not—may help you with your thinking.

Examples

The PTA of a high school serving a poor community on the outskirts of a big city is approached by a corporation that offers to donate the profits from all food-vending machines that they install on the school grounds, on the condition that no other vendors (aside from the school cafeteria) are permitted to sell drinks or snacks in the school at any time. Although it is tempting to think of the money this arrangement could provide, the PTA has heard about these kinds of corporate contracts from other schools and has discussed what would happen if a corporation made such an offer to them. Although at that time many parents thought the discussion was theoretical at best and a waste of time at worst, they all did cooperate in creating a fundraising philosophy that rejected any source of funding that did not promote the health and well-being of the students in the school. The high-fat, high-sugar snacks that are being offered to be sold through these vending machines do not meet their criteria, so it is easy to politely thank the corporate representatives but turn them down.

Across town, a wealthy developer who owns a small house offers to give it to an environmental organization to use as office space on the condition that they will not oppose a gated community he wishes to construct nearby. This new development will feature luxury homes surrounding a golf course. The land he wishes to develop is not environmentally sensitive and is slated to be developed. The organization's board and staff are divided as to whether to take the offer. Most feel that since the land is going to be developed anyway, it doesn't really matter that luxury homes will be the outcome. Others feel that a golf course, given the amount of pesticides and water it typically uses, is not an environmentally sound use of the land and that they should be working with local housing activists to ensure more low-income and affordable housing. Not being able to make a statement about this development will put them in an untenable position if the development becomes controversial. They spend hours, then days debating whether to take the developer's offer or not. In the meantime, the developer is denied permission by the county to build this gated community, and he withdraws his offer to the environmental organization. Although the situation is resolved for them, the bitterness caused by the disagreements it raised remains.

Answer these questions:

- What do you need to do to be as prepared as the PTA in your fundraising?

- Can you foresee any source of income or in-kind offer that would cause great division in your organization, as happened to the environmental organization, and what can you do to forestall that discord?

Policies That Help Create a Fundraising Philosophy

Many organizations start their philosophical explorations by creating a *gift acceptance policy*, which is essentially what the PTA did in the example just presented. A gift acceptance policy is usually very simple; for example, "People for Everything Good reserves the right to turn down any gift that we believe is not in the best interest of fulfilling our mission or that we know we cannot steward properly." The meaning behind such a policy, however, is much more complicated. The PTA had discussed what kind of corporate donations they would accept and what kind they would not. By being very clear that the health and well-being of the students is primary, they were easily able to turn down money that would result from promoting unhealthy snacks to students. Some would argue that the students will eat and drink high-fat, high-sugar snacks anyway and that someone is going to make money off of junk food and it might as well go to a good cause. The PTA, in their deliberations, undoubtedly acknowledged that potential but chose to have the school not be a partner in making junk food available.

In the second example, the developer is making a conditional gift. These are common, and many are quite innocent. "I will give you $10,000 if you match it dollar for dollar" is a useful conditional gift. "I'd like to pay for the children's section of the library if it can be named after my mother" is a reasonable request, albeit one that bears discussion among the library board. Generally, though, the presence of a gift acceptance policy would include the understanding that a gift conditioned on restricting an organization's work must be turned down.

ON THE
WEB   After your organization creates a gift acceptance policy (see premium content for more on gift acceptance policies), it is a small step to create a more encompassing philosophy overall. In this chapter, I have given the rationale for a grassroots fundraising philosophy; Exhibit 5.1 provides two examples of such a philosophy from the websites of two groups.

Exhibit 5.1: Samples of Fundraising Philosophies

Grassroots Institute for Fundraising Training (GIFT)
www.grassrootsfundraising.org

Mission Statement

The Grassroots Institute for Fundraising Training (GIFT) is a multiracial organization that promotes the connection between fundraising, social justice, and movement-building. We believe that how groups are funded is as important to achieving their goals as how the money is spent, and that building community support is central to long-term social change. We provide analysis, training, and resources to strengthen organizations, with an emphasis on those focused on social justice and based in communities of color.

We believe:

- Social justice organizations are more effective when they have a broad base of individual donors

- The leadership of people of color in fundraising is important for building a strong social justice movement

- Fundraising, program, and organizing need to be integrated so that all staff, board, and volunteers are aware of and involved in all aspects of the work

Santropol Roulant, Montreal
www.santropolroulant.org

Mission Statement

Santropol Roulant is an intergenerational Meals On Wheels program that uses food as a vehicle to create trust and build bridges between individuals in a city where isolation among the elderly is the highest in Canada.

Our [fundraising] philosophy is that *fundraising is not a job that someone does, but a program that we are all responsible for and in which we are all actively engaged.*

While all good ideas need money to thrive, the most important stereotype we break through our fundraising efforts is that it doesn't need to happen in the dark corners and shadows of an organization. We make it visible, accessible, fun and successful. Our "Fundraising for Social Change" program is grounded in our mission and provides meaningful opportunities for staff, board, volunteers, neighbors and donors to become actively involved in raising funds and supporting Santropol Roulant. These funds go directly to our programs and our vision, and it is our role to provide all participants with the skills or motivation they need to succeed.

Why? Because no matter how much money we raise, at the end of the year the funds are well allocated and well spent and the energy, excitement and sense of shared purpose is what is left. At Santropol Roulant, we have developed an amazing fundraising program that is built not on the heroic and solitary efforts of any one individual, but on the active support, participation and passion of many. This collective sense of accomplishment permeates everything we do.

Summary

Having a fundraising philosophy is key to having a successful fundraising program. It is a step that, historically, most organizations have skipped over, much to their eventual detriment. The discussion you will have in creating a fundraising philosophy or developing a gift acceptance policy will be rich, interesting, and informative. It is a great way to get buy-in from the board and other staff, and it will help solidify the place of fundraising in your organizational culture. Further, the issues that are raised as you create your own fundraising philosophy will help you begin to address the flaws discussed in Part One, and they will provide the basis and motivation for correcting the problems that are discussed in the rest of Part Two.

Chapter Six

Creating and Maintaining a Healthy Working Environment

When we analyze why a fundraising program is not working as well as it should, we often start with how staff are allocating their time among various responsibilities: interfacing with the board, communicating with donors, finding prospects. But often how staff are using their time is simply trying to cope with an inadequate work environment. In this chapter, we look at how much time and creativity is released when basic working conditions are addressed. Let's start with a story.

Western Counties Alliance Against Rape (WCAAR)

Western Counties Alliance Against Rape (WCAAR) has a small office in a trailer. The rent is very low, offsetting the fact that the trailer tends to be cold in the winter and hot in the summer, and if they use the photocopy machine and the microwave at the same time they will blow a fuse. WCAAR has two staff, Anna and Tiffany. Tiffany is in charge of development, public relations, and an outreach campaign into the schools. Anna conducts trainings for police, lawyers, and victim advocates, and provides technical assistance to rape crisis and counseling centers in the nine counties WCAAR serves. Both Tiffany and Anna spend a lot of time on the phone, and they find it hard to concentrate when they are both in the office. In addition, they have a number of volunteers, whose presence increases the noise and the density. But whenever the subject of moving to a more adequate space comes up, the WCAAR board insists that all extra money raised be put into developing new programs or doing more outreach.

As they expand, the group hires an office manager, Susan, to take care of the grant reporting, donor data entry, website updating, scheduling of trainings, and so on. There is not enough room at another desk, so Susan and Anna share a desk. At their wits' end, Anna, Tiffany, and Susan ask me how to prove to the board that they need better office space. I ask them to keep a time diary: write down what they are doing every hour for one week. The results are stunning: about ten hours of Anna's and Tiffany's time each week is spent dealing with the results of this office arrangement: finding places to hold meetings because their office is too crowded, telling volunteers not to come in because there is no room for them, returning calls that come in while they are working at home. "Plus," Anna sighs, "I can't keep track of how much time I lose in taking aspirin for headaches, or having to start a sentence over five times because I have lost my train of thought." The volunteers also report losing time: one says she could come in Wednesday afternoons, but there is no room for her. Another says that she spends a lot of time describing where the trailer is to new volunteers, and a former volunteer says she quit because she could not work in the "mayhem."

Although not scientific, our time-documentation project points to a lot of work not getting done and, in the case of paid staff, wages being wasted. I tell the board that they are not saving money on this arrangement. The few board members who also volunteer in the office agree. The real hurdle emerges: the board is afraid they won't be able to raise the money needed for the cost of a move and for increased rent. Never having estimated what these costs would be, they don't know whether these fears are realistic. Now they take that step, which makes it clear that the costs of moving and of paying more rent will be more than offset by the increased productivity of staff and volunteers, the ability to have more volunteers, and the increased visibility of the group.

WCAAR suffers from a common syndrome—fear of being unable to raise "enough money" (exact amount always undefined) for decent space, which leads to putting up with inadequate facilities or equipment, until the frustration is so great that they finally must question the wisdom of this scrimping and the price that is being paid.

In the end, WCAAR raises the funds needed by launching a mini-campaign among board and key donors. They raise enough for the move, for new furniture, and to upgrade their computers, as well as funds to cover the first nine months of the rent increase. This is not only the first campaign the board has ever done by themselves, but it is also the biggest they have ever done. The campaign shows them how much support there is for WCAAR and how relatively easy it is to raise this money.

WCAAR's move proves to be an important watershed, not just because the new offices are so much better, but because the organization, in the words of the board chair, "decided to act its age." "We are not a little start-up group that has to squeeze every penny, but we were acting like that," she said. "We learned that we have the support that comes with being a ten-year-old successful organization, and all we had to do was ask for it."

Elements of a Development Office

For many years, the thought of having a "development office" was ludicrous to me and to most of the grassroots organizations I worked with. We shared desks, typewriters (later computers), and phones in run-down apartments, large lofts, or old store-fronts. Sometimes we had offices in an office building (a novel concept!), where we either were squashed into cubicles or simply had two or three desks in each office. I began to notice that when I worked at home I got a lot more done and was much less tired at the end of the day. I became very interested in the science of time management, and I felt I had stumbled upon an insight worthy of a religious experience when I learned about "opportunity cost"—the cost of not doing what you would have been doing had you not been doing what you were doing. I have since helped thousands of organizations like WCAAR figure out what they need to spend money on in order to raise more money. One of the fundamentals of being able to run an effective fundraising program is to have a good work environment, and, as I discussed in Chapter Two, the cost of the kind of environment WCAAR and organizations like them tolerated did not save money but simply disguised the cost of doing business.

So let's explore all the elements of this space, which starts with the physical setup but also embraces an organizational attitude toward fundraising. First, even in the smallest and most grassroots organization there must be a space dedicated to fundraising that is used by the person primarily in charge of fundraising. This space has a desk, a telephone, a filing cabinet, a computer, and a printer that is not shared with more than three people. The chair and computer setup must be ergonomically correct and adjustable by different users to prevent developing serious physical problems. Backaches, repetitive stress and carpal tunnel syndrome, and headaches plague many office staff, whether in development roles or not. Much of this can be eliminated by taking the time to set up the chair and computer screen at the right height and make other ergonomic corrections.

The fundraising staff is afforded some privacy and quiet, either by this space being an actual separate office or cubicle or through some arrangement of furniture and curtains. This space includes the following, each element of which I describe in more detail later in this chapter:

- A master calendar, hanging in a prominent place, on which fundraising dates and timelines are clearly marked for all to see. This physical calendar may be augmented by a master calendar on the network for all the staff to consult or add to, but don't ever underestimate the power of a large paper or wipe-off wall calendar.
- A fairly up-to-date and well-maintained computer with easy-to-access, clearly named files of up-to-date rosters of board members, key volunteers, staff, key donors (major donors who also volunteer, foundation staff, and corporate contacts), vendors you use regularly, media contacts you talk to often, and organizations you work with routinely. Everyone in the organization has access to these rosters, either through a network or stored on the website or on paper copies. Regular updating is a shared and scheduled task. People who are in the office regularly (staff or volunteers) are familiar with these names, so that when these people call or e-mail, they generally do not have to explain who they are.

- A literature display by the entrance to the office, with copies of the latest newsletter, brochures, annual reports, a copy of your 990 tax form, and any other literature for people to buy or to take.
- An attractive website, the content of which changes frequently. Options for donating online are clear. The annual report is available as a PDF for downloading, as are lists of staff and board.

   In addition, the following essentials are in place:

- Data protection: access to electronic files is protected by passwords, and any paper files with donor information are in a filing cabinet that can be locked. Everyone who works in the organization has a clear sense of what information is confidential and what is not, or knows who to ask if they are confused.
- Although fundraising is the primary responsibility of one or two people, everyone in the office feels that fundraising is part of what they think about and participate in, and the development staff can ask for help when they need it or, for extra credit, may even offer unsolicited help from time to time. Even if there is a well-staffed development department, the executive director always plays a key role in fundraising.

A Room (or at Least a Desk) of One's Own

The first requirement for a healthy development office is for it to exist at all. The fundraising function of an organization, even if it is staffed by volunteers or is part of the job of the only paid person, must still have its own space and its own equipment. How much space, where it is located, and how fancy it is will depend on the organization. However, keep in mind that there is a mathematical relationship between money raised and money spent, which means simply this: little money spent will equal little money raised. The truth of this maxim is obvious in strategies like direct mail or special events, but it is just as important in setting up and maintaining an office.

The key factor in having a healthy development program is integrating fundraising into all the other work of the organization. This means giving the development function the same level of attention in terms of space, salary, time on the agenda, and so on that other programs or functions have. It also means seeing donors as part of the constituency you are trying to reach through your work—not as a sidelined group to whom you relate only when you need their money. On the other hand, if the development office is nicer and the salaries for development people are higher than everyone else's, this is a sure setup for resentment and lack of cooperation.

Other Signs of Health

Good development people are on the phone a lot, so they need a space in which they can easily hear themselves and the party they are talking to. There needs to be enough telephone lines into the office so that people can get through to them (as is true for any staff). When development people are not on the phone, they are often writing—thank-yous, appeals, newsletters, proposals, reports, and so on. They must have a good computer with a lot of memory and up-to-date programs, and access to a high-quality printer. They probably also need a laptop with wireless access or some kind of PDA for when they travel (even if just across town) to visit donors.

When they are not talking on the phone or writing, development people are most often out meeting with people, so they need to know that their papers, database, and files will be as they left them when they return. In many organizations staff share desks with a volunteer or someone who comes in irregularly, like the bookkeeper or a computer consultant. Because the development director is gone a lot, that desk becomes the one that people use, and they pile up everything that's on it and shove it to one side to clear space for their own work. When the development person returns, she has to take the time to recreate her work before she can begin working. This situation needs to be avoided as much as possible.

Master Calendar

The development function needs to be very visible. A calendar that shows board meetings, special events, proposal deadlines, direct mail drops, e-newsletter blasts, and major donor campaigns, along with the timeline leading up to each of these actions, helps other people see how much work and lead time go into fundraising. Organizing campaigns, rallies, conferences, and any other major program dates should be posted on this calendar too. Putting together a calendar like this calls for organizational planning. Too often, program plans are tacked onto fundraising deadlines, or vice versa, or the two are not planned together at all, leading to periods of intense overwork when, say, a programmatic event is scheduled the same week as the launch of a major donor campaign.

Current Roster

Organization-wide familiarity with board members, key donors and volunteers, foundation staff, and similar key players is imperative. It is unsettling to be on the board of an organization and not have your name recognized by the person answering the phone, and it can cause needless irritation when the cochair of the major gifts committee (himself a major donor) is automatically put through to voice mail because the development director is on a call with a friend.

Literature Display and Website

An organization with a healthy development office will radiate a sense of pride about itself. Even if its offices are run-down, they will be neat and there will be a display about the organization near the entrance. The display does not have to look professional, but it should appear well kept. A table with one yellowing copy of last year's spring newsletter and a dead plant gives the appearance of a group that is on its last legs, whether that is true or not. Ditto for your website and any other virtual media that you use. Advertising an event that has been over for two months or having an organizational blog whose last post is six months old, or having several broken links, does not give a good impression. More and more, people doing fundraising report calling a donor and having the person say, "Let me pull up your website" or "I read your blog faithfully" or "Your Facebook page is cool."

Confidence in Confidentiality

Part of the taboo about money is people's fascination with the people who have it. In fundraising, this can take the form of gossiping about major donors or sharing confidential information with someone who shouldn't know it. Because we are all human, we can be tempted to read things that were not intended for us if they come into our line of vision or are easy to find. Therefore, even with the most trusted coworkers and volunteers, information in the donor database must be protected somehow. One method is using passwords. One password lets you into the names and addresses of donors; this is used by anyone who is getting out a mailing or is making corrections to entries. Another password allows you to see the donors' giving history; the final one lets you have access to all the information. If this arrangement is not possible, then one person needs to keep tabs on who has access and who has used their access to the database.

This also applies to paper information that is kept in a filing cabinet. Just as personnel files are not available for everyone to rifle through, so donor files are off limits—and the easiest way to keep them off limits is to have a locked drawer with a key whose location is known to only the few people who need to know it.

Development directors must be careful not to leave sensitive information on their desks and not to use e-mail to send highly confidential information. E-mail must be regarded as something that can wind up anywhere and be seen by anyone. This is particularly important with regard to donors who want to be anonymous. An e-mail was forwarded to me a few days ago that said, "Mary Smith, our 'anonymous' donor, has given again!!! Yeah Mary!" As it turns out, Mary had told the executive director that she and the development director could know about her gift, but no one else. I am neither of those people, nor were the three other board members who got this e-mail.

Locked file cabinets, password-protected information, and cautious use of e-mail to convey confidential information—all this may seem to risk creating an atmosphere of mistrust, but it should not. We trust people to be human, and we are dealing with sensitive but very interesting information. Don't make a big deal out of all of this: although it is important to be careful with donor information, these are not state secrets, and we don't need to be paranoid. Just be prudent.

Everyone Understands Fundraising

Build in time at staff meetings, board meetings, and volunteer meetings to explain the fundraising plan and to keep people up-to-date on progress. During campaigns, put up a "thermometer" (or some more creative symbolic display) to show the goal and progress toward the goal. Thank people for anything they do to help or any idea they have (even if it is not a good idea, they took the time to think of it). Over time, people will move from thinking of fundraising as some awful combination of dreary and scary and begin to see that a lot of it is fun and creative, and that the dreary tedious parts are no more so than they are on any other job.

Because people spend their prime-time hours at work and are expected to do their most creative work during those hours, they must have a work environment that supports them. Ironically, this is more true in a small understaffed nonprofit than at a large corporation. In the small nonprofit, if one staff person cannot get her work done, there are no other people to pick up the slack. The work is simply not done. An organization that scrimps on the infrastructure needed will end up spending all the money it thinks it is saving in high staff turnover and lost staff time. Eventually this will erode the organization's functioning to the point that you are not raising enough money to keep your organization afloat. On the other hand, making simple inexpensive changes can make a world of difference.

A healthy work environment leads to, but does not guarantee, a happy development staff. In the next chapter, we look at what kind of person does well in development, particularly in a grassroots organization.

Chapter Seven

How to Be Happy in Development

I recently sat on the hiring committee for an organization that was selecting a development director. The most fascinating question asked of the candidates was posed by a board member who is the president of a successful investment firm: "Tell me about your biggest fundraising failure."

The first two candidates answered with stories about something that wasn't really their fault. One said that the board had committed to raising an amount of money that was needed by a certain date and then failed to come up with it. The other said that he was never able to get the executive director to go with him to see donors.

The final candidate said, "I persuaded the board of directors to spend $15,000 on a direct mail program that after three years still had not paid for itself." He described pushing the board to agree to spend the money and pleading with the executive director for a go-ahead. He had cast aside all caution, even forgoing testing the lists because he wanted to take advantage of a lot of publicity the group was generating.

The board member then asked this candidate, "What fundraising accomplishment are you most proud of?" He said that following this mail fiasco, he had gotten together with three board members and two other long-time volunteers and they had developed a plan to raise $500,000 for a reserve fund. The executive director was persuaded to go with the plan by the enthusiasm of the board members. They were able to raise the money in one year, while also raising the amount they needed for their annual operating expenses.

After this candidate left the room, the board member who had posed the questions said, "That's our person. Able to spend money, able to admit he is wrong, and able to pick himself up and try something else just as big." The organization hired him, and he has been superb. Taking risks that involve talking everyone into something they don't want to do is not the hallmark of a good development director, but admitting when you are wrong, then being willing to work with a team to develop a big project and providing leadership and enthusiasm for that project, is. Clearly this person had learned the difference. This person also walked into an organization able to use his talents. A good fundraising program and a good development director are related but not the same.

A healthy work environment still won't work for people who are unhappy in their line of work. Knowing whether you are suited to development is very important, as is knowing what makes a development job doable. In the current economic roller coaster, it is critical to examine yourself and your job to make sure you can keep doing it. Organizations continue to need both money to operate and people who will help coordinate raising that money. These are people who are excited by these times and see opportunities and challenges where others might despair. Board members, volunteers, and other staff will look to you for how they should be reacting to the economic news, and you have to remain calm and optimistic, so that you can help set realizable goals. To do that, you have to be fundamentally happy in your work—and this chapter helps you figure out how to achieve that.

A Healthy Worker Helps Create a Healthy Work Environment

Of course, much of what makes a person happy in a fundraising job is what makes a person happy in any job in a nonprofit organization. The person is able to balance setting boundaries with being flexible and to be a self-starter who also seeks input and advice from others; the person works well with a team and sees the mission of the organization as the benchmark for any decisions made. No matter whether you are the executive director, the lead organizer, the bookkeeper, the administrative assistant, the development director—whatever your title or responsibilities, you understand that all the work of the organization is based on its mission. The framework that informs all decisions, from what goes on the website to the contents of the agenda for a board meeting to staff salaries and benefits, is founded on the mission and the goals of the organization—not efficiency, not popularity, not convenience. Being very strict on this point is the best way to ensure a healthy workplace, happy and hardworking staff, and outstanding and important work.

Like all staff, the fundraiser should have a job description that allows him or her to do the job in forty to fifty hours a week. Staff should be required to take time off and to improve their skills by attending workshops and conferences, reading, and belonging to appropriate professional organizations.

For many development directors, fundraising presents three big challenges. The first—as pointed out by the late Henry Rosso, founder of the Fund Raising School—is that development is a job with little authority and wide responsibility. You are ultimately responsible for one of the most needed elements in running your organization—money—but you may have little say in what the money should be raised for. You may find yourself defending a decision that you don't agree with to a funder or a donor. Budgets may be created without proper consideration of the fundraising elements required to meet them. You may be expected to raise money without spending any money. However, an organization that has integrated fundraising into its programs and has made the development director an integral part of the staff in terms of planning programs will avoid much of this problem.

The second challenge is that your job performance is usually measured by dollars raised, particularly in organizations unfamiliar with all that goes into creating an ongoing, successful fundraising program. The number of donors acquired, quality of materials, adequate records, thorough research—none of these are taken into account in evaluating your performance if the cash isn't present. If you are really doing your job, you will increasingly rely on your board of directors and other volunteers to actually raise the money from the community. This means that when they do a good job, they get the credit—as is appropriate—and you must smile graciously and be happy for them. If you are not genuinely happy for them, you are not cut out for this job.

A third challenge is that the time required to make a strategy pay off is not understood. Board members or the executive director will say, "We could get that money faster from a foundation" or "I don't think it is worth developing an online program; it takes so long for that to add up to anything." The development director is constantly educating the rest of the organization about the long-term nature of fundraising: even to get a grant from a foundation involves a process that takes six to eight months. Just as for a special event, there are a lot of costs in grantseeking: the staff time researching, writing, and negotiating with the foundation and the time and accounting to fulfill the grantor's reporting requirements. Just as the gross income from a special event will be higher than the net, so the total amount of the grant received is not the true amount you have available for the program. Acquiring individual donors is also a long-term undertaking. To receive $35 from a new donor will cost some money, and the $35 doesn't go that far. But if the person gives money year after year—for only the cost of the newsletter, thank-you note, and renewal notice—the return on investment is very high, even if the person stays at $35. If that $35 donor eventually gives $100, or $1,000, or possibly a capital gift, or even a planned gift, the return on investment could be very high.

Many development directors get tired of having to explain this basic principle over and over and are often in the position of fending off unrealistic and get-rich-quick ideas without discouraging the enthusiasm of the idea-maker. "How about a golf tournament? A Sting concert? Let's get on a talk show! Take out a full-page ad in the *New York Times!* Buy an airplane and visit all our donors!" If you get too much in the habit of talking people out of ideas, you may accidentally turn down a really good one. That's what happened with the Penny Change Can idea. After three other groups rejected the idea of putting spare-change cans on local bar counters, an AIDS organization took it up and collected $80,000 in spare change in three months. Finding a good idea in even the most seemingly hare-brained scheme is an important skill for keeping people involved and engaged in fundraising. Over time, as people understand fundraising better, the ideas proposed become more realistic and the time you have put in educating the rest of the staff and volunteers clearly pays off.

Some of this experience changes if you are the director or the only staff person. You have more authority, and you are given credit and support for more than just money raised. Of course, you also have more work.

The solution to these challenges is to accept them as part of the job. Every job has its trade-offs; these are yours. If you are truly successful in the most important part of your fundraising job, which is integrating fundraising into the work of the organization and developing a fundraising team from board members and volunteers, your burden will be shared and lightened. You will also see that these issues of authority and responsibility are ones that most people in nonprofits wrestle with, particularly if they want activists and community leaders to have some ownership over the goals of the organization. And things improve. As the whole organization becomes more familiar with fundraising and more comfortable with it, your position will be evaluated not just on money raised, but also on all the aspects that make a good fundraising program.

The Association of Fundraising Professionals, which is the trade association for professional fundraisers, estimates that people leave development jobs every eighteen months. They usually move on to another development job and then another and another. And even in times of very high unemployment, with people desperate for any kind of a job, development jobs often go unfilled for months, or the organization may wind up hiring someone who is not very experienced.

There are several reasons for the frequent turnover; here is one that's all too common. I often encounter development people who believe they could be happy in development if only they worked in a different kind of organization. Over the course of one three-day period I had three such conversations. First, a woman working in a peace group said she felt fundraising would be so much easier in a service group, such as an alcohol- and drug-addiction program. "You can tell donors how many people you helped, and what exactly happened to them. Peace work seems so vague compared to that." Not long after that, a man working in a counseling program for IV drug users told me, "I wish I worked in the arts. No one likes drug addicts or cares what happens to them. Everyone loves the arts—you work with beauty and passion and greatness all the time." A few days later, the development director of an art museum confided, "I am thinking of getting into social change fundraising, like peace work. Arts are so fluffy and unnecessary compared to these revolutionary struggles—you could really raise a lot of money for that kind of work."

I don't know if any of these three left their jobs based on their unfounded belief that another issue would be easier or more interesting to raise funds for, but I know many people do. Unless your boss is a controlling, moody, mean person, or the board is utterly incompetent, or the organization's programs don't work, you should try to stay in a fundraising job for at least three years. It takes a full year to understand the organization and how best to present it to donors, which strategies work best, and so on. It takes a year for the board and executive director to place full confidence in your ability and trust in your judgment. Just as fundraising strategies often take more than one year to hit their stride, so too do development directors. Many people leave a job just when it was about to get easier, and it was about to get easier because of all the work they had put in up to that point.

Some organizations are in fact more difficult to raise money for than others, depending on the issues the group addresses, the community response to an issue, and, most important, how systematically the organization has been raising money over its lifetime. Nonetheless, if you want to raise money for social change, however broadly you define that, changing the issues you work on within that universe is not going to make that much difference.

Many of us got into fundraising because we cared deeply about a cause and fundraising became the thing we did to help promote that cause. However, fundraising is a "behind the scenes" activity. If you love the arts, fundraising for an arts program will be rewarding, but not because you will be doing any art. If you believe in saving the wilderness, fundraising for the money to buy property for preservation or to pressure the government to save acreage will be satisfying, but you will almost never be out in the forest, unless you are showing a donor around. If you want to raise money for groups helping to rebuild countries destroyed by earthquakes, or fund freedom struggles, or help stop militarism, you will do that from your office, and when you leave your office, you will be visiting donors or funders in their homes or offices. Your front lines will not be the art, the wilderness, or the struggling country. Your front lines are the donors it takes to fund change.

However, there are ways to keep in touch with the issue that propelled you to the work. To remain passionate about the work and become familiar with it, I recommend that organizations give all the staff and board members a direct sense of the program. Crisis lines staffed by volunteers often require board members and staff to go through the training and take a shift. I have known of administrative staff (including the development director) at a small theatre who have walk-on parts in some of the plays or help build the sets whenever possible. I have known development directors to do substitute teaching, deliver meals to seniors, register people to vote, attend demonstrations, and testify at public hearings, all as part of their jobs. It is important that development directors know all aspects of the program, preferably through some personal experience, not only so they can represent the program well to donors, but also so they can best figure out how fundraising can be part of all the jobs in the organization.

Although people should try to stay at least three years in a job, I also recommend that they don't stay for much longer than ten years. You don't want to become an institution yourself. You need to move on to other organizations and shake yourself up. If you are in a job too long, the job begins to be molded around you and you become harder to replace.

Work Well with Your Executive Director

What will help you stay in your job for that long is working with other staff you like and respect, particularly the executive director. The development director usually reports directly to the executive director, and much of the work of visiting donors and funders will fall to the executive director. The fundraising work of the executive director is usually managed by the fundraiser, who is in the odd position of telling the executive director what he or she must do to ensure the success of fundraising while being supervised by that person. If the executive director is uncomfortable asking for money or does not understand the long-term nature of fundraising, your job will vary from difficult to miserable.

Here are some ways you can develop a productive working relationship with your executive director. Establish regular meeting times early on, and learn what your executive director's working style is. Does she like a written outline of what she is to do, or does she prefer to talk a plan through? Is he a hands-off manager who prefers that you create your work and come to him only when you have questions or concerns, or is he someone who likes to see every letter before it goes out and know what you are doing every day? There is a wide range of healthy work styles; your style needs to mesh with the director's.

The most important element for good working relationships is trust. Does the director trust that you do your best, that you thoroughly evaluate strategies before undertaking them, and that you are good with other people? If he trusts you and you make a mistake, it will be just a mistake, and you and he will go on and not make that mistake again. If the director does not trust you, the mistake will become an open sore and will decrease your willingness to take risks. If you trust the director, then when she isn't able to finish the work she agreed to do, you will know that something more pressing came up and both of you will regroup. If you don't trust her, you may interpret lapses on her part as disrespect or incompetence. Mutual trust allows for honesty and even confrontation when necessary.

The success of any fundraising effort is contingent on having reliable, dedicated volunteers. Understanding why people volunteer, what the pressures are on volunteers, and how to make volunteer efforts satisfactory is imperative for fundraising professionals. There is no better way to keep the situation of the volunteer in mind than to be one yourself. The experience you gain will later help remind you, for example, that it is not always possible to do all you said you would do; that it is easy to feel left out of the loop of an important decision; that anxiety can overcome you as you set out to ask someone for money.

Volunteering, especially serving on a board, is also an excellent way to get perspective, to learn about other issues, and to express other parts of yourself. It makes the time you put into your own job more effective, allows you to network with others in your community, and is the right thing to do.

Don't Make Work Too Important

Studies of work habits show that people who consistently work more than sixty hours a week often become irritable and defensive, lower their immune systems, sleep badly, and cease to be as productive as they once were. As I have said earlier in this book, from an organizational point of view, a job that takes sixty hours every week to accomplish is a job that requires another half-time staff person. People who constantly overwork disguise the cost of doing business and make themselves impossible to replace. Although we have often interpreted the comment, "It took two people to replace her" as a compliment to the person who left, we actually need to see it as a result of bad planning and bad work habits that drove the person to leave.

Development has a never-ending quality about it. Few organizations (none that I've ever met with) think they have enough money. Money is spent as fast as it is raised, and you always feel you could have raised more if you had only done this or that task longer or better. But you have to set boundaries on your work. Time is your best boundary. Each day, decide when your day will end. Take weekends off, and when you have to work weekends, take a weekday off. Make sure the organizational goals are clear and that they can be accomplished in the time allowed. Letting the time you spend on your job stretch somewhat is appropriate, but remember, being a rubber band is not in your job description.

Staying in Fundraising for the Long Haul

As you can see, if you take the initiative, you can make development an interesting job year after year. Find a group where initiative is encouraged and where the organizational culture is collaborative and supportive. Volunteer for other organizations to remind yourself that there are often many ways to raise money. Take time away from work to remind yourself that although work is important, it is not everything. Above all, remember why you do this work, and be mission driven yourself.

Chapter Eight

Analysis and Evaluation

With the fundamentals of the previous chapters in place, you are now ready to examine what is working and what is not in your fundraising program. This will enable you to see what permanent changes you need to make in your fundraising to face the future more confidently. The analysis can be done all at once or piecemeal as time allows. Of course, you will need to set priorities for the changes you need to make. (Be sure to take the quiz at the end of Chapter Ten for help in setting priorities.) You can't make all the changes that need to be made all at once, and it is possible that you can't make some of them for quite a while. You may also become aware of other changes in your organization unrelated to fundraising that must be made before more dramatic changes in your fundraising can occur. However, if you do not make these changes, even over a period of time, you will sink into a crisis. A roller coaster economy affecting almost all parts of the income streams for an enormous nonprofit sector means that thousands of nonprofits may go out of business in the next five years. If you don't want to be one of them, you will need to figure out what changes you need to make, make them, and make sure they stick. This is the nonprofit version of what they say in the health world: you don't need to go on a diet so much as you need to change your relationship to food.

Look at your fundraising overall. Not only do you need a diverse set of income streams, but you also need to evaluate whether your sources of funding will be able to sustain your organization for years to come. This requires a broad base of individual donors, or a very hardy income-generation program, or both. No matter what happens in the economy, foundations are not going to be an ongoing source of revenue except for a handful of organizations. As our government ceases to be run by a handful of antitax, pro-war multimillionaires, government funding will eventually become an important and stable part of some organizations' budgets. In the meantime, public funding is not reliable and may require too many compromises in mission even when it is available.

Your goal is to expand those sources of funding that are expandable and reliable. The following are some of the things you need to look at.

Rates of Response

All too often, a development director reports that a mail appeal made X amount or a phone-a-thon netted Y dollars. They are surprised to learn that these numbers by themselves are almost meaningless. What is meaningful is to measure what percentage of response you got compared to what you might have expected. For example, a mail appeal sent to a list of good prospects who have not given before should yield a 1-percent response. Supposing you send an appeal that yields a much smaller response, perhaps 0.5 percent. But in that tiny number of people, a staff person's grandmother who was on the list wanted to be supportive of her grandson, so she sent $5,000. Your appeal was a major flop, although you do have a generous new donor. Focusing on the fact that the appeal raised $5,000 will lead you to send the same appeal package again, which is a mistake.

Start by knowing what we have learned most organizations can reasonably expect from any particular fundraising strategy, and then see how your organization compares to the "norm." With this information, you can decide how to get more money, visibility, donors, long-term gifts, or whatever from the strategies you are using.

Acquisition: Response to First Mail Appeal

To a list of people who are chosen because they are known to have given money to a cause like yours, with no personalization and sent by bulk mail, you can expect a response rate of 1 percent.

If you send the mailing first class, you can often improve your rate—to about 2 percent or 3 percent—possibly enough to cover the cost difference between first class and bulk.

If you personalize the letters, especially by adding a personal note—which is what you want to do with names given to you by board members or other volunteers—you can move your rate of response to 5 percent and sometimes more.

Requesting an Extra Gift in the Same Year the First Gift Was Made

From people who have given to you once, you can expect a 10-percent response to a request for an extra gift in the same year. In a crisis that is clearly not the fault of your organization or one in which your organization is David to the adversary's Goliath, you can get that rate up to 15 percent. For example, organizations that work with political prisoners or have been accused of being unpatriotic or that are in big fights with corporations over environmental or health issues will often elicit a lot of sympathy from their donors.

Conversion Rate

This is a very important concept, particularly for organizations greatly expanding their donor base. In mail parlance, *conversion rate* is the percentage of first-time donors who gave a second gift. Many organizations have been able to do well in recruiting new donors but are not able to keep them. A healthy conversion rate is around 40 percent. In other words, if you have a thousand donors and two hundred of them have given for the first time, you will expect eighty (40 percent) of those givers to give a second time.

If your conversion rate is lower than that, make sure that your systems for thanking people promptly are in place, your thank-you notes are personalized, you have spelled all donors' name correctly, and you have sent a newsletter, annual report, or some other kind of correspondence between requests for money.

Retention Rate

For donors who give two years in a row, your retention rate for the third year should be about 70 to 80 percent. Among those who are major donors, the retention rate should be at least 80 percent, giving you an overall retention rate of about 66 percent. In other words, if you have 1,500 donors, you will need to replace one-third of them—or get 500 new donors every year. If you have a higher retention rate, it may be that you are doing an excellent job or it may be that your donor list is too small. However, with more personalization, including phone follow-up on renewal efforts, you can bring your retention rate up to 70 percent or so.

One factor that can temporarily depress your retention rate is the people we call "crisis donors." Fires, floods, famine, and the like attract a cross section of big-hearted people who want to help but are not going to make an ongoing commitment. If your crisis is something very dramatic and well publicized, you will see an influx of these donors. They are a wonderful boost to cash flow, but you need to monitor them so that you do not spend their entire donation trying to get them to give again. How do you know who they are? Obviously you don't know all of them, but if you have a dramatic event that attracts these donors, create a field in your database for unsolicited gifts. Donations that do not come in through a mail appeal (they do not arrive in a return envelope you sent) or donations that come in with a note, "Mary Smith told me about your fire/theft/police raid; here's something to help out" should be noted as such. These people are entered into the database, and they get a newsletter and whatever other mailings anyone else would get during the year, but when it comes to renewal mailings, they will get a special one referring to their help with the crisis and asking them to become an ongoing supporter. If they do not respond to this letter, remove them from getting regular mailings. You can keep their names and write to them from to time when you have a dramatic need (which does not have to be a crisis), but it is not worth spending money on keeping them up to date with your ongoing work. The same holds true for people who give you memorial gifts. They are memorializing someone for whom your organization was important, but your organization may not be important to them.

Fulfillment Cost

Fulfillment cost is what it costs you to keep a donor. Costs include staff or volunteer time to enter the donor's name onto your database, the cost of sending a newsletter (paper, printing, postage, staff time), and the cost of renewal mailings. These costs should be between $3 and $10 per donor per year. Many organizations have hundreds and sometimes even thousands of people on their mailing lists who are not current donors (they have not made a gift in the last sixteen months) or may never have given at all. Because the cost per person of keeping these people on their rolls is minimal—or, more likely, the organization has never figured out the cost—most organizations do not pay attention to the cost of carrying these people. They see this as a form of outreach.

One sometimes hears stories of a person who gave $35 five years ago and never donated again, but kept on getting the newsletter, then died and left the group $10,000. I am sure this does happen, but keeping hundreds or thousands of people on your list for years and years in the hope this will happen is not a fundraising strategy. In fact, even if that did happen, the entire value of a bequest could easily have been used up by the cost of keeping all these people on your list for years. One organization had four thousand people on their mailing list, with only nine hundred of them current donors. They figured out their fulfillment cost at $3 per person per year, meaning they were spending $9,300 a year ($3 x 3,100) on people who were not giving money. That money could be freed up and actually used for real outreach. Every year, you need to go through every name and know why these people are on the list.

Cleaning Up Your Mailing List

Here are the people who can stay on your mailing list:

- Donors who have given any amount at least once in the past sixteen months.
- Donors who have ever given more than $1,000 at one time. (If they have never given again, they should be approached personally to find out what is going on.)
- Volunteers who give time but not money.
- Current and immediate past funders.
- People who have requested to be on the list, but who cannot pay. This request needs to be made every year.

- Vendors, if they request it.
- Politicians who have been very helpful to your organization or with whom you work on some of your projects.
- People who used to give regularly (in any amount) but have now stopped. They need to be approached personally also.

Who does not need to stay on the list and why:

- Former board members and staff who do not contribute time or money, unless they specifically request to be on the list. People may have had a great time being on your board ten years ago, but they have gone on. Their interests have changed. If they show no desire to be on the list, take them off. If you want to make sure they don't want to be on the list, call them. The same goes for staff. Many people work for five, ten, even fifteen or more organizations in their lifetime. They may have loved them all, but they are not people who want to get your newsletter.
- Funders who have not given you money in three or more years. Funders get a lot of mail; most of it goes unread. Newsletters and annual reports are often dutifully placed in the library or in a file, but funders hardly have time to keep up with the groups they are currently funding or thinking of funding, let alone all the organizations they used to fund.
- People who you think "should" give and will do so if you just send them enough stuff.
- People who no one knows, and no one remembers why they are on the list.

Cleaning Up Your E-List

An e-list does not have to be kept as clean as a snail mail list because it doesn't cost any more to send to a thousand people than it does to send to a hundred. But you still want to keep this list clean by handling unsubscribe requests promptly (preferably by setting up your e-list so that people can unsubscribe themselves), and by adding new people regularly. Once a year, you should ask people to confirm whether they want to stay on your e-mail list, so you are not inadvertently sending spam. Pay attention to your open rates and your click-through rates so you know how many people are actually reading your e-mail, which is far more important than how many people are on the list. Finally, make sure it is obvious how to unsubscribe, and honor that wish immediately.

How Many Donors Could You Really Have?

In the corporate world, the answer to this question is called *market penetration*. How many customers are there for your new widget? Who else is trying to sell a similar widget? Nonprofits for social justice particularly need to look at this issue if their work is controversial or geographically specific, or if they work in rural communities. Once in a while, I find an organization that probably has attracted all the donors it can and now needs to focus on upgrading donors or even moving into earned income strategies to continue to expand their organization's income. The vast majority of nonprofits, however, are not in that position. You can hire people to help you figure out your market penetration, or you can make an educated guess. Here's how to do the latter:

In the United States, on average, seven out of ten adults, or 70 percent, give away money. Some states have done surveys of giving and discovered that their state varies from that. For example, in Hawaii, 90 percent of adults give away money, whereas in Colorado and Alaska, only 60 percent do. Your local community foundation or Association of Nonprofits may know what percentage of people give in your state or even your county. If you can't find out, go with 70 percent and assume that seven out of ten adults in your giving area is the maximum number of donors that are available. From this seven, subtract two whose giving is fixed. They have a certain set of charities they give to, and they are unlikely to add or subtract any. Subtract one more who is a crisis donor—who may give you money once but will not be an ongoing donor. Subtract one more who gives only to very well-established, mainstream organizations and is distrustful or completely unaware of smaller or more grassroots groups. You are now down to three out of seven as possibilities for your group. Now think about how well known your organization is in your community. How old is it? How many people does it reach in a year? If we were to stop people in the street near your office, how likely is it that they would have heard of your organization?

How many other organizations do work like yours? How controversial is your organization? In answering these questions, be realistic, but also think about how your situation might work in your favor. Being controversial will attract donors as well as repel them.

If there are a lot of organizations like yours in your community, this can also work to your advantage. In towns with a large number of arts organizations or environmental groups, these nonprofits often find that they can raise more money than if there were just one or two of these kinds of groups. Awareness of their issue is greater, and sometimes a community's reputation as an "arts community" or a "green community" is built from the presence of these nonprofits. Taking all these factors into account will give you a rough sense of what your maximum donor base is, and you can compare it with the one you have now and see how much room there is for growth.

Exhibit 8.1 provides two examples.

Exhibit 8.1: Figuring Maximum Donor Base

Small-Town Montessori School

A twenty-year-old Montessori school in a rural community of five thousand full-time residents has two hundred donors. Because their fundraising has been limited to parents, grandparents, and friends of students and board members, they have a fairly high attrition rate, as parents of graduating kids stop giving. A handful of former students are now donors, but they are young, and it will be a while before there is a critical mass of alumnae to raise money from. In figuring out the maximum number of donors they hope to have, the school calculates that out of 3,000 adults in their area, 2,100 (70 percent) are donors to any group, and 40 percent are already not available to them; this leaves them with a maximum of 900 potential donors.

They are well known in the community and well respected, but they are in friendly competition with the public elementary school and high school, which have recently had to slash their art and music programs and have embarked on their own fundraising programs. In looking at their situation, the Montessori school fundraisers realize they already have 10 percent of the donors in the community and, given their niche appeal, it seems unlikely they can gain more. Moreover, a

➤

demographic shift is occurring as families move away to places where they can get jobs, so enrollment is down.

They need to create another income stream besides donors. This information keeps the Montessori fundraisers from putting a lot of effort into widening their donor base. Instead, they focus on upgrading existing donors and on creative uses of the school. The town does not have a community center, and the Montessori school has a fairly large cafeteria/gymnasium/library with moveable walls, lots of tables and chairs, and a nice playground and grassy area. They decide to make this space available as a community center in evenings and weekends for a rental fee, and on Sunday mornings they rent the space to a church that had been meeting in a private home. They are continuing to explore joint use of space as an income stream and community service.

Alliance Against Poisoned Rivers

Alliance Against Poisoned Rivers (AAPR) is organizing in communities downstream from a paper mill that has been polluting their water for many years. The mill is a major employer, and efforts to get the mill to use cleaner practices have always led to the mill's threatening to move overseas. Most residents get their water from wells and have thought they were safe from the toxins in the stream. However, water tests show that some toxins are now leaching into the well water. A foul smell from the stream wafts over the community nearest the mill, and fish and wildlife have been diminishing.

AAPR has four hundred people on their mailing list, many of whom are donors, about a hundred of whom are from out of state. Their records are not very accurate, as they have been primarily supported by foundations and have done very little individual donor fundraising. One of their main funders, a family foundation, has given away all its dwindling assets and gone out of business. Some funders have notified the organization that they will no longer be funding them because their funding priorities have changed or because they have had to cut back on the number of grants they are making. The board—made up of activists and scientists —is not interested in fundraising. The organization is convinced that they are too controversial to be able to raise money from a broad base of individuals. However, a cursory analysis shows that they have never approached people in the many communities up- and downstream from this mill.

There are about thirty thousand adults in four communities downstream from the mill who can smell the effects of the mill. There are two very environmentally conscious communities with about five thousand adults upstream from the mill. A member of the family that had the family foundation has a background in marketing and offers to bankroll a mass mailing to these communities. He thinks the group should be able to build a donor base of five thousand over a couple of years, which would be about 12 percent of the adult population—far fewer, in his reasoning, than those who are adversely affected by the mill.

Using a reverse directory (a list of people by address rather than name), AAPR is able to get the name and address of every household in the six communities. They tailor each letter and envelope to each specific community, even putting a small map on the front of the letter showing where the town is in relation to the mill. The results show that this organization has seriously underestimated its support. Their mailing receives a 2 percent response, remarkable because it was sent to all households—30 percent of which, we know, do not donate to anything. With seven hundred new donors, the organization realizes that they have far more support than they have ever mobilized.

This organization is saved from a serious financial problem not so much because of the money raised, although that is certainly helpful, but because they developed a clear sense of their potential. They have among their current donors people with skills and talents to help them, of which their former funder is one. He also helped them focus on raising money, rather than cutting the program, as the board might have been inclined to do. AAPR has a way to go to thoroughly strengthen its fundraising program, but the momentum and improved morale they generated will carry them through.

Time In for Money Out

Another aspect of fundraising analysis is to look at how much time it takes to produce how much money, and whether the time could be better spent on another strategy that would bring more money in, or whether you are getting enough collateral value (publicity, new donors, visibility) to make the time worth it. In instances involving a longer-term strategy, such as planned giving, you wouldn't expect a lot of money just yet.

Your Fundraising Team

Anyone in fundraising knows that follow-up is key. A board member says he will call five people, but he won't unless someone reminds him—and probably reminds him more than once. But at what point do the reminders become less than cost-effective? This analysis is very important. If it takes a staff person two hours in phone calls and e-mails to a board member who actually makes five calls that take her two hours and bring in two gifts of $1,000, it has taken four hours to earn $2,000—put another way, the group has earned $500 an hour. This is clearly worth it. If the two donors give $100 each, then the group has earned $50 an hour, which may or may not be worth it, depending on the opportunity cost. However, if a staff person has to spend only thirty minutes in follow-up and the board member spends one hour calling for two gifts of $100, then we are averaging $133 an hour. If, after two hours of reminder calls and e-mails, the board member never does anything and the staff person winds up doing it herself, it almost doesn't matter what the donors give because we have undermined the whole idea of being a team.

Without driving yourself crazy, try to keep track of the time it takes to accomplish fundraising tasks. At the end of any campaign, look at the time in for what you got out of it. See whether there are ways you could use less time next time—often, just knowing *what* to do saves time. What do you wish you had known ahead of time? Make sure you tell the next campaign chair that information. And do your best not to work with volunteers who waste your time.

Foundations

A recent study showed that an organization spends, on average, a hundred hours on every grant proposal—this time includes identifying the appropriate foundation, contacting them, writing the proposal, perhaps hosting a site visit or other meeting with foundation personnel, and writing the required reports. Even with low salaries, this is an investment of $2,000 to $3,000. In good economic times, this investment of time has to be amortized over the life of your relationship with the funder, who, with much less effort, often makes a grant three or four years in a row. However, when the market is down, foundation giving is also down. Getting new foundation support is very hard, and even getting repeat grants is not at all assured. Thus, there is little point in applying for a grant of less than $5,000, because you could direct the same investment toward a special event, a mail appeal, or a major gifts campaign that would bring in as much money—or more—year after year.

Meetings

Many people in nonprofits love to meet, especially if that means delaying actually doing the fundraising. People complain about the number of meetings they attend and the time meetings take, but a meeting is often the de facto "next step" for any project, and nothing can proceed without a meeting. A meeting is a place to process feelings and vent frustration. Meetings can be comforting and even fun. At the end of a meeting, you feel like you have done work, whether you have or not. Certainly meetings are a critical feature of getting work organized, but be sure you use them for that; don't get into the habit of having a meeting just for the sake of it or because the group is procrastinating in doing its fundraising. Every meeting should have a purpose, an agenda, minutes, and a brief evaluation. If you track the person power that goes into meetings, you will be sure to use them wisely. Twelve people in a three-hour meeting have just spent the equivalent of a week of work (thirty-six hours)—ask yourself if that time (which you will never see again) has significantly helped your organization raise money.

We have to use our time wisely; to do that requires paying attention to how we use it and how we could use it better.

Summary

Paying close attention to what is working and how to make it work better; what isn't working and how to fix it or whether to let it go; who is working and how to help them work better and feel good about their work—these actions are all part of analyzing your fundraising to make positive and lasting changes. It takes time to do all that I am suggesting, but it takes far more time *not* to do it.

Chapter Nine

Developing a Donor Base

There are two reasons organizations decide to develop or expand a donor base: (1) they can't get foundation funding any more (because foundation funding has become more scarce in this economy) or (2) they understand that having a broad base of donors is the most reliable way to sustain their organization over time. Loyal donors are, of course, the lifeblood of successful stable social change nonprofits: whatever you can do to increase both the number and the loyalty of these people is critical.

However, if your sole reason for developing a donor base is that you can't get foundation funding or some other kind of funding any more, you won't be very successful. If you think that when the economy recovers and foundation funding goes up again (as it will eventually), you will get back on the foundation wagon and make grants your main source of income, then you might as well scale back and wait for that day. Some day there will be a lot of foundation funding again, and then some other day, there won't be. That is the nature of foundation funding. It is designed to help start things, to experiment with new ways of doing things, to help expand things, but it is not designed for—and never will be good for—providing the ongoing costs of doing business.

A broad base of individual donors, on the other hand, is not only the one source from which you can continue to raise money now but also a test of community support; a source of ideas, volunteers, and bigger and bigger donations; and a pool of ambassadors educating the public, in the form of their friends and colleagues, about the issues your organization addresses. A broad base of donors has intrinsic value and is something to pursue, whatever the economy or the government is doing.

Building a Donor Base

To build a donor base for the long haul requires looking for people who believe in the work of your organization. In the beginning it is fine to ask friends, relatives, neighbors who may or may not care a lot about your cause, but who like you and want to support you. This is how most organizations get started. But that set of people quickly falls away, leaving behind those who are truly interested in your work. These are the people you will go to as you begin building your donor base.

One of the not-so-secret facts about fundraising (and possibly life itself) is that people know people like themselves. If a person loves public radio and can give $100 to the local station, he or she will know ten other people who love public radio and can also give $100. That person will also know two or three people who could give $250. What you have to do with all the people who give you any amount is ask them who else they know who can help you. Some people will help you in this way and some won't. Sometimes you will ask for more contacts right away; other times, you will wait until you know the person better. You will also have to find out how the contacts of your donors like to be contacted themselves.

The following exercise will help you find those donors who will lead to other donors.

Make three lists of people as follows:

1. *Who cares deeply about your organization and would be very upset if you had to close?* List twenty people by name and note what types of people they are. Donors? Clients? Volunteers? Parents? Union members? Lawyers? Teachers? Clergy? Every organization will have a slightly different list. Don't censor a name because you think the person has no money to give. We will cross that bridge later.
2. *Who cares about your organization, but not as much, perhaps, as those on the first list?* Again, come up with twenty names and note what type of people they are.
3. *Finally, who supports your organization in a more casual way?* List those people.

Some people in the first category may have already contributed, if not money, then time, advice, stuff. Those who have helped financially should be asked if they know other people who have never given who would be interested. In many organizations, people in this first category do not have much money, but they do have friends and colleagues. If they generate ten or twenty names each and two or three of those contacts do the same, you could be recruiting a dozen or more donors each week.

For example, in one organization, ten of the twenty people on their #1 list each gave ten names of people they thought could give $25, $50, $100 or more. The organization generated personalized e-mails to them—personalized meaning the e-mail began "Dear Mr. Jones" as opposed to "Dear Friend" and started off with a sentence such as, "Your friend, Mary Smith, gave me your name ..." or the subject line read: "Mary Smith suggested I write." In the first week, a hundred e-mails went out directing people to the website and the "Donate now!" option, and ten gifts came in. Each of those ten donors was contacted and thanked by the person who had given the potential donor's name in the first place. They were also asked if they could think of other people who would give. Four of the ten gave a total of fifty names among them. Letters or e-mails went out and ten more gifts came in. In the meantime, one of the original twenty people, excited by the response she was generating, asked more friends for more names and brought in another hundred names.

In the first few weeks, the organization sent two hundred e-mails and three hundred first-class letters with personal notes and brought in sixty new donors. One person who gave $2,500 was contacted and agreed to host a small party at her house, which raised another $5,000 from five other people. Over the course of two years of systematic (and, to be sure, somewhat tedious) work, the organization has built a base of donors from twenty people to one thousand, with an accompanying healthy income stream. Every donor was asked for more names, and any of those people who gave were asked for more names. By personalizing all their mail and e-mail, they receive a very high rate of response and a good-sized median gift. They were able to find a hundred people who were able to give $500 or more, including the person who gave $2,500. It took a lot of work on the part of four volunteers and the backup support of a staff person. However, if they keep up their personalized fundraising, they should be able to raise more money with less time each year.

When I tell stories like this, I always hear, "Well, good for that group, but no one in our organization knows anyone who could give $2,500." Perhaps, but you don't know who everyone in your group knows. People are often surprised themselves at who they know when they really put their minds to it. The issue is to keep at it and not get discouraged by the people who choose not to either give money themselves or provide other names.

What you will often notice is that the people on the #1 list start pulling in people from the #2 list. However, the people on the #2 list should be asked to open doors for you to larger groups of people. Their support for your organization often comes because they support any organization working on the issue you are working on, or because they have a general belief in your work. They are usually not personally affected by what you do, and they are generally not personally involved. This means they move in other circles and so can help your fundraising branch out. Perhaps they can get you invited to their Rotary Club or give you access to their union members. They may be willing to bring your organization to their house of worship for a second collection or for a donation from the "domestic missions budget" or something similar.

In either list, some people will be able to lead you to other people, one person at a time, and some will be able to get your organization in front of a group of people—a house party, a service club, a bar association, a conference. You need to take advantage of any opportunity because you don't know where it will lead.

The third list is very interesting. It includes people like landlords, computer salespeople, restaurant owners, conference center managers—people who have received income from you. It may include researchers, journalists, politicians—people who have received useful information, political support, pithy quotes, or great stories from your organization's work. If yours is a direct-service organization such as a rehabilitation program, it may include employers of your clients. People on this list may help you with a donation and should be offered that opportunity, but they can also help you raise money from other institutions—small businesses, corporations, professional associations. They may also help you figure out an earned income strategy.

For example, an organization providing a range of services for homeless people has one program that helps formerly homeless people learn how to interview for a job by helping with resume preparation and teaching interviewing skills. In coalition with another organization, they provide clothing for a job interview and, for those who get the job, two weeks' worth of clothing to wear to work. Several corporations often call this organization when they need to hire people, as they have found reliable workers through this program. But recently this organization has lost half of its city funding.

A corporate executive on list #3 suggests that the group offer résumé writing and interviewing skills for a small fee to anyone who needs them. She offers a meeting room in her office building to hold the class. With unemployment skyrocketing, the organization finds it is not hard to fill the classes. People pay on a sliding scale from $10 to $250. Those who get jobs often make an additional donation. The organization has expanded its repertoire to new college graduates and has now been asked to teach this course as part of the Adult School curriculum. The classes themselves bring in a small but steady income stream; more important, the graduates now form the basis of the group's donors. The group has expanded their donor base from one hundred people giving a total of $1500 to three hundred people giving a total of $15,000 in just one year. Classes in the first year bring in additional funding. Although this income will not fully replace their city funding, the group has developed a strategy that is relatively easy to put in place.

Sometimes people in this third category help you raise money by helping you save money. Groups have worked with landlords who, fearful of being unable to rent out their space in a down market, have lowered rental fees. A service club donated the proceeds from their annual pancake breakfast, and a specialist in marketing became a volunteer webmaster for a year. He spiffed up the group's site and continues to change it so it is fun to visit, and he has registered the organization with a wide range of search engines and gotten them set up to take credit card donations on the Web. The group is beginning to see the fruits of that effort, with their web income doubling every quarter. Catching the spirit, two volunteers started a bimonthly e-newsletter, which drives more traffic to the website.

As you can see, building up a base of donors from scratch is a slog. However, not having money is a drag, so choose: slog or drag? I hope you will choose slog, because individual donor fundraising gets easier and it grows geometrically. It is stable and secure, and after you get the hang of it, it is fun. Honest.

Expanding Your Donor Base: Ability, Belief, Contact

We appreciate all gifts and all motives for giving. But our best chance of getting a donation year in and year out is by building a relationship with the donor—a relationship that transcends any of the people currently working for the group and that continues through any number of changes the group may undergo.

Let me explain further.

People who are new to fundraising tend to focus on finding donors who "have money." They will say, "I don't know anyone who has money," or "My brother-in-law has money, so I should ask him." Their sole criterion for identifying prospective donors is how much money they are reputed to have. As soon as people learn that what a person has and what they will give are almost unrelated, they move to the next level of learning. People are fascinated by the studies that show that Mississippi has the highest per-capita giving of any state, or that people with incomes under $10,000 give away a higher percent of their income than people with incomes of $100,000 or more. They are generally most fascinated by the fact that when people are asked to remember the last donation they made, and why they made it, 80 percent of them will say, "Someone asked me," but only 50 percent of that group can remember what organization did the asking. They see clearly the vital importance of personal connection in fundraising. People do give to causes, but they are more likely to make significant gifts to causes that involve people they know. At this stage of learning, people are likely to ask all their friends for money, and they are likely to have success. Through house parties, personal letters, and phone calls, a team of people will build a donor base. If an organization stays at this learning level, they are going to have a lot of donors whose loyalty is not to the organization but to a person in the organization. When that person leaves, these donors may leave also.

Look for Very Clear Evidence of Belief in the Cause

People will often say, "But my friends do believe in the cause—that is partly why we are friends. We have values in common." Certainly that is true. But we have to look more closely at our friends, because all of us care about far more things than we can give money to. We all know organizations that we hope someone will support. We believe in them, we think our community is a better place because of them, but we are not going to give our money to them, because our charitable dollars are directed elsewhere. Most people who give to nonprofits give to between five and fifteen organizations. Some people support as many as thirty to forty organizations. But almost no one cares about much more than forty issues. So we are looking for donors who will place our organization and our cause on the list of those they give money to, regardless of who is involved, as long as they have confidence in the good work of the organization. We focus our upgrading and intensive renewal energy on those folks. Some people are loyal enough to our cause, but they really love an annual event that we put on. We focus on getting them to keep coming to the event and on adding income streams to the event, rather than appealing to them several times a year by mail when all they ever give to is the event. Let's look at an example.

Mary is involved in Feral Cat Rescue. This is an all-volunteer organization: it spays or neuters and vaccinates feral cats in the community where Mary lives, and it tries to tame feral kittens and place them in homes. Mary spends most of her evenings and weekends working for this group, as does a core group of ten other volunteers. Although they don't have staff, the group needs money for cages and educational materials, and to reimburse veterinarians for medicines, spaying, and other expenses. Their dream is to get a mobile van where they could both treat cats and display those ready for adoption at shopping malls.

To develop into the organization they envision, they need to raise about $50,000 per year. On top of that, the van will be a major capital expense of $30,000 plus upkeep. Mary and her friends have built an impressive donor list by asking all their friends and friends' friends for money. But they notice that the donors tend to keep giving at the $25 and $35 level, and no amount of asking seems to move them up. Feral Cat Rescue also has a lower rate of donor retention than is healthy—about 55 percent. (A healthy rate is 66 percent.)

A handful of donors give more, and two or three give large gifts of $2,500 and $5,000, which is how the group can do as much as it does. Mary approaches me for help in upgrading her donors, and we quickly realize the problem. Mary has a lot of donors who like her and admire her, and who probably like cats, but who are not really that loyal to this cause. I ask her and her volunteers whether they know the favorite causes of the donors to Feral Cat Rescue. The answers are illuminating: "Middle East peace," "the local repertory theater," "music programs in the schools," "civil liberties." Very few of their donors even give significantly to environmental causes, and none of them seem to give to other animal rescue or animal rights organizations.

A lot of the regular small donors come to their annual event, "Cattin' Around," a progressive dinner and dance where people have the option to dress as cats and go from a bar for drinks to two restaurants for main courses and dessert and then to another bar for more drinks and dancing. The bars and restaurants are all in the same two-block area, and the event, which takes place in the summer, is fun and attracts a cross section of the town. With tickets at $35 each, the event nets about $10,000.

I suggest they think about their donors as falling into three categories:

1. Those who are primarily loyal to the event
2. Those who will always give something, but will not increase their giving
3. Those who might make Feral Cat Rescue one of their top giving priorities

I suggest they then create a committee of people from their most loyal and committed donors whose job it will be to recruit more of the same.

Mary and her friends cast a wide net and haul in everybody they can. Now it is time to take that broad base and work with a small cross section of people who might give more.

They identify from their donor list twenty people who have given $250 or more each year for three years, and they send them the letter in Exhibit 9.1.

By promising it will be both fun and a one-time-only thing, they get seven people to come to the meeting. All agree that Feral Cat Rescue is not that well known and that expanding the donor base is a good idea. One person says that she thinks most people have no idea how much the organization costs to run

---

Exhibit 9.1: Invitation to a Fundraising Brainstorming Meeting

Dear (name of donor),

You have helped Feral Cat Rescue for the past several years. We are so grateful, and even though cats don't show gratitude, in their own way our rescued feline friends are grateful too.

Today I am writing to ask you not for money, but for a different kind of help. You are one of our most loyal donors, and we need more people like you. As you know from our newsletter, we want to buy a mobile van to be able to treat cats and show the cats that are available for adoption. To do this, we need to ramp up our fundraising.

Would you do me a great favor and come to a focus group to help us brainstorm the best ways for us to raise money? We need the help of our community in thinking through various ideas we have and coming up with more ideas. I promise the following:

- There will be good food.
- The meeting will last only two hours.
- We will have pictures of our latest rescues on the wall.
- We will have fun.
- We will not ask you for money at this meeting, and there is no obligation to come to future meetings.

Your presence will make a big difference. I'll call you in a few days to answer questions and see if you can come.

Best wishes,
Mary Catlady

because it is known as an all-volunteer group. Another says she has always wanted to be involved but not with the rescue part of the work.

In the end, five people pledge to help with coming up with names of prospects and with other work. After six months, one of them has gotten the mailing list of subscribers to cat magazines in their area and is sending a letter to those people; another has put together a list of people who have adopted their cat from Feral Cat Rescue but are not on the donor list, and she is calling them; the other three are approaching their own friends, with the caveat of looking for people who really care about this issue.

The people who mostly give out of loyalty and respect for Mary or her friends are still asked, but now they are asked only once a year, and there is no attempt to upgrade them. They are now renewing at a higher rate than they have in the past. "Cattin' Around" became a bigger event because the advertising focused on the quality of the food and the fun of the dancing rather than the cause, so it attracted more people. They also raised the ticket price to $40.

By being more systematic with their donors and more clear about who was loyal to what about the organization, Feral Cat Rescue has been able to raise more money and focus their upgrading efforts more on people who care about feral cats—and not so much on people who care about Mary and her friends.

Identify Why People Give and Find More People with Those Beliefs

To get further clarity about who your supporters are—and therefore where you might find other, similar supporters—it is helpful to make a list of types of people who support your group and reasons they might be giving. Think about the different motives people have for giving, then see where your group fits. Some people will give because they share your philosophy. They think your approach to the issue is the correct one. Others will give because they have been personally touched or know someone who has. Others will give because they are community minded and think that your group or service is a good addition to the community.

People can fit into all these categories and many more. But, going back to Feral Cat Rescue, George and Monica give because they love the fat tabby they got from the rescue. They do not have strong opinions about spay and neuter clinics. In fact, they are mostly involved in the arts. Esmeralda gives although she has no cats. She cares about birds, particularly those that nest on the ground, and she wants to protect them from feral cats. She wishes the cats would all find loving homes, but mostly she wants to keep them from breeding. Harry and Carl have just retired to this community. They have always supported animal groups wherever they live, and they give money to national animal rights organizations. They have two dogs and are actually not cat people. Amina is a veterinarian and gives both time and money to the group.

Insofar as these people represent a cross section of people like them, they should be treated differently. Harry and Carl, who don't have cats, may well be better major donor prospects than George and Monica, who do, because Harry and Carl care about this cause. Esmeralda will be a good person to lead the group to other people who care about the specific project of the spay/neuter program.

Staying in Touch with Donors

Asking for money cannot be the only way you are in touch with donors. You need to make sure you are telling the donors what you do and helping them be ambassadors of your work with their own friends. There a several ways to stay in touch with donors.

The Newsletter, or Just a Newsy Letter

One way your organization stays in touch with donors should be through a newsletter. So often, a newsletter is slapped together with little thought about who is reading it and what they will think about it.

The newsletter should be a priority. It is a public statement of who you are, what you do, and why people should help. It needs to have a balance of articles that inform (as opposed to overwhelm), articles that touch the heart, and articles that make the donor pleased with the organization and happy to be a giver. More and more it seems that donors don't care so much about having their names listed in the newsletter; instead, they want to give that space to more information, or even to have a shorter newsletter. Many organizations are having good luck with a newsy letter—a three- or four-page letter with subheads and bullet points, which begins "Dear Donor" and ends with "Thanks again." It is a letter that is actually fun to read.

Anything that can convince the donor that their money is well spent will be worth the space. Profiles of board members and stories about donors are always useful for pulling in more people. Frequently asked questions or analysis and news about your issue are always appreciated. Short stories, with a longer version on your website, drive traffic to your site and allow people who want to know more to find out more without overwhelming those who are satisfied with the brief teaser.

Most organizations have moved to using e-newsletters for quick and more frequent contact. Many donors prefer an e-newsletter, but you will still want to occasionally send out a paper newsletter. Even donors who will sign up for your e-newsletter may be more likely to read a paper newsletter, and although donors will forward an e-newsletter, they will leave a paper newsletter in their dentist's or doctor's office where it will reach a wider, untapped audience. You can give people a choice between paper and virtual presentations, but keep in mind that e-mail is a different culture from paper. E-mail newsletters should be short and pasted into the body of the e-mail. Links should be used to take donors to your website for more information, the rest of the story, or photos and graphics that might take up too much bandwidth for e-mail. A paper newsletter as short as an e-mail one will seem skimpy. An e-mail newsletter as long as a paper one will be overwhelming and too text heavy.

E-mail and paper newsletters have different functions; most organizations find that using both works well. Environmental organizations often find that donors have a high acceptance of e-newsletters, but organizations working with seniors or organizing in communities where computer use is not so common may experience some resistance to an e-newsletter—or find that it simply doesn't reach people. As of 2009, about 75 percent of American families have access to a computer and know how to go on the Internet. Younger people are far more likely to be online than older ones, and a generation from now there will be very few Americans who don't know how to use a computer. You will want to know what is true for your audience now and in the future. If you have historically had trouble getting a newsletter out, think about sending a smaller e-newsletter once a month and lifting the burden of doing a paper newsletter from your shoulders.

Annual Report

An annual report is another opportunity for either building loyalty or boring the donor. Fancy and expensive-looking is not in style for nonprofits these days, which ironically makes the report harder to design. It has to be readable and accessible without looking expensive. Pictures are still important—in black and white. Captions can be used to tell whole stories. The financial information should be explained, not just copied from the audit. Donors do not know how to interpret this information, and a friendly page from the treasurer of the board will go a long way to reassure them that their money is well spent; donors need this reassurance in order to keep choosing your organization. The annual report is a great opportunity to educate donors about what to look for in assessing the honesty and financial management skills of an organization as well as what vital functions administrative costs pay for. Use your annual report to advance understanding not just of your issues and your accomplishments, but also of the way the organization operates. You should also post your annual report on your website.

Your Nonprofit's Website

Having a website is not only a way of recruiting new donors, it is also a great donor retention strategy. You can drive donors to your site by reminding them of the site in every piece of correspondence. Put your web address everywhere. In your letters to donors, refer to them to your website for more information. Your newsletter and e-mail newsletter should always refer people to your site. Make sure your site is linked to those of other organizations like yours and that it is registered with search engines. Try finding your site from other organizations' sites and by typing in your name or your issue in various search engines to test how likely it is that someone surfing the web would find you.

For most organizations, although all online efforts may not provide a big income stream right now, it is one good way of being in touch with the public and will become more and more *the* way as time goes on. You will want to get ahead of the curve on this strategy. There are many volunteers who hate asking for money in person who may love working on your website or your other online strategies, so these do not have to be a major expense.

Persistence and Patience

Building a broad base of donors requires using a wide variety of strategies, and keeping close tabs on what is working and what is not. This will change over time, so testing and evaluation must be part of your fundraising program every year. Expanding a donor base takes patience; donors have many choices, and they do not always choose you. Having chosen you once, they don't always choose you again. You cannot take any of this personally or get discouraged. Persistence is key. Here's a personal story to illustrate:

For years, people would tell me that if I exercised every day, there would come a day when my body would rather exercise than not exercise. I always thought to myself, "Well, I must have quit the day before that was going to happen." Then I got a dog who need- ed to be walked every morning and evening. One day after walking her daily for several years, I realized I looked forward to walking. When I was out of town I walked even though I didn't have to. I see this as parallel to the effort people put into fundraising—keep at it and one day (in the not-too-distant future) you will wake up and realize you have a strong, vibrant, individual donor program.

Chapter Ten

Segmenting: The Key to Maintaining Relationships

Once you have developed a sizable donor base using the techniques discussed in the previous chapter, the key is to figure out a manageable way to build the organization's relationship with each person on the list. Having a donor is not like having a pillowcase or a table. Donors take maintenance. They are living, breathing beings with feelings and attitudes, and they are being sought by 1.5 million other nonprofits in the United States alone. Certainly, they gravitate to organizations they believe in, but if they have a choice between two organizations they believe in, and one pays attention to them and one doesn't, it is not hard to guess where they will go.

As soon as you have more than a few dozen donors, you will find that maintaining and expanding your donor base, and particularly upgrading donors to the next level, requires "segmenting," which means dividing the donors into smaller batches according to various criteria so you can treat each category of donor most appropriately to their giving practices and preferences. Clearly, Clara Jones, who has sent a check for $25 twice a year for ten years, should not get the same letter as Max Smith, who sent $250 as his first and only gift, or the same letter as Sarah Brown, whose yearly $2,500 gift comes through a donor-advised fund at a community foundation each December. Should these donors be in three different segments? And how many segments should an organization have? I met with an organization recently that has 310 donors allocated to 20 segments. They were so busy thinking through their segmentation (even remembering all those segments was beyond my mental capacity) that December snuck up on them, and then, in a panic, they sent all 310 donors the same year-end appeal letter. Clearly this was not the point of segmenting!

The Purpose of Segmenting

The primary purpose of segmenting donors is to help build appropriate relationships with a large number of people. Segmenting is helpful for organizations that have more than a hundred donors, and it will be most helpful for organizations that have a few thousand people on their list. If your organization has fewer than a hundred donors, you may want to think about what segments you will eventually want to have, but instead of segmenting now, you could just look at each donor record and decide what to do next with that donor, while also spending a fair amount of time bringing in new donors.

High-Touch Fundraising

Almost everyone appreciates thoughtful personal attention, but donors also have individual likes and dislikes, which we accommodate to the extent that we can. For example, someone sends you $35 with a note that says, "I only give once a year, so please only ask me once a year." You should be able to code this donor in your database so that their name is suppressed for any other mailing during that year. That person will not be invited to an event or get the spring appeal. Similarly, someone who says on their reply card, "Absolutely no phone calls" is never phoned. This information is in their donor record. In fact, even if you have their phone number from their check, don't enter it into your database. If you don't have it, you are much less likely to make a mistake and call.

However, most donors *don't* tell us directly what they want. They may still have opinions, and they indicate their preferences by their behavior. We need to make an informed guess about their behavior before they decide not to give us money any more. Segmenting allows you to take their preferences into account and saves your organization time and money because you are not aiming strategies at people with a track record of not responding to those strategies.

You must have a good database to do segmenting easily—in fact, to have an efficient fundraising program you must have a good database. So even if you have to stand on the street and ask for money, find the money to buy a decent database. There are many very adequate databases designed for fundraising, starting from about $90. There are even some that are free, although it is important to make sure that a free one is actually worth more than that. You should not need to spend more than $2,500 for an excellent database, not including the technical support—and that should not break your bank either. (For excellent and up-to-date reviews of databases, go to www.techsoup.org.) Before you can segment your donors, you must have their information entered into your database so that you can get the output you need. Exhibit 10.1 discusses what a good database can do.

Size, Longevity, and Frequency

The first set of segments is very simple. Donors should be sorted by *size* of gift, *longevity* of giving, and *frequency* of giving.

Size: Determine what amount of money is more than most people in your constituency can give and create a list of donors who give that amount or more. In some organizations the amount may be $100, but for most it will probably be $250 and up.

Longevity: This is the most important variable—you want to identify those who have stayed with you for three or more years. Create a category for those people. If you are an old organization and your records are very good, you may want to create other categories for five or more, or even ten or more years.

Frequency: Although there are many donors who only give once a year, there are many who give every time they are asked. Create a category for those who give two or more times a year.

Now draw from these segments to make up a list of people who have given $100 (in one gift) or more for three or more years. Note which of those people also give more than once a year. (Some of

Exhibit 10.1: What Your Database Should Be Able to Store and Retrieve Easily

For every donor:

- Full name, correctly spelled, with preferred title (Mr., Ms., Dr., Your Holiness, and so on)

- Address where the donor prefers to receive snail mail

- E-mail address

- Date, source, and amount of first gift

- Date, source, and amount of every subsequent gift

- Additional involvement in your organization (such as board member, activist, vendor)

- Whether you may rent or exchange donor's name and address with other nonprofits

- Whether donor responds to phone calls

- Any other segmenting information: monthly donor, or ask only once a year, or event donor

Additional information about major donors or major donor prospects:

- Family, including name of spouse, partner, children

- Additional work or home addresses

- Special programmatic interests

- Likes or dislikes that affect raising money from this donor

- Other organizations this donor supports, and how much

- Names of people in your organization who are able to contact this donor personally

- History of all contact with this donor

Additional information you may want to track about a subset of your donors:

- Willingness to volunteer

- Have named our organization in their estate plans

- Contacts this donor has that may be helpful to us

these people will already have appeared on the list of people who love your organization the most, as I discussed in Chapter Ten.) Your personal solicitation efforts should be aimed at this group. They care about you and have shown that they value your work for several years. Show this list to trusted board members, volunteers, and people who know your community who also have some discretion. Ask if any of the people on this list are capable of giving a lot more than they have given already. Perhaps Jane Smith gives you $250 a year and has done so for three years. A volunteer may know that Jane Smith gives $1,000 to an organization similar to yours and that Jane always speaks highly of both organizations. With this information, you should be asking Jane to upgrade her gift.

Donors who give only once a year should be asked for gifts only once or twice a year, whereas those who give every time they are asked might get an extra appeal during the year or be asked to join a pledge program to become monthly or quarterly donors. If there are people on your list who always renew by phone, you will no longer send them three renewal letters before phoning them; instead, you will send one renewal letter and then call them. By observing patterns among your donors, you can save yourself a lot of time and money and increase your fundraising income with very little more work on your part.

Other Segments

In addition to the Size, Longevity, and Frequency segments, begin to create others. Note those donors who only come to events or perhaps only come to one event. They should not get regular appeal letters unless you have evidence that they give to those appeals as well. If a donor gives only when she comes to your signature event, does so for three years or more, and does not give in response to any other request, that is a sign that he or she is loyal to the event, not to your organization. The other appeals are wasted. If that donor misses the event one year, then you could send her a letter after the event describing how well the event went and how she was missed, and asking for a contribution.

Note which donors give only to appeals for specific things (playgrounds, scholarships, demonstrations) and do not respond to general appeals. If you have a specific need, approach these donors more personally for that need. These people are often your best prospects for capital campaigns. All donors should be offered the chance to pledge every time they are solicited, but donors who give frequently should be offered that option in a special invitation about the advantages of pledging.

Our goal in doing this kind of segmenting is threefold:

- We will give donors the kind of attention they want.
- We will save ourselves from phone calls or letters from frustrated donors saying, "You send too much mail," or "I can't stand being phoned," or "You are using all the money I gave you to ask me for more money."
- We will be able to focus our primary fundraising energy on donors who are loyal to the organization, as opposed to donors who are loyal to a person in the organization or to an event.

Every organization will find the segments of size, longevity, and frequency to be helpful, but each organization will also have to create segments that make sense for the issues they are working on. Segments can also change over the years as your work evolves. Eventually most organizations will have a segment of donors who have shown interest in planned giving; organizations using a lot of technology may have segments of donors who are into social networking. Make sure you actually use the segments you have created and that you keep track of responses to the ways you tailor your fundraising to each segment. Over the course of two or three years you will discover what is important to keep track of and what isn't.

The recommendations in Chapters Eight and Nine and this chapter may seem overwhelming for a one-person development office, which is why you need to recruit more people to help you. The next chapter explores how to build a fundraising team. Before you read it, though, go through Chapters Eight, Nine, and Ten again and highlight what you can do with some effort, but not at the expense of the insights you gained in Chapters Seven and Eight. Then, with the list of what you *can* do, decide what you will do this month and this year and what will need to wait.

Even the most perfect fundraising program has details that need to be fixed and things that need attention. A donor base is like a garden—it does best when tended to regularly and properly, but it will continue to grow, and some plants will flourish, with very little attention. Overall, what everyone wants—donors, board members, volunteers, and staff—is that your organization be able to accomplish its goals and fulfill its mission. Take the quiz in Exercise 10.1 to see how to keep your nonprofit strong.

EXERCISE 10.1: QUIZ: KEEPING YOUR NONPROFIT STRONG AND HEALTHY

Take the following test and give your organization a score. Sometimes it is useful to ask each staff member to take the quiz separately and then compare notes. Use the results of this quiz to help in setting priorities for your work. You can't fix everything at once, but you can make a start. What do you agree on? Where are your differences? Can you arrive at a consensus about where to start?

On a scale of 1 to 5, with 1 being "not in place at all" and 5 being "about as good as it could get," rate your organization on the following elements of your fundraising program.

Your Fundraising Goals

1. We have a fundraising plan broken down into specific goals based on our program plans and budget.

    1   2   3   4   5

2. We have a fundraising goal, which we could express as follows: We need to raise $ _____ in _____ period of time to accomplish .

    1   2   3   4   5

3. Staff members are all aware of the fundraising goal _____.

    1   2   3   4   5

4. At any given time, the staff knows how much we still need to raise to meet the fundraising goal.

    1   2   3   4   5

5. All board members are aware of the fundraising goal.

    1   2   3   4   5

6. At least every month, most board members know how much we still need to raise to meet the fundraising goal.

1   2   3   4   5

7. The fundraising goal and our progress in reaching the goal are visible in the office in the form of a thermometer or other representation.

1   2   3   4   5

Now add up your score and see how you rate:

Maximum Total: 35

Healthy Organization: 28–35

Needs Improvement: 20–27

Fix This ASAP: 12–19

Start Here: under 12

Your Fundraising Strategies

1. Based on our fundraising philosophy, our fundraising plan calls for expanding (or creating, then expanding) a broad base of individual donors.

1   2   3   4   5

(If this is not so, skip this statement and #2 and move on to #3.)

2. Our fundraising strategies are all chosen because they either acquire donors, retain donors, or upgrade donors.

1   2   3   4   5

3. Our fundraising strategies are evaluated at regular intervals to make sure they are performing adequately.

1   2   3   4   5

4. Fundraising staff and key board and volunteers understand the function of each strategy in our fundraising plan.

1   2   3   4   5

Now add up your score and see how you rate:

Maximum Total: 20

Healthy Organization: 15–20

Needs Improvement: 9–14

Start Here: under 9

Your Communications With Donors and Other Interested Parties

1. Donors receive information (newsletter, action alert, e-newsletter) at least three times a year.

   1   2   3   4   5

2. Staff, board, and volunteers feel confident telling people to check our website to learn more about our organization or to keep updated on our programs, projects, and fundraising.

   1   2   3   4   5

3. All donors receive a personal note or phone call or a personalized appeal at least once a year.

   1   2   3   4   5

4. Thank-you notes are sent in as timely a fashion as possible: generally between forty-eight hours and one week after receipt of gift.

   1   2   3   4   5

   Subtract three points if you thank only larger donors.
   Subtract five points from your total if you do not send thank-you notes at all.
   Now add up your score and see how you rate:
   Maximum total: 20
   Healthy Organization: 15–20
   Needs Improvement: 10–14
   Start Here: under 10

Your "Back Office" Functions

1. You have a database that you like, and at least two staff people (paid or unpaid) know how to use it.

   1   2   3   4   5

2. You back up your data at least twice a week, and daily if you enter data daily.

   1   2   3   4   5

3. You store your backup data on the Web or on a disk drive that is not in the office.

   1   2   3   4   5

4. You have a reason for keeping someone on your mailing list who is not a donor (other than "outreach" or "maybe they will give some day"), and that reason is recorded.

    1   2   3   4   5

5. You have systems in place for keeping track of responses to mail appeals, newsletters, renewal mailings, and all other requests.

    1   2   3   4   5

Now add up your score and see how you rate:

Maximum total: 25

Healthy Organization: 15–25

Needs Improvement: 9–14

Start Here: under 9

Evaluating Your Results

Each of the questions here relates to fundraising functions that require a number of details to be attended to, representing some work. Obviously, no organization can work on all elements of their fundraising program at once, so this questionnaire is designed to help you set priorities. Note which section got the lowest score and why. You will probably give priority to the work required to improve that section.

It is possible that you will pick one element of each section as your priority. Be realistic and do what you can. Fix one thing every week or two. Creating and maintaining an interesting website takes more time than starting to send thank-you notes promptly. Getting a database you like could take a couple of months, but if you don't have a good database, you will need to make that a top priority in order to fix other things that are weak in your program.

The important thing is to start somewhere and make a plan to keep going until your organization comes into the healthy range for all these elements. This can take up to a year, so don't get discouraged.

Chapter Eleven

Building a Volunteer Fundraising Team

Building a team of volunteers requires the same patience as building a donor base but uses a slightly different set of skills. It requires starting with the assumption that there are volunteers who are reliable and willing to do the work, some of whom will come to like fundraising. Ironically, that assumption is what we have in place when we start our organizations, but we tend to move away from it as the organization grows. Before I explore exactly how to work with volunteers successfully, let's look at an example of what typically happens as organizations grow without paying attention to maintaining volunteer involvement.

A small, countywide organization focused on the rights of nursing home residents has had three board chairs in four years. The executive director, JoEllen, who also does all the development work for the group, explains to me that she does everything she can to make the board's job easier. "I write the plan and bring it to them for approval. Then I tell them what tasks they need to take on. But most of the time they don't do what they say they will, and I end up doing the work." She sighs. "I don't know what they think their job is besides coming to meetings and asking me a bunch of questions about the budget."

JoEllen has been at the organization for ten years and is widely credited for saving it from near bankruptcy. She works long days and often works on weekends. She and her current board chair acknowledge that JoEllen cannot continue to work at this pace, so she has applied for and received a capacity-building grant from a foundation, and she asks me to help the organization.

Before I take the job, I interview the current board chair and one former chair. They each paint a similar picture. The current board chair describes JoEllen as very talented and committed and a hard worker. They say she tells the board what to do, but seems to get frustrated easily and takes the work on herself, then complains at board meetings that she doesn't have board backup. She e-mails the chair three or four times a week with new tasks and ideas. The rest of the board members also call or e-mail the chair frequently to complain about the process. "I spend all my time either calming JoEllen down or calming the board members down," explains the current board chair. "It is just not fun or satisfying, and I am not good at it."

I ask the previous board chair with the longest record as chair how it went when he headed the board. "When I first started working with the group, the board was really involved and we worked as a team. Then some board members rotated off and some new ones came on, and the program got bigger. JoEllen got busier, and the new people didn't do as much. Gradually she took on more and more fundraising and we did less and less, and she seemed to get more and more frustrated."

JoEllen and the current board chair think the solution is to hire a development director to ease the workload. JoEllen has far too much to do, she feels she can't rely on the volunteer board members, and the board chair feels the board members don't have time to do the work. Their fantasy is that a staff person will do all the fundraising, relieving both JoEllen and the board from having to worry about it. They are willing to pay such a person a good salary, reasoning that after a few months, the extra fundraising being done will cover the expense.

Hiring a development director may well be the right thing to do, but not to do the work that JoEllen and the board chair imagine. The only way a development director will really be helpful is when JoEllen, perhaps with the help of a coach, examines her work style, stops being a martyr, and helps the board get back on board with fundraising.

This scenario, with slight variations, plays out over and over again in small organizations all over the world. The solution that most organizations propose for any fundraising problem is to hire a development director. As often as not, that person can't do the work by herself; when that happens, she is replaced, or, if the agency has a little more money, it hires more staff or outsources specific pieces of work to consultants and freelancers. Some grass-roots organizations will have a tiny staff of one or two full-time people, but then they will also be paying another five or six people who work varying numbers of hours managing the website, writing grant proposals, designing materials, organizing special events, and so on. The amount of time it takes to manage these freelancers and coordinate their work is never calculated—never mind that freelancers will always be more expensive than staff. The organization never seems to get ahead, and the director is always stressed, but, in a common symptom of insanity, the group keeps trying the same thing over and over, hoping for a different result.

The general consensus that underlies this self-defeating behavior is that no one likes fundraising and it is so hard to get people to do it that you should just pay to get it done. The fact that it is hard to find experienced development directors for these jobs is attributed to how few of these people there are, not to the fact that an experienced person would know better than to apply for such a job! This model is problematic even in the best of economic times, and it is impossible to maintain when the economy is down and whatever money there might have been to pay all these people disappears.

So what is the solution? It is to recognize that no one person can carry out all the development tasks for an organization; that responsibility for fundraising should be shared among staff, board members, and volunteers, with the development staff person initiating and organizing the work and supporting the staff and volunteers who are helping to carry it out. The organization described in the beginning of this chapter needs to step back and rethink its entire approach to fundraising. That thinking won't take long, but changing the habits of the board and director may take a while.

It is hard to maintain fundraising volunteers, but it is easier than the other solutions, which include burning out talented staff, alienating willing but tentative board members, using a variety of freelancers who cannot make your organization a priority because they work for so many other organizations, or simply cutting back on expenses until there is virtually nothing going on in the organization.

Examining Core Beliefs

Building a team of volunteers who can do effective fundraising requires some practical steps, which I outline later in this chapter, but the very first step is a philosophical reexamination of several false assumptions, many of which you will recognize as springing from the problems in the nonprofit sector outlined in Part One. Here they are, each followed by its more truthful corollary.

False: We have to run our organization as if it were a business and be more professional. Tiny neighborhood groups can run with mostly or all volunteers, but organizations of any real heft must be run in a more businesslike way. Businesses hire people to get things done.

True: Although there is much to be learned from the business sector about how to run nonprofits, hiring more and more people to do portions of the work is not a lesson we can import. In fact, the belief that this is how business works is actually a myth about business—particularly small businesses, which are the most comparable to small nonprofits. Many small businesses run on the blood, sweat, and tears of the owner (in nonprofits, this would be the founder) who is not paid for the time he or she puts in, particularly when the business is getting started. Family members and even friends work for little or nothing to get the business going and help to keep it going in hard times. Businesses often borrow money to expand. We in the nonprofit sector borrow time from volunteers. The idea that people must be paid in order for them to work hard and effectively is actually not true in the business, corporate, or nonprofit sectors.

False: Volunteers can't be fired. They work for free and you have to be grateful for whatever they do. You can't expect much because they are working for free.

True: Volunteers do not receive money from the organization, but they do cost an organization money. How much money will depend on the organization and the volunteers, but here are some common hidden costs of volunteers:

- Staff hours to supervise them, send them thank-you notes, and otherwise show appreciation

- Food at meetings
- Space for them to meet
- Materials to orient them to their tasks and keep them up to date
- Phone expenses to call them and remind them of their tasks

Of course, the cost of a good volunteer is far outweighed by the volunteer's contribution, and many volunteers are also donors, so there is often a large net gain to the organization. But the total cost of all volunteers needs to be in an organization's budget, and the volunteers need to be aware of it. The real cost is time: theirs and yours. Time is our most precious nonrenewable resource; when time is wasted, we cannot get it back. This is a real cost, and people who waste our time (and possibly our money) are not truly "volunteers." Being a volunteer is a job, and people need to either do their job, renegotiate their job, or leave their job. It is both patronizing and infantilizing to not hold volunteers accountable for their work, and it wastes precious resources.

False: "I could do it more easily myself," and its corollary, "I could do it better myself." By the time a volunteer is brought up to speed, we (the staff) have invested the same amount of time it would have taken to just do the job, and the job still isn't done. Moreover, volunteers just aren't going to be as thorough or as careful as a staff person, and because we feel we can't fire them, we are stuck with inferior work.

True: You probably *could* do it more easily and better yourself. But if you always do it yourself, you will always do it yourself, and you will burn out. You cannot keep up with all the tasks that must be done; you *must* delegate. Once a volunteer learns a task, she can teach another volunteer. You don't always have to be the teacher. Also, keep in mind the expression, "The best is the enemy of the good." Sometimes a perfectionist staff person insists on a level of quality that is not necessary for the task. Good enough is good enough. The truth is that a person who feels she must do everything herself is a person who lacks skills in setting priorities and delegating.

False: People just don't have time to volunteer any more. Furthermore, they don't like fundraising, so what little time they have, they are not going to use in raising money. The only way to get fundraising done is to pay people to do it.

True: Some sixty million Americans would beg to differ with the idea that people don't have time to volunteer. And in hard times, with high unemployment, we often see much greater numbers of volunteers. People have as much time as they ever had: twenty-four hours in their day. There are more demands for our time, but a large cross section of people in every country believe that taking some of their time to volunteer is a high priority. Your job is to use precious volunteer time wisely.

False (mostly): Fundraising is more complicated than it used to be. You can't just have a yard sale or get ten friends to each give $20 and run your organization with that. People may have been able to operate that way in the 1970s, but those days are long gone. We need big money, and unless you have really rich volunteers, you can't raise the kind of money we need with volunteers.

True: You never could run an organization of any size with the proceeds from a yard sale! Fundraising *is* very different now from how it used to be. Some things are much easier, such as keeping and sorting data about donors, and keeping in touch with people. It does cost a lot more to run a nonprofit organization than it used to, but the need for a disciplined, systematic fundraising program is more clear now than ever before. For success, this has to include using volunteers.

As you can see, there are two fundamentally false ideas underpinning all these assumptions:

- Fundraising is a horrible job, and asking someone to do it for free is just not realistic.
- Accountability and reliability come only when you pay people.

The false belief that fundraising is a horrible job brings us right back to the taboos about money discussed in Chapter One. The extension of this idea is that the only way to get the job done is to pay well. In fact, however, fundraising is a series of hundreds of tasks, all of which have to get done. Some tasks take specific skills, some are tedious, some require quick decisions, others require methodical thought and research, but "fundraising" is so many things that even to use the phrases "Fundraising is hard" or "No one likes fundraising" is meaningless, almost like saying "Driving is hard" or "No one likes food." Driving where? Eating what? We must stop using these phrases and reframe our attitude toward this work to a more accurate view.

The notion that volunteers cannot be held accountable is unfair to the millions of volunteers around the world who not only do extraordinary amounts of work but also do it extraordinarily well. We need to reframe how we think of the remuneration of volunteers. They don't work "for free." True, they don't work for money, but they work for a number of rewards that for most of them are more important than money, or at least equally important. They believe in the cause they work for, they want their communities to be better places, they want to learn more about the issues and the organizations, they want to share skills they have developed in a different work environment, they want to meet like-minded people, they believe in giving back, they enjoy socializing and see this as part of their social life, they like recognition and appreciation—the list goes on. In fact, all of us who volunteer have multiple motives for doing so. Moreover, as I discuss later in this chapter, it is completely possible—and in fact necessary—to create accountability structures for volunteers.

There are also some grains of truth running through these false assumptions: in decades past, many people had more time to volunteer than they do now, and it did cost less money to run even a small nonprofit. From the 1950s even until the late 1980s, many families with two adults were often able to live on the salary of one adult, freeing up the other adult to volunteer or work for a low salary. Many middle- and upper-class women volunteered many hours of time each week and developed skills and talents that were then marketable. Many women grew with their organizations, working first as a volunteer, then as a board member, then as a board chair, and then as the first paid staff person. Both men and women founded organizations, built them with hundreds of unpaid hours, and then became the first paid director. (For more on this, see Chapter Nineteen on founder's syndrome and generational change.)

Another grain of truth is that technology, which has made our lives easier by making communicating faster and easier, has also added great expense to running even a tiny organization. Just two decades ago a budget of $100,000 was enough to run a staffed and well-equipped organization, with an office, phone lines, an adding machine, and access to a copy machine. Today a setup like that would seem positively Pleistocene, not to mention completely inadequate. New phone systems, voice mail, computers and computer networks, e-mail accounts, databases, photocopy machines, scanners, software, websites—all these are just the most obvious costs that all but the smallest and most local organizations must incur.

The solution to coping with these changes is not to give up on volunteers, however. Rather, it is to rethink how volunteer energy can be mobilized, to stop perpetuating the idea that asking for money is awful, and to make sure when we hire development staff that they have a job that can actually be done by one person—and a cadre of volunteers—in a reasonable working time frame.

The way we build, maintain, and expand a core group of volunteers who will help with fundraising is not so different from how we build a base of donors. (In fact, one place to look for fundraising volunteers is in your donor base. Here are people who give you money, know how *they* like to be asked, respond to *your* requests—so, in addition to caring about your cause, they surely also think that the way you raise money is OK, and chances are they know other people among their friends and colleagues who would be interested in your organization.)

Another grain of truth is that hiring a development director is often a good idea, and can be a good solution to many problems. However, the development director leads by pushing from behind. Their message to board, staff, and volunteers is this: "You can do it. I'll help you. I'll coach you, I'll provide materials. I'll take care of the back-office functions—thank-you notes, newsletter, great website—so you can be proud of the organization. But you, Mr. and Ms. Volunteer, need to be out in front asking, along with me, the executive director, and anyone else we can round up."

Start with What, Not with Who

Before we look for *who* can volunteer, just as with donors, we start with *what* we want our volunteers to do and what is reasonable to expect from them.

ON THE
WEB
Start by dividing the activities on your year-long fundraising plan into shorter segments. Of course you are seeking major donors all year long, but pick a period of time in which you will focus on that strategy intensively. (See also premium content "How to Raise $50,000 in Six Weeks.") It is easy to see how this works with special events, as they start with a few volunteers, then recruit more and more until the day of the event. But almost all our fundraising can be designed this way.

Your list might look something like the one in Exhibit 11.1, although it will be much more detailed.

Next, identify all the tasks that a reasonable, intelligent person, with a minimal amount of training, could accomplish. For example,

---

Exhibit 11.1: A Year's List of Fundraising Tasks

Spring Gala April 1: Begin planning in Oct, soliciting sponsors in Jan, selling tickets in Feb. Deciding logistics of place, parking, table decorations, auction items takes place from Oct to April. Final thank-you's and evaluation April 2–10.

Major Donor Campaigns: Sept 10–Oct 30: recruit new major donors by asking existing donors to upgrade and asking friends and colleagues of volunteers to become major donors. Nov 1–Dec 15: renew all current major donors. Dec 15–31: final follow-up calls and thank-you's. Early new year: evaluate year-end campaign.

Mail and Online New Donor Drive: Mar, Sept, and Dec: Ask all new people who came to the April event to become donors, send appeal to everyone who attended educational events and rallies, keep website up to date and interesting, use blog to recruit new donors, make sure we have a new blog post twice a week. Keep Facebook profile up to date and keep adding friends.

Renewal Drives: Feb, May, July, and Oct: ask current donors to renew their gifts. Late Nov: Final renewal appeal to anyone who hasn't responded. Early Dec: Phone-a-thon for lapsed donors.

in our example list I would consider assigning the following tasks to volunteers:

- Almost everything related to the event. Events should not require staff time; they should be volunteer driven. If an event is too complicated for volunteers to reasonably coordinate, you should hire an event planner.
- Major donor drives: Review lists of donors who have given the same amount several years in a row and decide who should be asked to give more; edit appeal letter written by staff, or write appeal letter to be edited by staff; write, call, and visit donors to ask for upgrade. Call all volunteers and board members individually to compile list of prospects and to decide who will ask and how much to ask for.
- New donor drive: Create a team of three people who maintain the group's Facebook profile; help get appeal ready to go to event donors and other names as acquired.
- Renewal drive: Help with the mailing or e-mailing to current donors four times a year. Phone-a-thon: Create a team of five to ten people to conduct the phone-a-thon in December.
- Year-round tasks: Write a personal note on thank-you letters, write blog posts on a regular schedule, be available for speaking engagements.
- Sporadic, time-intensive tasks: Get newsletter and appeal letter mailings ready to go (for small mailings; for mailings over two thousand pieces, use a mail house).

With this list of tasks in hand, we now look for people who are suited to doing them. Taking a page from the book of individual donor fundraising, we build relationships with our volunteers. We don't ask brand-new board members to chair the major donor campaign: it is too much work, they don't know the other volunteers that well, and they will quickly burn out. Similarly, we don't ask a long-time reliable person who loves to speak in public and has a lot of knowledge of our issues to come in and help with a newsletter mailing. A good writer who dislikes social gatherings and is perhaps a little shy is not asked to chair the gala committee but may take on coordinating the blog posts.

Sometimes it is obvious what a person should be asked to do and should not be asked to do, just as sometimes it is obvious who should be asked for $10,000 and who should be asked for $500. But often it is not quite that simple, so the next job of the staff or even of longstanding volunteers is to go to your potential volunteer pool and ask what they would be willing to do. Give them a list of choices, and if you think there is something they would be particularly good at, ask them to consider it. Encourage people to move past their comfort zones, but don't guilt-trip them into agreeing to do something they may not really be comfortable with.

The overall goal here is to sort out what can only or most effectively be done by paid staff (or even paid freelancers) and what can be done by the volunteers your organization is able to recruit. Every organization will have a different set of tasks taken on by volunteers. In some organizations, especially those with a lot of young people, everything related to Web 2.0 is handled by volunteers: the website, the e-newsletter, social networks, and so on. In other organizations, all public speaking and all press relations are taken care of by a core of trained volunteers. Your volunteer base will change as volunteers come and go; the key is being flexible to take advantage of the talents and skills being offered. In areas with high unemployment, we often have far more volunteers, many of them highly skilled. Volunteers also tend to be seasonal, with more people available in the winter and fewer in the summer.

Once you have a set of tasks that could reasonably be done by volunteers, begin to match tasks with specific people. If you have a lot of disparate tasks, you will want to cluster them into types of skills, talents, or knowledge. Here's a sample of such types:

- Enjoying public speaking
- Knowledge of faith-based institutions
- Having friends and colleagues in the business community
- Being well organized and detail oriented
- Being a good writer or a good editor
- Understanding specific computer programs

Under each heading, list the tasks that require that attribute. Some tasks cross several types—you can cross-list if you want.

(If you can put yourself under the heading "Understands Excel spreadsheets" or similar computer programs, you may want to use that software for this step.)

After What, Now Who

Now we look at *who* could do the task. Again, there are many ways to get people involved, but usually the most reliable and fastest way is to ask them individually. This is very like fundraising: the best way to raise money is to ask a specific person for a specific amount that must be given in a specific time frame for a specific reason.

Start with the board of directors. Presumably your budget includes a fundraising plan that the board has approved and for which it is willing (sort of, more or less) to participate in fundraising. Each board member has made her or his own gift, so there is 100-percent giving from the board. (See also Chapter Eighteen: The Truth About Boards and What to Do About It.) At a board meeting, the chair or someone on the development committee (if you have one) should announce, "In keeping with our commitment to help with fundraising, someone from the staff or board will be in touch with each of you individually to discuss some ways you can get involved." Then you will follow up with each board member and reach agreement on a strategy and a set of tasks.

Each board member ends up with a simple agreement that looks something like the one in Exhibit 11.2.

Exhibit 11.2: A Board Member's Agreement

Name: Blanca Ramirez

I am giving:

   $1,000 to be paid in $250 installments in Jan, April, July, and Sept.

I will:

   Chair the winter Major Donor Campaign, which goes from Jan 15 to March 1; help find thirteen volunteers and take twenty-five names to solicit; help keep in touch with the other volunteers and work closely with the development director to ensure that we make our goal of $100,000 during this time.

   Attend the fall gala and sell ten tickets.

The secret of making these agreements work is that they require lots of work in a short amount of time and then there is time off. Blanca will be putting in massive amounts of time for about nine weeks, and then she will do nothing with regard to fundraising until the fall, when she will sell ten tickets to a gala. Along with her donation, this is plenty of work. As a staff person, you know that you will be working closely with Blanca in the winter. Otherwise you will not be in touch with her that much, except as is appropriate for maintaining that relationship.

Once you have gotten agreement from each of the board members on their assignments, you can see how many tasks are left and begin to parse them out to other volunteers. If you are commencing this work in the winter, don't feel you have to have lined up all the volunteers you will need in the summer. Let the work of each season be sufficient for that season.

Finding Other Volunteers

If you already use volunteers for other work in your organization, look through that list, and particularly look through the list of former volunteers. Organizations that have trained counselors, legal or medical advocates, or reading or math tutors, or that pair adults with children, often have volunteers with very fond memories of those experiences. These people may not be able to devote as much regular time as they used to because they have children now or their job changed or they moved too far away. But they would welcome a time-limited and very specific opportunity to get involved again. Technology allows many tasks to be done remotely, so geography is no longer such a barrier. Some of your current volunteers may want a different kind of involvement or may just be interested in some particular aspect of fundraising. The volunteer coordinator should announce that there are many fundraising opportunities, and the list should include some examples that don't fit anyone's stereotype of a fundraising task, such as public speaking, managing the organization's blog, creating visuals to show progress toward a fundraising goal, data entry, and prospect research. Another way to advertise is to ask for specific skills:

- Are you comfortable selling products?
- Can you explain our organization quickly and easily?

- Are you good on the phone?
- Do you have nice handwriting?
- Can you learn a database quickly?
- We need you! Call 510-998-9988 or e-mail Irene@rightmakes-might.org

In addition to former and current volunteers, or if you don't use volunteers now, send an e-mail to your regular donors, starting with those you have already met. If you think that a particular donor would be good at something, tell them. "I think you would make a great chair of this year's gala. People like you and they want to be around you, and you know everyone in the small business community. It would be a lot of work, but also a lot of fun!"

Follow-Up

There is an old saying in fundraising: "Fundraising is 10 percent planning and 90 percent follow-up calls." The ways in which getting volunteers to do fundraising can fail are predictable and can be easily fixed; they usually come down to three things:

1. Failure to be specific: what do you want the person to do, by when, for what purpose?
2. Failure to let people rest between tasks. Far too often the reward for a volunteer's doing her work is to be asked to do more work. People need to have a sense of "their share" and to know that when they have completed what they agreed to do, they won't be asked to do more for the time being.
3. Failure to follow up.

The last element in successfully getting volunteers into fundraising is to make sure that you stay on top of the time frame that they have agreed to.

Let's take an example:

Mae-Lin agrees to ask ten people for $500 each in the next three weeks. She goes to a training in how to ask for money, she chooses ten people she is willing to ask, and she knows the deadline. She has the materials she needs. To make sure Mae-

Lin completes her task, here is what the development director or other appropriate person would do:

- Ask Mae-Lin how she is going to start.
  - Will she e-mail all ten people, then call? (Make sure she has the sample e-mail letter that has been developed.)
  - Or, preferably, will she start with four people this week, then three more in the second week, and then the final three in the third week?
  - If she is going to e-mail her prospects, ask her to blind copy you on those e-mails so you can see when they go out. If she is using snail mail, ask her to e-mail you when she sends out the letters.
- Ask her which people she will start with.
  - The day before she is to have completed this task, call and ask if she needs anything from you. This is a gentle reminder but will help surface any obstacles she is running into.
- E-mail her to see how her follow-up calls are going.
  - At the end of the first week, make sure she is one-third of the way through her asks and see what she needs to get there.

Mae-Lin is not the only person working on this campaign, so once a week send a group e-mail with a description of progress:

> Eric has called three of his prospects and one has pledged. Wanjiru has already met with two people and brought two checks over to the office. George had a bad fall on the ice, but will catch up next week. (He's going to be fine, just bruised.) Mae-Lin has sent all her letters and has left messages with three people.

Conclude the e-mail with,

> We are 15 percent of the way toward our goal, which is great for the first week, but means that next week we have to reach more people. So, go team!

Firing a Volunteer

Do not even think of taking a task away from a volunteer until you have reminded her of her task at least three times. Then try honesty first. "It seems like you are not able to keep up with the deadlines we set. Should we redo them, or is there another way to get this task done?" If there is still no movement from the volunteer, tell her or him, "I am going to ask someone else to finish this because it has to get done." And do that. You don't have to be huffy and righteous or martyred and beleaguered. Just be straightforward. Often the person will say what he or she thinks happened: "This is much harder for me than I thought," or "I got caught up in the enthusiasm, but I really hate this task." Sometimes the person searches for someone to blame, and you will be convenient. "You said it would be so easy, but it isn't," or "You didn't get me the stuff on time," or "When I said I would help I didn't realize you were going to make me do this." No matter what the person says, don't be defensive. If you can take any responsibility, do so, and apologize. You might ask, "What could I have done differently?"

Remember, what you are trying to do here is to preserve a relationship and also create a reliable pool of volunteers you can count on. Again, just as in fundraising we have to ask far more people than the number of gifts we need, with volunteers we will start out with more people than we end up with.

People who don't follow through on one task shouldn't be written off—perhaps it wasn't the right task for them but there are other things they actually would do.

When you ask someone for money and they don't give, it is rarely personal. When you ask someone for time and they don't give it, it is also not personal. We all say we are going to do things and don't do them. Think about it: the person you disappoint most often is probably your own self. "I am going to stop smoking/lose weight/call my mother more often"—if you can keep in mind that you have a long list of tasks you have promised to do but didn't, you will have much more compassion for your errant volunteers.

The time involved in training, motivating, mobilizing, reminding, and evaluating volunteers, although significant, is always going to be less than the time it takes to do every task yourself. Each year, working with the volunteers will get easier and you will be more practiced in knowing how to assign jobs and predicting who is going to do their work and who isn't. In the best of times, building a base of volunteers to help with fundraising is a skill worth developing. In hard times, only organizations with a core of dedicated volunteers—some of whom are willing to do fundraising—will be able to grow and thrive.

Chapter Twelve

All Roads Lead to
Personal Asking

Let me repeat a lesson from all the fundraising books ever written, including this one: *the purpose of fundraising is to build relationships.* And no relationship is complete unless the parties in the relationship meet each other from time to time. Generally, we are better friends with people we see in person from time to time than with those we only phone, and we are definitely better friends with people we see and phone or even e-mail than with those we only correspond with by mail. As it is with friends, so it is with donors: if you want someone to really think of your organization as their favorite, then you must get to know them more personally. Yet most organizations stop just short of this step, which means they have done a huge amount of work and now will not receive any reward.

Let's take an example:

Independent Artists Collective (IAC) runs a gallery for emerging visual artists, whose work is chosen for showing by a jury of artists. During their five years of existence, the IAC gallery has become a "go-to" space for collectors looking for emerging talent and exploring cutting-edge artistic concepts. In addition to artist fees for submissions and gallery shows, IAC also raises money from donations—through online requests—from artists, art collectors, art appreciators, and small businesses in their neighborhood that appreciate the traffic the gallery generates. IAC's donor list of five hundred people is generated from their e-mail list of six thousand, whom they solicit for donations a few times a year. All of their correspondence with donors is by e-mail.

The downturn in the economy has meant fewer sales and less sponsorship from local business, so IAC seeks my advice on how they can raise more money to operate. Because they have meticulous records and know that some donors have been giving money ever since the gallery formed, and because donors who have visited the gallery have written notes offering to help, I recommend a major donor campaign. Nonetheless, they are resistant to personal asking for the simple reason that they don't like the idea. But they also know that they have gone as far as they can with online fundraising. Everything they have done up to now makes them well prepared to take the step of personal face-to-face asking so that they can generate larger gifts.

When they finally, reluctantly agree to do a major donor campaign—to call all their donors who have given, in any amount, more than three times and to ask for a personal visit with all their donors who have given more than $250—they are amazed by the positive response. The six-week campaign brings in more money than they usually raise in a year with all other strategies. "I wonder why we didn't try that before?" a member of the collective asks during the evaluation of the campaign.

IAC is typical of many successful small nonprofits. They earn enough from the strategies they use to keep going, but these organizations will be unable to grow if they don't move into personal asking. During periods of economic decline, even successful organizations like these will have to make cuts if they are not willing to get closer to their donors.

Some organizations don't move into personal asking because they are uncomfortable with the idea of it, and because they don't know how to stay in touch with their donors.

Getting Comfortable with Asking for Money

In Chapter One, I explored our societal taboo about talking about money—especially, about asking for money. It is worth revisiting that chapter and talking within your organization about how you wish you had been raised to think about money. Start the conversation with these questions:

- In the best of all possible worlds—a society with zero poverty, with only a small gap between the richest and poorest citizen, with universal health care and a clean environment, with a thriving arts and culture, and [add here other things you would want to see]—what would people be taught about money?
- To build a better world, what do we need to start thinking and saying about money and what do we need to teach our children about it?

As you move through this and other conversations about money, remind yourself that we are grown-ups. We do not have to maintain the beliefs and cultural norms we were taught. We have the right to form new beliefs and to create new cultural norms, and we have the obligation to do so when what we have been taught is oppressive and counterproductive.

Whether you take the time for philosophical conversations at this point or not, your inability (and/or the inability of your group's board and volunteers) to go to your organization's donors and to prospective donors—people who like what you do and who give away money—and ask them for money in person also has to be addressed very practically and immediately. The following are six tips to keep in mind about asking for money; follow them, and you will be able to ask anyone who is appropriate.

1. Success in fundraising is defined by how many people you ask, not how much money you raise.

Because we have to ask many more people for money than the number of gifts we need, we cannot measure our success only by the amount of money raised. I go to meetings where one person proudly reports, "I raised $2,000," and another, more shyly, says, "I raised $200." But the truth is that the first person asked his Aunt Sophie for a donation and she gave it because she thinks her nephew needs some encouragement, whereas the second person brought in her $200 by asking fifteen friends to give

$25, to which eight said yes. Clearly the second person was more successful: she asked more people, some of whom will keep on giving. Instead of measuring success by the amount raised, think of ways to measure by the number of people asked. You can have an "asking thermometer" that shows how many people will need to be asked in order to raise the money needed. Or you could have a "No" report: "How many people turned you down since we last saw each other?" If the answer is "No one turned me down," then you know this person has not been out asking enough.

2. Be OK with "No."

Clearly the corollary to #1 is that you have to be unfazed by having people not make a donation when you ask them personally. Few, if any of us, can afford to make donations to all the causes we care about. We say no not just to causes we don't believe in, but also to causes we do believe in. We say no not just to requests from strangers, but also to requests from friends. Your job is to ask, to invite people to contribute to your organization. Their job is to say yes, or maybe, or I have to think about it, or maybe later, or no, and then your job is to thank them for whatever they said and to move on to your next prospect. Their no is not about you, and most of the time it is probably not even about your organization.

3. Your belief must be bigger than your anxiety about asking.

No matter how long we have been in fundraising and no matter how many people we have asked in person, there is still a little part of all of us that hesitates, even just for a moment, when asking for money in person. That hesitation is normal. No one seeks rejection, and we know, once the question "Will you help with a donation of X?" has been asked, that we may be turned down. We are afraid the whole conversation will be terribly awkward and negatively affect our relationship. Because most of us, especially women, are raised to make everyone feel comfortable, in the moment of asking we are battling our taboos about money and our conditioning to be "polite." To ensure that your hesitation is only momentary and that it doesn't stop you from asking altogether, you have to focus on why you are doing this.

What is at stake? What will your organization be able to do with the money that it won't be able to do without it? Choose an image or a story from your organization; review it in your mind and hold onto it until you can do this even if you are afraid. It doesn't matter if you are uncomfortable asking for money or if you don't like asking for money; what matters is whether you will do it anyway. Is the cause important enough to you?

4. You don't have to ask everyone.

I notice an interesting pattern in people who are new to fundraising as they think about who they might be willing to ask. Many people immediately think of family members: "I'll ask my brother, cousin, mother, great aunt." An equal number immediately rule out their family; they will ask almost anyone before they will ask family. Either pattern is fine. Similarly, some people are more comfortable asking friends, whereas others prefer to ask people they don't know. Again, either is fine. Don't fight your personality on this. You need to ask some people, but you don't have to ask everyone.

Here are some people I recommend *not* asking:

- People who work for you, unless you can be completely confident that there is nothing coercive in the request, and that they won't read anything coercive into it.
- People you don't like. When someone gives your organization money, they make an assumption that the person asking them likes them. When they see you, they expect you will be friendly and interested in them. If you didn't like them to begin with, and every time you see them you feel you must be friendly to them, you will feel slimy and hypocritical. Better to get someone who does like them to ask them.
- People who are just going to turn around and ask you. This is called *fund trading*, and it is not fundraising. To some extent, friends support each other's causes, but this quid pro quo can quickly spin out of control. In the same way, don't ask someone who you think owes you a favor or someone whose cause you have recently supported unless you truly believe they are going to be interested in your organization.

5. Start with yourself.

The first time you ever ask for money in person, you should get a yes, because the first person you should ask is yourself. Then every subsequent request is simply, "Join me. I've given and I hope you will too." Watch yourself as you decide what to give: certainly what you can afford is a primary consideration, but also note that what you can afford is determined in part by what you give to other causes. Your decision may also be influenced by how well you think the organization uses money or how badly they need it right now. Whatever leads you to choose $500 instead of $250 or $50 instead of $35 will give you compassion and insight into how others might make a decision.

6. And above all, keep this in mind: Givers give.

People who give away money are going to give it away, in good times and bad, and they are going to give it to your organization or somewhere else. If you want some of it, you will have to ask for it.

The six tips in Exhibit 12.1 will help you remember the important things about asking for money.

Photocopy these tips, or write them down. Post them on your computer, above the sink in the bathroom, put them alongside pictures of friends and family in your wallet, take a picture of them and keep the picture in your cell phone. Saturate your brain

---

Exhibit 12.1: Six Tips on Asking for Money

1. Success is asking.
2. You have to be OK with "No."
3. What you believe in has to be bigger than what you are afraid of.
4. You have to ask some people, but you don't have to ask everyone.
5. Make your own gift first.
6. Givers give and will keep on giving, no matter what.

with them and, with these tips and with practice, gradually you will become comfortable with the process of asking.

Expand Your Definition of a Donor

Next, to really be flexible in your fundraising and to ride the ups and downs of external forces successfully, you need to broaden your definition of *donor*. When you see a donor as more than someone who may give you money, you immediately expand your possibilities of finding more donors.

So although a donor is traditionally someone who gives your organization money (and that remains a key definition), a donor can also be someone who:

- Gives time
- Shares ideas about how the organization can succeed
- Says nice things about the work you do
- Opens doors for you
- Expresses gratitude for the services you provide

All of these people can be invited to give money, of course, and therefore they meet the traditional definition of donor, but all of them can also be asked for names of other people who could give your group money. They should also be invited to keep helping your organization in whatever other ways they can.

Here's an example of this need for inclusiveness and flexibility: someone who gave you $5,000 two years ago was not able to give any donation last year because she lost her job and then her house was foreclosed on; nonetheless, she volunteered a lot of time. This year, she's in a new job and introduces your cause to new colleagues and friends, but she may be able to afford a gift of only $250. This person's consistently supportive actions make her a rock-solid, committed donor.

Another example: a couple may be grateful that your group successfully organized to keep the music program as part of the school district's budget; they give $25. They may also mention your organization to their book group; another member has a child in the school district, so she also gives $25. She goes on to mention the organization to a friend, who happens to be the building manager where you have your office, and he agrees to let your group have one month rent-free this year.

You will never even know all the permutations that led to some of the donations you get, but to ensure that everything "permutates" positively, you have to have a broad definition of *donor*, an ability to maintain relationships and follow up on offers of help, and a great capacity for expressing gratitude.

The Hundred Most Important People

Using this broad definition of *donor*, make a list of the fifty to one hundred people your organization could not exist without. (We hope you could exist without any one or two of them, but all together these are the most important people for you.) This list will include major donors; long-time donors of any size gift; some current and former board, staff, and volunteers; some program officers at foundations; and possibly some clergy, vendors, neighbors, and so on. These people are each connected to dozens of other people, so by keeping in touch with them, you spread the word about your organization.

Make a master list of these people and a calendar of scheduled times to be in touch with them. In the record of each of these people, make a note about what they most like about your organization or what they might be most interested in, and also what is going on with them that might be appropriate for you to inquire about or comment on—a birthday, a child's graduation, a new job. Someone from your organization should be in personal touch with each of these people two or three times a year. Ideally, at least one of these times is a personal visit. Personal letters or e-mails count toward being in touch if they are truly personal—that is, written to that person alone and not as part of a group. The goal of this personal contact is not just telling the donor about what you did with their money, but also finding out what is going on with them, which is why a visit and a phone call are the most preferred forms of communication. Letters and e-mail can augment those communications. It is likely that many on this list are people someone in your organization sees frequently anyway, so it won't be hard to keep up with them. The rest require a plan, but that is not as hard as it sounds. Some will be seen by your major donor campaign team; some will come to events anyway. Just make sure that these people hear from you and are asked by you to do something two or three times a year, and that they are thanked for whatever they do.

Some databases have an excellent contact management feature that allows you to keep track of contacts made and results of those contacts in the donor record. A Microsoft Excel spreadsheet can work; so can a list kept in Microsoft Word. With a smaller number of people, the low-tech paper list is fine. If your database is web-based, trusted people can enter information about their contacts with these donors from their own home or office.

Here is an example of a contact record from a friend of mine who is a board member of an organization focused on low-income seniors. He has been assigned ten people to keep in touch with over the year; he keeps this list in a Word document on his computer. Once every two or three months, when prompted by an e-mail or a call from the development director, he sends in the most recent information, such as shown Exhibit 12.2.

Exhibit 12.2: Sample Contact Record

Contact record: Paula Olgilvy

Notes: Likes our economic education work and our advocacy on anything related to senior housing. Has served on various fundraising committees for three years.

12/15/08: Called to tell her that we got her mother's donation of $500 and to thank her for asking her mother again. Found out her mother is having a lot of dizziness and vision problems. Paula will go to stay with her until February, but will check e-mail.

3/15/09: Sent a letter with a copy of the op-ed about our work from the paper, and inquired about her mother. (3/25: Got an e-mail saying things were really up in the air with her mother, and thanks for asking.)

6/15/09: Called to ask if Paula would work on the summer house party campaign again. She said she would host a house party but could not be part of the campaign committee this year. Her mother has moved in with her and needs a lot of care. Sent Paula's name to Marita, who is chairing the house party program.

Note: Marita said Paula also asked two friends to host parties and one agreed. Marita thanked Paula.

9/15/09: Called to see if she wants to come to a special screening of *Thirst* and help us explore whether we should take on working on water issues, since water quality is so bad in most of the neighborhoods we organize in. She said she can't come and is concerned this would take us away from a focus on senior housing. Would like to hear how it goes.

The contact person will note when he calls her about the screening and will be sure her concerns and interests are passed to the person who will solicit her for a year-end gift. Paula also gets the e-newsletter, the annual report, invitations to events, and anything else that the whole list receives.

We cannot maintain this intensive a relationship with very many people, so it is important that this list is well chosen and reexamined every year. If it grows, then you will need to recruit more people to help keep up with it. Over time you will learn who likes a lot of contact and who is happy with just a phone call at the end of the year. As in a big family, some members are more needy than others, some are more fun to be around than others, some take initiative whereas others wait to be invited to do things, some are reliable and others less so. But all are important in one way or another. These fifty to one hundred people are mini-ambassadors for your organization: they speak highly of it to friends, they forward your newsletter, they post facts they have learned about your group on their Facebook page and link to your website, they think of you when someone says, "In lieu of gifts, give a donation to your favorite organization." But you are in charge of staying on their radar screen and on *their* list!

Seeing Your Donors as Whole People

A mistake many nonprofits make is not to recognize their donors for more than the money they give. Let's look at an example. Pam is a real estate broker who gives to an organization called Coming Home, which helps former prisoners reintegrate into society. In addition to her monetary donations, Pam helps find housing for ex-prisoners who need it, sometimes even loaning them a security deposit until they can pay her back. For several years Pam has also given to a choir, Caged Birds Sing, made up of local prison inmates. Although she likes what they do, she is much more moved by and involved in Coming Home.

A new executive director of Caged Birds Sing notices Pam's long-time, if modest, support of her organization and invites Pam to lunch, where she learns of Pam's interest in Coming Home. A few weeks later, the executive director calls Pam with an idea: Caged Birds Sing could made a CD and split the proceeds from it with Coming Home if both groups put up some money and help sell it. Pam likes that idea and, after talking with the executive director at Coming Home about it, raises money from her friends to support it. As the years pass, the two organizations collaborate on other projects.

When the bottom falls out of the real estate market, Pam's income takes a hit. She e-mails both groups to say she can't give very much money this year. The executive director of Caged Birds calls to thank her for her e-mail and to ask if Pam would be willing to come to a meeting to discuss some ways the organization could augment their donor income by earning income through fees or sales. She is happy to. Meanwhile, the executive director of Coming Home doesn't quite know what to say, but sends a brief e-mail: "I'm sure this economy is very hard for you. Keep in touch."

The difference in the two executive directors is simple: one saw Pam as primarily a donor of money and when that wasn't true anymore, the director didn't know how to relate to her. The other saw her as a collection of talents and possibilities and when Pam couldn't give money for a while, the director simply moved to make another aspect of her talent useful to the organization. Pam likes to give, whether it's money, time, or opinions. She is entrepreneurial and willing to go out on a limb for what she believes in. Coming Home's failure to recognize all of Pam's talents eventually cost the group her involvement.

Challenges Ahead

 There are many fine books and articles on how to ask for money; I recommend you consult them for detailed discussions on the topic. "The Fine Art of Asking for the Gift" is posted as premium content, and many books are recommended in the Resources.

All those who work with donors in your organization should familiarize themselves with the process of asking for money in person, but they should also keep in mind that we need to be prepared to meet the new challenges of asking that are particular to this time and that will arise over the next decade. The main challenges are:

Competition: Donors have a massive number of nonprofits to choose from; there are 1.5 million nonprofits in the United States alone. For your organization to be chosen to receive a donation, you need to have a very clear and compelling message and current examples of your work. You need to be exact about how much you need and what you will do with the money you raise.

Collaboration: You also need to be working with other nonprofits on joint fundraising and programming efforts. Many nonprofits must break their unfortunate habit of trying to convince themselves and their donors that they are unique and that they, and only they, can do the work they are doing. Except in the most extraordinary circumstance, this is not true, and now donors need to see evidence of your group working with other organizations. In choosing your organization, the donor must feel that she is actually helping a whole movement and indirectly helping other organizations doing similar work. (See also Chapter Twenty-Two: Our Main Job Now and into the Future.)

Communication: This refers to the ways that donors get information about your organization. Even the tiniest organization needs far more than simply a brochure, some return envelopes, and a willing set of volunteers to raise money. Donors look at your website, they read about you on Facebook, they may even check you out on any number of charity watchdog sites. But they will also respond to truly personal appeals, and a personal high-touch element must be part of your strategy. Moreover, if they don't hear directly from you, they will forget about you.

The financial realities that donors juggle: When donors think about making their donations, they are not just considering their current income; they are also concerned about how much they should have in a retirement fund, or how much they should save before they start a family, or what it will cost to send their children to college. Many U.S. jobs (including, disgracefully, 30 percent of nonprofit jobs) do not pay for health care coverage, adding either another financial burden or the worry of being uninsured. In communities with high unemployment, many people face the reality that they will never be employed again unless they retrain for another skill. People will continue to give away some of their money, but your organization will not only have to do good work to get it but will also have to show that it is financially sound in a world that is really not.

Public confidence: Organizations are going to have to practice a very high degree of transparency to win and maintain donor confidence. Board, staff, and volunteers need to be as schooled in budget information as they are in program outcomes and to know as much about cash flow as they do about clients. Board, volunteers, and, increasingly, management staff (which for most small organizations is the staff who give orders to themselves and then follow them) will need to make not just a gift, but a significant gift: to really test the proposition that the organization is worth supporting and that it uses money—their money, along with other money—wisely.

Changing demographics: Your organization may need to make some profound changes to reflect the changing demographics of your community. The racial makeup of the entire organization—staff, board, volunteers, and donors—should reflect the racial composition of its community, or there should be a clear rationale about the racial makeup of your staff and board. With rare exceptions, communities are increasingly multicultural; in a number of states—including California, Texas, Colorado, and New Mexico—the population has no racial majority or the majority is made up of people of color. The nonprofit sector has lagged behind every other sector (government, business, and corporate) in diversifying its work force and its donor pool. Dealing with this reality not only calls you to look at numbers and percentages; it also requires shifts in organizational culture.

Generational change: In addition to race, another fundamental change in the world and in nonprofits is generational change. As baby boomers move out of positions of leadership in organizations, the groups must deal with the effects of that change and what it means to their organizational structure. In addition, groups need to account for age-related demographic changes in their constituents and donors (see also Chapter Twenty-Two).

Summary

Personal face-to-face asking will always be the most lucrative strategy—and the strategy whereby the results of building relationships will be most keenly felt. But as people get closer to your organization, they will ask more questions, they will know more about your operations, they will see more about your results. This is all good, as long as you make sure your organization is set up to welcome more inquiries, more questions, more visits, more suggestions—and more donations.

Even though many organizations are shy about moving into personal solicitation, they often find it far easier and more fulfilling than they had imagined. Donors become volunteers, advisers, and friends, and they bring in their networks. Just getting started is almost half the battle, so pick a few people to ask, find a few people to help you, and begin.

Chapter Thirteen

Don't Leave Money on the Table

The expression that we caution against in the title of this chapter means, according to *Webster's Dictionary*, "to refrain from taking the utmost advantage of something; to not address every aspect of a situation; to negotiate a deal that is less financially beneficial than is expected or possible." I see organizations engaging in this behavior in a number of ways: in what they ask of their donors, in what they charge for their services, in what they propose to foundations that a project will cost. In many ways, we undersell ourselves and ignore signs that people would give more or pay more. Let's look at an example.

South Gloucester Literacy Council (SGLC)

South Gloucester Literacy Council (SGLC) serves a primarily immigrant neighborhood in a large Midwestern city. Housed in an old YMCA, their large but deteriorating building holds a wide range of classes for people learning English, studying to become citizens, preparing for college entrance exams, and so on. In addition, a core of volunteers offers recreational activities such as ballroom dancing, basketball, aerobics for seniors, and some art classes. Now forty years old, SGLC started as a program funded by the War on Poverty under the Johnson administration and has been supported over the years with a variety of federal, state, and city grants, as well as donations, fees, and rental income.

The staff include a multitalented man named Fred who has been at SGLC for twenty years and who serves as director and maintenance man, a development director and finance manager named Frances who returned to the neighborhood and took the job two years ago on graduating from college, and an assistant named Titus (no one has a formal title, although they all have broad job descriptions) who has been at the center for ten years and does whatever isn't getting done. All three are underpaid and overworked, but they love their work, and there is a general air of joy in this organization. There are two other part-time teacher coordinators who have also worked at SGLC for many years. A core of volunteers and a board active in everything except fundraising keep the organization humming along.

Now some financial problems are beginning to surface. Health insurance premiums have doubled over two years. A number of deferred maintenance issues really shouldn't be deferred too much longer. Their largest individual donor has fallen victim to a Ponzi scheme, and a funding source is requiring an audit before renewing their grant. Altogether, they need to replace about $30,000 of annual income, and their capital needs will run in the $500,000 range.

I am asked to help them think through their fundraising options, so I meet with the board of directors, the staff, and some volunteers from the community who want to help. Over the course of six months and a six meetings, plus numerous e-mails, along with surveys to current users, we create a plan:

1. *Raise fees for the classes and charge different fees for different classes.* Class fees are currently $10 for the entire session; a survey shows that the students would happily pay much more. Give the teacher coordinators discretion to lower or waive fees to ensure that the classes remain totally accessible.
2. *Ask all donors who have given $100 or more for three years to increase their gift.* Nearly two hundred people fall into this category, some of whom give $500 and even $1,000. A handful (including their largest donor, who has been giving $15,000) give more than $1,000, and these donors have received more attention from the Council, but no donors have never been asked to increase their giving.
3. *Make a list of capital needs and distribute it to local contractors and suppliers.* Query interested contractors about whether they

would work with students and other volunteers interested in learning construction to do the repairs. As business is slow, they may well volunteer or cut their prices significantly.

Fred isn't convinced this plan will work. "The people who use this place are really poor, and I am afraid we'll just drive them away," he says. "The donors will be offended to be asked more personally—they like to be asked once a year by mail. And no contractor will want to help with this building, especially working with volunteers and kids."

Frances, whose parents are originally from Pakistan, disagrees. "There are poor people here, but this place is convenient and friendly for people. Some people come because the programs are low cost, but a lot of immigrants like how they are treated here. My parents told me this is the only place where they are always treated respectfully, especially after 9/11. I know they would give as much as they could if they thought you needed it."

Titus says his mother has offered to pay to renovate the women's bathroom on the first floor because that is the one she uses.

Reluctantly, Fred agrees to give the plan a try. Three years later, the building is in much better shape, fees generate almost 50 percent of operating costs, and donations are way up. Fred concludes, "This old dog just learned a bunch of new tricks."

To understand how this organization was leaving money on the table, let's examine it through that lens.

Fees

The amounts they charged for their services were far lower than the local market. In fact, there was no other place in this neighborhood where people could take citizenship or English classes. On the other hand, a brief survey of the students indicated that up to half came from outside the neighborhood, naming "price" as the draw—which proved Frances correct that SGLC was seen as a bargain. Their mission was not to be the cheapest place in town for classes—it was simply to be accessible to their own constituents. Organizations that provide services need to ask themselves, "Are there people who would pay more for what we are delivering for free or low cost, and can we bring them in without diluting our mission?"

Major Donors

Although their biggest donors were solicited every year with a lovely personal letter, there was no phone follow-up or visit. During the new fundraising campaign, many donors expressed surprise that their gift of $250 or $500 was significant enough to the organization to warrant a personal contact, and many indicated that they gave much larger gifts elsewhere. All were very positive about SGLC, and almost half of the donors contacted increased their gift, many doubling or even tripling what they had been giving.

Capital

Titus told me later that his mother had told Fred several times she would pay for the women's bathroom to be renovated, and that "Fred couldn't hear it. He is a good guy, but he thinks all immigrants are poor as church mice. In fact, my mother has socked away a lot of money and made very wise investments, and she is quite well off." Titus and Frances both remarked that although there are a lot of low-income people in the neighborhood, there are also a number of people who are both generous and well off. Fred's preconception about immigrants kept his organization from benefitting from their donations.

All of us from time to time find we have fallen victim to our own preconceptions of who has money and who doesn't, who will give and who won't, what people will pay and what they won't. These preconceptions and unexamined assumptions cost us money. Coupled with a reluctance to ask, these biases cause our groups to lose thousands of dollars every year.

Write Down All the Ways You Are Passing Up Money

Anyone who has taken a money management course will recognize the advice to write down all your spending and see where your money is really going. In fundraising, I offer a similar piece of advice: find out whether you are not collecting money that is being offered to you or that would be very easy to raise. Here's how.

First, list all the ways you raise money now. Note beside each source whether what you are charging is at or below the local market for comparable services or goods, whether other organizations similar to yours make more money in these areas (this may take a bit of research), and whether anyone has ever offered to help you with any of these strategies. Are you making any untested assumptions about your fundraising? Here are some of the most common ways we leave money on the table.

Appealing Too Infrequently to Current Donors

Except for the few donors who may have requested to be contacted only once a year, you should be asking more often. This rule of thumb is especially true during times of economic volatility. For example, a donor gets an e-newsletter request the day she learns that people in her corporation are going to be laid off. Not knowing if she will be one of them, she is too nervous to even think of giving. Three months later, she gets an invitation to a special event. Grateful not to have been laid off, she sends a donation even though she can't be at the event. Three months later she gets an appeal in the mail. Earlier that week she learned that her car would need a new transmission. But she likes the content of the appeal, so she sends in $10 with a note, "Hope this helps." The thank-you note she receives three days later says, "Of course your gift helps, and your ongoing support is most appreciated." At year end, when she is phoned for a gift, she explains that, in fact, she was laid off in a second round of cuts and can't give a year-end gift. Her solicitor says, "I am so sorry to hear about your job and hope you find something soon. Thanks for all you did this year—it really helped! We'll be in touch."

In this example, the donor had money to give for two appeals and none for two others. Had the organization asked only once, they would have gotten, at most, one gift, and they stood a good chance of getting nothing. By making the donor feel appreciated all year long, they are very likely to get a donation the next time this donor is in a position to give one.

Too Big a Gap Between Donor Categories

Many organizations lurch between two extremes: believing that what they do must be free or so low-cost that no one is left out, but then setting the price of admission to the higher donor categories so high that people can't afford to join them. Here is the donation string that appears on the return envelope of the mail appeal and on the website of an organization working to end gender discrimination in the workplace.

Friend: $35–Supporter: $250–Advocate: $1,000

The problem is that many people who could give more than $35 are unwilling or unable to go to $250; similarly, of those who could give more than $250, few could reach $1,000. This organization's mail and online appeals are mostly aimed at acquiring new donors or renewing smaller, habitual donors. It is unlikely that a stranger, reading about this organization for the first time, will give $1,000. People who have given $35 for some years may well give $50 or $100, but the organization makes no invitation for them to do that. Further, although donors are offered benefits for giving, the benefits are all the same until they give $1,000 and up. When the organization changed their donation string, as shown in Exhibit 13.1, they increased their income by 30 percent in one year.

Some organizations seek to solve the question of how much to ask for by not suggesting any amount at all, but this is also counterproductive. People need to know what you want, but you have to make your choices sensible and accessible. Obviously donors can give whatever they want, but people tend to follow the suggested categories, so these need to correspond to the reality of people's giving abilities.

Exhibit 13.1: Sample Donor String

Friend: $35–99: e-newsletter and action alerts

Supporter: $100–499: all the benefits of a Friend, plus an invitation to join our monthly conference calls updating donors on the progress of the cases we are working on

Advocate: $500 and up: all the benefits of a Supporter, plus an invitation to a reception with our honorees before our annual gala.

All gifts are received with thanks; we promise all our donors that we will use your money wisely and well. Thank you for whatever you can give!

This problem of huge gaps between donor categories is even more commonly found with special events, where a ticket might cost $35, but becoming a sponsor starts at $500, with no gifts in between these two numbers suggested.

Upgrading That Is Too Aggressive

Similar to having vast gaps between one donor category and another is asking current donors to greatly increase the amount of their gift without acknowledging that you are asking for a big jump. I am all for enthusiasm and boldness, but it needs to be handled sensitively. For example, I have been giving $250 a year to a peace group for several years. Recently, I was called by someone from the group whom I don't know personally; after describing some exciting work they are doing, he said, "You have been giving the same amount for several years, and we need you to increase your gift." Putting a demand in your close is not a good idea. "We need you to"—or what will happen? Is this a threat? I like this organization, so I let that go, and said, "What do you have in mind?" The caller replied, "At least $1,000." As you can see, the language is the problem as much as the amount. He could actually ask me for $1,000 (although that would be a big upgrade) if he phrased it like this: "I'm glad you like what we are doing. As I explained, we have to raise a lot more money this year, so we are approaching all our long-time donors with some really bold requests. Do you think you could go as high as $1,000? Keep in mind that you could pledge it over the course of the year." In that case, he's saying he's going to be bold and then he is, but he is clear that if I increase to that amount, I have done a lot. He is also giving me a few ways to say no or to say, "I can't go as high as that" or "I don't want to commit for the year because things are so uncertain." Stating that all long-time donors are being asked for such increases also lets me know I am not alone, and I could say no because I am imagining that some of them will say yes.

Even better would have been to have had someone who knows me call me, but we often don't have the option. The secret of bold asking is to give donors some way to say no that does not embarrass them or you. Phrases like "at least" or "as little as" or "a little stretch" make donors feel embarrassed if they find the amount you are naming is too high for them.

Letting Untested Ideas About People Guide Your Fundraising

Challenge yourself and the people around you to look out for assumptions about who will give what, and find out what is really true. I hear people make all kinds of false statements about the willingness and ability of immigrants, young people, women on welfare, lawyers, old white men, Native Americans, and high school dropouts—among others—to make a donation. The only way you know that any particular person is not going to give is when he or she tells you that. We do a disservice to our constituents when we make decisions about their giving for them. In the story at the beginning of the chapter, many assumptions were in play, and all of them turned out to be false—which led to the organization's disregarding offers from donors, vendors, and volunteers.

Many people make the mistake of thinking that those who say, "Call me if you need anything" or "I can't volunteer regularly, but if you had something time-limited that needed to be done, I'd be happy to help" or people who hand you their card and tell you how interested they are in your work are just being nice. Of course, some are not expecting you to follow up. But many more than you realize actually mean that they want to help, and that they would do something if you asked them.

When someone says "Call me," tell them you will be calling, and then call. Create a list of specific, time-limited tasks that people could do for you with little training or supervision required. Create another list of things you need, and ask for discounts from your vendors. If you regularly buy at chain stores, ask about their corporate giving policies and pursue those.

Not Making It Easy to Give

In addition to not giving donors enough choices of giving categories, nonprofits often start their giving categories too high and don't help people understand what the money is for. Just as people are spending their money more carefully and feeling they do not have as much money to give as they used to or would like to, they will also look at your spending; you need easy ways to help them understand what you need money to do. In addition you need to create some strategies that make $5 or $10 the right

---

Exhibit 13.2: Sample Program Cost Breakdown

Paying staff transit costs:

Roundtrip ticket on the subway for staff supervisor to visit satellite office: $3.50

Number of trips needed to ensure our programs are of the highest quality: 52

I'd like to sponsor _____ trips × $3.50 = $ _____

Providing each field staff member with a cell phone to use in their organizing efforts:

Number of staff needing a cell phone: 3

Cost of cell phone plan per month to cover three phones: $6 per day =
   $180 per month

I'd like to pay for _____ number of days of cell phone
   use × $6 = $ _____

---

gift. For example, break some of your program costs down into very small increments, as shown in Exhibit 13.2.

Make sure your examples are accompanied by a description of an accomplishment that will result from the donations given. In these examples, the story might be of a satellite office serving constituents who could not make it to the main office, or where it's possible to have staff who speak the languages spoken in the neighborhood. The cell phone example could include stories of being able to call the press right from an action taking place, or being able to photograph building code violations and send the photos immediately to the proper authorities. The idea is to help donors understand that small amounts of money can have big results. Such an approach also lets you educate people about what it takes to run your organization.

Taking a page from magazines that offer trial subscriptions, some membership organizations are offering the option of giving $10 to cover one quarter, during which the donor receives one newsletter. At the end of the quarter, the donor receives an appeal for $30 to extend the membership for the rest of the year. This approach allows people to join for a short time and then decide whether they want to stay on as a member. Raffles and door prizes are also good ways to legitimize $1 or $2 as a gift.

Systems That Don't Work Well

Organizations lose a lot of money when they don't thank their donors, don't follow up on pledges, don't give the option to donate using a credit card, don't offer the choice to have ongoing periodic donations withdrawn automatically from a person's bank account, and don't keep good records.

Keep revisiting your list of income streams every few months. Make sure board members and other staff are familiar with the list and are paying attention to what other organizations are doing and charging. Keep coming back to this essential question: How can we acquire, retain, and upgrade our donors more effectively? Are there ways we can we create earned income streams that are not donor dependent? Making sure there are no gaps in what you do will ensure that you don't leave money on the table.

| Creating Financial Security

As they age, most organizations, like most individuals, seek some level of financial stability. For many years, the conventional wisdom was that organizations should create an endowment and use the investment income to augment their other annual income. When the stock market is doing well, this seems like a good idea, but when the market plunges, it doesn't seem so smart. Going forward, small organizations need to find fresh ways of thinking about their financial stability. In this chapter, we look at some conventional ways to provide a measure of financial security for your organization, and we explore some other approaches. We conclude by looking at what needs to be in place for an endowment to make sense as a strategy to pursue.

There are three ways nonprofits can ensure an appropriate measure of financial stability:

1. Maintain a savings account with few or no restrictions on its use.
2. Maintain a reserve fund (or funds) whose intended use is defined.
3. Establish a formal endowment with very clear guidelines for managing the principal and using the interest.

The differences that distinguish these from each other are important, and the way you finance each of them will vary. Some organizations use all three vehicles for saving money, some use only one, and some groups do not have any money set aside at all. Let's look at each strategy.

Savings Account

After your organization has been around for a few years, and the donors who helped get you started have moved on to start something else, and the foundations that granted you money have passed their honeymoon period and are less and less likely to give you new grants, you start experiencing financial ups and downs that are no longer related to being a new organization. You realize that no matter how carefully you budget for expenses, there are unexpected costs. No matter how cautiously you put together your fundraising projections, you sometimes fall short.

At the same time, you begin to experience some predictability. Some donors give year after year. You can expect a certain level of response from your mail appeals. Some board members always call their prospects. With enough asking going on, you can count on a certain amount of money coming in. At this point, if they haven't done so already, smart groups open a savings account. They can literally open an account and move money into it steadily, or they can simply create a line item on their books indicating money that is in "savings." The money thus set aside can be used xfor any unexpected expense, shortfalls in the general operating budget, or cash flow problems. Generally, it is not used to fund specific programs.

Reserve Funds

Money in a reserve fund is usually designated for opportunities to respond to expected but not always predictable events. Community groups use reserve funds for big campaigns, to fight Strategic Lawsuit Against Public Participation (SLAPP) suits if their insurance won't cover those costs, to generate media attention, to mount a strong response to something that has happened in their community (an oil spill, an incidence of police brutality, exposure of a corrupt government official), or to have front money for an important event.

Endowment

Money in an endowment is set aside for an organization's permanent use. The principal of the endowment is invested, and only a percentage of the money earned as interest is designated to be spent. Legally, the principal of an endowment can be spent under extraordinary circumstances, but this step is to be avoided if the endowment is going to continue to do its job of providing a steady income stream.

Let's look at one group that has done a good job of putting all three of these savings vehicles into place.

Community Concern, a health advocacy group focusing primarily on health education in the poorest neighborhoods of their city, rents a storefront office for $1 a month on a street where most businesses have had to close. The landlord leases the space to them because he can't find other tenants but he doesn't wish to sell the building. The rent is kept at this token amount on the condition that the landlord doesn't have to do any internal repairs beyond replacing things that wear out. Repairing the broken water heater or electrical wiring, painting, dealing with insulation, and the like are up to the group.

The storefront is perfect for this group. It is wheelchair accessible and near a bus line, and it gives them visibility in the neighborhood they serve. The group has put the money they were paying in rent on their previous space into a savings account. They don't know what will go wrong with the building or when, but they know that eventually they will need to make some repairs. They also use the money they've channeled into their savings to improve their offices. They have painted the rooms, bought a new refrigerator for the staff kitchen, and purchased decent chairs for the meeting room.

The director has discretionary use of the savings account up to $1,000 before a vote of the staff is triggered. Expenses must be reported to the board and cannot exceed the amount in the savings account.

Community Concern also has a reserve fund. They use these funds to rent billboards advertising "Soda Free Summer," a program aimed at reducing obesity as well as to pay tuition for members to go to trainings, to get two community gardens up and running, and to cover other expenses incurred during organizing campaigns. The reserve fund is called the Oh My God! Reserve Fund, named after what the mayor said the first time the group bused two hundred people to city hall to protest the closing of a city-run health clinic in the neighborhood. Money for the reserve fund comes from an annual membership appeal describing how they have used the money in the past and asking people to make an extra gift to maintain the Oh My God! Reserve Fund. It is one of their most popular appeals.

Like the savings account, the Oh My God! Reserve Fund can be used by staff for any expense of less than $1,000; greater expenses must be approved by the board or its executive committee, whichever is meeting first. Because the board members are often involved in the decisions leading up to spending money from the reserve, a board member usually presents the idea to the rest of the board. The reserve fund money cannot be used for anything that the savings account would normally cover, but the savings account can augment costs incurred under the auspices of the reserve fund.

Two years ago a long-time donor to Community Concern died, and the group found that they were named a beneficiary of his life insurance. They received $10,000. They were touched both by their donor's generosity and by the size of the bequest. They decided to use the money to begin an endowment, and they set a total endowment goal of $100,000 before they would use any of its earnings. Then they designated that half of the earnings would be used for general operating expenses and the other half reinvested. The board was empowered to tap the principal only in the most extreme circumstance—if the organization was in danger of closing—and only by unanimous vote.

Community Concern advertised their endowment fund in their newsletter, asking donors to help reach the goal by including Community Concern in their wills. They approached a few donors for one-time large gifts for the endowment, which resulted in one gift of $20,000 and two of $5,000. They spend little time on raising money for the endowment, seeing it as a long-term process that will be funded largely by bequests.

Because their savings and reserve fund give them a measure of financial security, Community Concern would probably not have started an endowment at the time they did without the initial bequest. But they realized that one-time-only gifts like this bequest shouldn't be easily spent.

Community Concern is unusually thoughtful in its financial planning, but almost any organization could follow their example, particularly in regard to having a reserve fund.

How to Think About Financial Stability

Nonprofits face two problems when looking at ways to be more financially stable. The first arises from the standard of care that board members are expected to exercise in making financial decisions. Nonprofit law says that board members are to be "prudent" and tells them they have "fiduciary responsibility." The concepts of prudence and fiduciary responsibility are often explained by the recommendation that board members treat the nonprofit's money with the same care they would use in dealing with their own. Some books call this care "stewardship."

However, many otherwise good people are not that careful with their own money, and the standard of care they exercise is not one we wish to impose on a nonprofit. Few people are taught about responsible money management, and most live in a commercial culture that constantly urges them to buy on credit. As a result, most people carry credit card debt, and few having savings outside of their retirement plans, if they even have these.

The second problem for nonprofits is that financial security is always measured in terms of money: how much we have, how much interest we will earn, how much we have been promised by this foundation or that donor. We need to see other elements of our organization as assets that also earn predictable amounts of money. For example, a ten-year-old organization with a thousand donors monitors their attrition rate carefully. Every year they know exactly how many new donors they will need in order to replace those who have lapsed. For the past five years they have netted at least $50,000 from donors giving less than $250 and $150,000 from their major donor campaign aimed at donors giving $250 and up. Last year, even with all the economic turmoil that surrounded them, they had their best fundraising year ever. They netted $58,000 in gifts of less than $250 and $160,000 in gifts of $250 or more. Over the years, they have begun to build an endowment, which at its height had accrued $500,000, yielding about $25,000 per year, which they used for operating expenses. Because the value of that asset has dropped to about $300,000 and it is earning only minimal interest, they are not drawing from it this year.

This organization, like many that I work with, complains that now they have no "predictable income" because the market is in such upheaval. I point out that they already have predictable income; every year, if they invest a certain amount of time and money in their donors, they will net at least $150,000 and probably more. To be able to take $150,000 a year from an endowment would require principal of about $3 million and a growing economy.

Donors are always our best source of financial stability. If your organization knows it can raise a certain amount of money from its donors, the questions before you are how much more money do you need, and how many new or upgraded donors will it take to raise that amount?

Once you understand that income from donors is predictable, your fundraising plans become built around acquiring and retaining more and more donors and offering them more and more ways to help you. These ways may include asking them for capital gifts, bequests, or other planned gifts. Some of the donors will want to contribute to a reserve fund or an endowment if they think your organization will be strengthened by having such vehicles.

Organizations that have not previously had much experience with setting money aside should start with something simple, like a savings account. The discussion of what it is to be used for, who can decide when it can be spent, and how much can be taken out at any given time, as well as how the savings account is to be financed and invested, will give you practice for the much larger discussion you will have to have if you decide to begin an endowment. You may find that a savings account gives you enough stability to eliminate the need for more complicated strategies.

Owning Property

Another form of stability that older organizations often seek is owning their own office space. This has many advantages:

- Your monthly costs are fixed and will not go up.
- You can do whatever you want to the space (within the zoning laws).
- You cannot be evicted.
- You can borrow against this asset or even sell it, should either of these become necessary.

- Donors often like organizations to own their space, feeling that the money they are giving is not supporting a landlord and is adding value to the organization.

Organizations that have commercial leases with clauses that increase their rent every year are particularly conscious of the advantage of owning their space when the value of real estate goes down, but their rent continues to go up.

The problems that come with owning property can be daunting and must be considered before leaping into buying:

- The property has to be maintained by you—no calling the landlord when the toilet overflows or the roof leaks. Major repairs can be very costly.
- Your property may not increase in value, and if you need to move to, say, a bigger space, you may not be able to sell or rent your property easily.
- You may not agree with your neighbors about laws pertaining to property in your area. For example, a service agency working with homeless people saw the people they helped as constituents, whereas their neighbors saw them as vagrants. Neighbors blamed this organization for an uptick in crime, and dealing with complaints from the neighbors has consumed massive amounts of time.

If you have enough money in a reserve fund, savings account, or even an endowment and you are thinking about buying a building, make sure you discuss the following questions:

- Do you believe in owning property? Do your donors and constituents believe that property ownership is a good move for your organization?
- Do you intend to stay in this neighborhood for at least ten years? Are you willing to be part of this business community and participate in the decisions that property owners must make? Do you feel good about who is in the neighborhood with you?
- Do you want to consider buying a building with other nonprofits and sharing not only the initial costs but also the upkeep?

- Do you have enough money not only to buy a building but also to maintain a reserve fund for repairs?
- Is building management on the list of competencies of any of your staff?
- Can you afford to have so much money tied up in something that is not liquid?
- Any other considerations?

Starting an Endowment

Many organizations that have taken the first steps of having a savings account and a reserve fund may now want to consider an endowment. Like owning property, there are advantages to having an endowment (besides just having the money):

- An endowment allows—actually, even forces—an organization to think in terms of long-range planning, because an endowment means you have committed the group to exist in perpetuity.
- Endowments provide a vehicle for people to make larger gifts to an organization than might be appropriate for an annual gift, and they allow people to make larger one-time-only gifts with assurance that the gift will provide for the organization for the long term.
- An endowment is a vehicle for people to express their commitment to an organization through their wills; few people will leave money to an organization that does not have some kind of permanent fund.
- Endowment principal can be used for capital expenses and as collateral for loans, if ever needed. Some organizations have used some of their endowment principal to buy a building for their offices.

For every good thing you can say about endowments, you can also find some drawbacks. Here are the most common concerns about having an endowment:

- Because they allow an organization to exist permanently, endowments may support organizations that ought to have gone out of business.

- When endowments are very large, they allow organizations to become unresponsive to their community and constituency. With a large amount of investment income, organizations may cease to try to involve their community and may be impervious to criticism.
- Endowments can provide a false sense of security; in reality, interest rates can vary, stock markets can fall, and money can be invested badly.
- The existence of an endowment may discourage some donors from giving annual gifts if they perceive that other organizations need the money more.
- When donors endow certain programs, the work of the organization can become donor-driven rather than mission-driven. This is, of course, a problem with foundation and government funding or any large single source of designated funding. However, the complication with an endowment is that the donor is usually dead by the time it is clear that the program is no longer needed. Changing the terms of how the money can be spent is often complicated, legally messy, and expensive.

Most of the problems involved with an endowment can be avoided if an organization thoroughly debates and unanimously answers two questions:

- Does everyone in the organization agree that it should exist permanently?
- What will endowment income be used for?

Most organizations are formed with the idea that their work will be so successful that they will put themselves out of business. When domestic violence programs, food banks, and homeless shelters seek to be endowed, they give the message that they have ceased trying to eradicate the problems they were formed to solve, and that abused, hungry, and homeless people are a permanent feature of our society. Organizations working for a just society must maintain the idea that they will be able to address the root cause of social problems and eventually eliminate the problem they are focused on.

However, there are many organizations that can envision a society in which their work would not be needed and that are working for the creation of that society, but they must admit that this society will probably not exist for at least fifty years. That means that people not yet born will someday be sitting on the board or working as the staff of these groups. The current board feels an obligation to its future leadership to make life a little easier financially—and a permanent source of funding to augment fundraising efforts would certainly do that.

Other organizations are designed to be permanent features of the nonprofit landscape: arts and culture groups, alternative schools, independent publications, community centers, historic preservation societies, land trusts, parks, libraries, and the like are designed to exist forever. The degree to which they should be supported by tax dollars rather than private charitable contributions might be debatable, but an endowment would be appropriate for any group doing work that will always be needed or wanted.

If your organization decides that permanence—or at least a few generations of existence—are required, it should then discuss how the principal of an endowment will be invested and how the interest will be used. These questions don't have to be entirely sorted out in order to start an endowment, and you'll need to build an element of flexibility into the answers. But certain discussions are bound to arise: some people will imagine that their fundraising burden will be lessened by the income that is generated by an endowment, while others will see the endowment income as a vehicle for expanding programs beyond what they are currently able to raise funds for. This discussion about what to do with the interest will inform the size of the endowment the group aims for and the methods it will use to raise endowment funds. Will you go the route of Community Concerned and simply let the endowment grow? Will you conduct a full-scale endowment campaign? The how-to's of creating an endowment are explored in a number of books, including my book *Fundraising for Social Change*.

The questions of what financial stability would look like for your organization, what strategy to use in pursuing it, how to make sure your financial planning is mission-driven, how to think for the long term—and how long the long term *is*—are all important to discuss. It may take months to achieve consensus, but it is worth the time spent. These kinds of discussions strengthen the only really lasting endowment your organization has: the passion and commitment of the activists (whether staff or volunteers) and the creation of similar passion in new people.

In this part of the book, we have explored what you can do to maintain stability in your organization and to correct any problems before they turn into a crisis, and finally, how your organization really can grow and thrive, regardless of what is happening in the economy.

Some organizations, however, are already in crisis. In the next part, we will look at what that means and what they should do.

Part Three

What to Do if You Are in a Financial Crisis

Your organization may not be able to do the detailed work recommended in Part Two to strengthen your fundraising program because you are actually in a crisis right now. The crisis may have been brought on by some aspect of the economic turmoil the world is in, such as being in a community that is experiencing extremely high unemployment or having lost the majority of your funding with the loss of foundation or government support. Or it may have been brought on by a scandal or mismanagement. However you got there, you now have to figure out how to get out of it.

In this part we explore how to handle a crisis. It's useful to keep in mind that every problem an organization has will eventually show up in its fundraising and ultimately its financial health, leading most organizations to think that their problem has to do with their fundraising. However, difficulties with fundraising are often simply symptoms of a problem or part of a larger problem. To solve the problem requires correctly identifying it; otherwise, the solution will be only a temporary fix.

As you analyze what is going on in your organization, remember that a problem is not a crisis. Even a serious problem may not be a crisis. Determining whether you need to avoid a crisis or deal with one requires knowing the difference.

In general, these are the identifiers of a crisis:

- *No easily identifiable problem.* If an otherwise healthy organization starts to have a serious cash flow problem, or a serious disagreement arises between the board chair and the executive director, or the group receives bad publicity about something, it may get into a crisis. But it probably won't, for the simple reason that the organization can focus on the single problem, figure out the possible solutions, and solve it. It may not be easy and it may not be pleasant, but it is not likely to turn into a crisis.

- *No easy solution.* A crisis is often the result of leaving problems unaddressed or denied. This blinkered approach not only causes the problem to get worse but also often spawns other problems, so the solution won't be a one-step action. In a situation in which it's difficult to identify a single problem that lends itself to a straightforward solution, an organization needs to do something quickly to get out of crisis mode, but it can't be the wrong thing, because the group doesn't have the luxury of making more mistakes.

- *If the organization continues on its current path it will have to close.* In situations in which the forecast of more of the same will lead to ruin, the people running the organization have no choice but to change. But what kind of change, how fast they can change, who is going to lead the change, and, above all, how the change can be made permanent, are extremely serious considerations and will need careful thought and appropriate action.

To make the point more clearly, let's look at two examples of organizations. The first has a serious problem:

> A social service agency serving a wide range of low-income clients is told by their government funder that unless they verify the immigration status of the people they serve and stop serving any undocumented persons, they will lose their funding. As government funds account for 30 percent of their budget, this group does not have an easy decision. However, in looking at the budget of their state and the kinds of cutbacks that are going on all around them, they realize they will quite likely lose their funding—or much of it—anyway. Rather than comply with regulations they feel are unjust and unprincipled, they decide to do an organizing campaign to call this issue to the attention of the general public.

Although some people agree with the state requirement, most find it unfair and burdensome. The group uses the momentum from this campaign to broaden their individual donor program, and the public pressure that the campaign brings to bear results in the group's losing only about 10 percent of their state funding. They are able to replace that funding in two years by focusing on their new individual donors. Result: they have stayed within their mission (to serve all clients regardless of immigration status) without diminishing their overall income.

The second organization is in a crisis:

A community group in a poor section of a big city organizes on issues of greatest concern to their constituents, including lead paint in the schools and insurance companies redlining their neighborhoods. The group has won some impressive victories. Their success has attracted foundation funding for several years in a row, with foundation funders even approaching them to offer grant money. As a result, the staff expands over several years from two to fifteen. As they hire staff from outside the neighborhood, more and more work is done by the staff and less by community volunteers. Over time, staff salaries become larger than the salaries of most of the people living in the neighborhood. Many of the activist members, feeling that the organization is not focusing on its base, volunteer less, putting more burden on the staff.

As the economy sours, some of the funders do not renew their grants, and the group's income plummets. The executive director lays off five people; five others apply for unemployment insurance and continue to work as volunteers while looking for other paid work. Nonetheless, the group's financial situation continues to deteriorate.

When this organization first started, their fundraising included special events, membership dues, and even a small major donor program. In the early years, foundation funding never exceeded 50 percent of their income. Paid staff and activists worked side by side. As they attracted more foundation money, however, they stopped doing their events. People in the neighborhood who weren't volunteers no longer gathered to celebrate victories or help identify issues. Foundation funders, rather than community members, suggested issues the group could work on, and researchers, rather than neighborhood meetings, provided information for organizing. The executive director was invited to national conferences and had less time to meet with local leaders. The development director's time was spent writing proposals and reports to funders, so the newsletter came out less and less frequently. Membership dues were given up as being too hard to collect.

This is a classic crisis of organizations that were formed in the 1990s, when increasing numbers of foundations and their growing assets were focused on funding social change work. When this organization loses its foundation funding, it discovers that it has also lost its greatest asset—its membership. It may well be able to recover, but the group will need to recognize to whom they belong and to whom they are accountable. (See also Chapter Five: Creating a Fundraising Philosophy.) Fundraising can help solve this problem. By reinstituting membership dues and going door to door to collect them, the group can reintroduce themselves to their constituency. Holding a special event in the community will reenergize activists, and holding some town meetings will help identify issues that the group can work on. It will be a rocky road, but this group can recover and move forward if they are able to permanently institute the changes they need to by looking back to their original mission, philosophy, and constituency.

Why is it important to know whether you are in a crisis as opposed to a serious cash-flow problem or a serious personnel issue? For two reasons: first, a crisis requires a plan that causes a fundamental shift in the way an organization does business, a shift that makes a permanent difference. A problem—like loss of funding, as for the social service agency—can grow into a crisis if it causes an organization to lose sight of its mission and principles and if the organization does not see in it an opportunity to build or rebuild its grassroots fundraising program.

Second, a crisis requires mobilizing help from a variety of people who will rally to the crisis but will not be available very often. It requires a profound response to a deeply troubling situation. Donors will respond generously to one or even two organizational crises, but they don't like it when an organization seems to lurch from crisis to crisis. They begin to think that either you are not telling the truth ("crying wolf") or your organization is incompetent. Whatever they think, they begin to stop giving, so you don't want to be in a crisis very often, and you don't want to exaggerate something into a crisis that is not one.

To determine whether you are in a crisis, ask yourself these questions:

- If left unchecked, will what is happening result in our having to close our doors?
- If left unchecked, will what is happening result in our having to change our mission significantly?
- Do a lot of people around the organization feel that the situation is hopeless?
- Is immediate drastic action called for?
- Is there no clear immediate solution?
- Is this crisis the climax of a series of events that have led up to it, even if it is precipitated by one major event?

If you answer yes to two or more of these questions, you are in a crisis. Mobilizing to solve a crisis is different in scale, in depth, and in outcome than mobilizing to solve a problem, so if you are going to employ all the suggestions in the next few chapters, make sure you are in a crisis. Your best bet, of course, is to stay out of a crisis; using the suggestions that follow, modified to suit your particular situation, may help you do that.

Chapter Fifteen

Immediate Steps for Handling Your Crisis

Once you have established that you are indeed in a crisis, there are immediate steps you must take. This chapter walks you through the details of those steps.

Create a Crisis Task Force

First, establish a *crisis task force.* This is a group of three to five people who will act as "mission control" for the next two months. Their job is short-term but will require a fairly intense time commitment. If the organization has staff, a staff person should be on the task force; at least one member should be from the board, and at least one should be an "at-large" person with no other affiliation in the group except a commitment to the cause. This person could be a loyal volunteer, a friend of a friend with some expertise in fundraising, a consultant willing to donate time—any of these people will round out the task force nicely. As much as possible, they should come to the task force without a lot of judgments of their own about how the group got into this crisis. They need to have a calm and reassuring presence, be able to keep focused on the big picture, and be able to keep decisions from being made based on anger, resentment, or other negative (albeit understandable) feelings. The crisis task force should be made up of people who are eminently trustworthy. Because they will need to know everything about how the crisis happened and what has been done so far, they will have to be able to keep information confidential. Finally, they need to believe deeply in the organization and the need for the organization to continue.

The crisis task force relates to the board and the rest of the staff through the board member or staff member who is on the committee, but it also does some direct reporting to the board. Because the task force is not an official body, its members need to be clear that they make recommendations but not decisions. The board can give them some authority and allow them to make certain decisions, which I will discuss later. To ensure that those members of the committee feel their time is being used well, the organization's formal authority structure (board, executive director) must take their recommendations very seriously and act on them in a timely manner. Because the group is in a crisis, this should not be hard to arrange, as any delay tends to worsen the crisis.

Choosing the Task Force

Ideally, the chair of the board and the executive director put the task force together, and they attend the first few meetings, but it is not required that they stay on the task force. The executive director will be taking a lot of direction from the task force, and the chair will be reporting about their work to the rest of the board. Obviously, if the crisis is a scandal, no one directly related to the scandal should be on the task force. Don't spend a lot of time choosing the task force. If board and staff cannot agree among themselves who should be on it, this should be seen as part of the crisis. Among all of you, you should be able to identify three, four, or five people whom everyone trusts to do this particular job.

Other Considerations in Choosing the Task Force

If the crisis is strictly about funding cuts, the task force will be composed of people who will focus on immediate ways of raising money and who will create a longer-term fundraising plan. If the crisis has legal elements, you need at least one member who is a lawyer with nonprofit experience. If the crisis is about financial mismanagement or poor budgeting, then having a bookkeeper or accountant as a member will be helpful. The aggregate skills present on this team need to add up to a group of people able to help the organization change course and save itself. Don't ask a lawyer or an accountant or a business person just for the sake of having someone with those qualifications on the team. You don't want people making the crisis into something it is not. For example, one crisis task force with a lawyer among its members spent a lot of time discussing the fact that a donor who was not able to pay his pledge could be sued for the money. A pledge is legally binding, but you really don't want to sue your donors or even spend more than one second talking about this situation. The lawyer's presence in this case was not helpful.

You may wish to start the task force with two people and add one or two more people once you are clear on what kinds of skills you need.

Work of the Task Force

The crisis task force is not an investigative body. They are concerned not so much with whose fault this is or what should have been done differently as with what needs to be done now and what must be done differently in the future. This is not to say that investigating what happened or figuring out what should have been done differently is not important, but it is not the main work of this committee.

The crisis task force meets frequently (possibly as often as weekly in the beginning) for one or two months—three months at most. The meetings will probably last two or three hours, and there may be one or two longer meetings of a day or so. In addition, the members of the task force will be making phone calls, meeting with staff and other board members, and answering questions as they come in. People have to be willing to make the time to do this job, which is why the length of the task force's life must be kept short.

Information the Task Force Gathers

Here is the information that the crisis task force will need to begin developing in their first meeting. If this information isn't available, then one of their first tasks will be to get it. The rest of this chapter and the next discusses these elements.

1. Are people committed to keeping the organization going? If the answer to this question is yes, then the rest of the questions are considered.
2. What happened to bring the organization to this point?
3. What is the cash flow projection for the next six months?
4. What fundraising plans are already in place?
5. What, if any, financial reserves are there, and what are the terms of using them?
6. What is the *immediate* financial need?
7. What are the organization's other immediate needs? (Examples: to reassure staff that their jobs are safe or to figure out layoff plans; to hire an interim director, negotiate paying bills late, deal with the media)
8. What do the funders and donors know about what has happened, and what do they think about it? Equally important, which funders and donors should be told and how much?
9. How, how often, and to whom does the task force communicate what it is doing?

The job of the crisis task force is to keep the group alive during the crisis, as well as figure out a fundraising plan, begin implementing that plan, and put in place steps to ensure that the crisis does not recur. Remember that a crisis is not a one-time-only unfortunate event in an otherwise smoothly functioning organization; it is the result of a series of missteps and miscalculations that have led up to the crisis. There can be a precipitating event, but the event alone cannot plunge the group into a crisis. Therefore, it will undoubtedly take a multilevel process to resolve the crisis and restore confidence.

In cases in which the crisis involves dealing with the media, the crisis task force will delegate those tasks to a few of the people on the task force or to another small committee, or possibly a public relations consultant. If the crisis involves dealing with the Internal Revenue Service or a state revenue agency, those contacts should be made by another small committee or auditor.

Answering the Questions

In collecting the information that will enable them to answer the key questions above, the members of the task force will see what steps need to be carried out.

1. Are people committed to keeping the organization going?

This is the most important question—and the answer is not always obvious. The tendency of organizations is to say, "Well, of course we must keep going. What will happen to the children/ trees/clients/research if we don't?" But the task force has to be clear from the get-go: feelings of *should, must, ought* will not sustain an organization. When people on the task force hear any of those three words, an alarm should go off in their heads.

The answer to the question needs to be a resounding, passionate, unhesitating "*Yes!*" When it is a lukewarm yes, an obligatory "Yes, it is our duty," or a kind of "I guess so" yes; or when you don't have at least a handful of people willing to put in the time—not only those on the task force, but also board members, volunteers, and staff—then that's another red flag for the task force members. An organization takes up a space that another organization could fill. Obviously, if the task force realizes that the organization is using up resources while giving the impression that a particular issue is being addressed or a service is being provided when it is not, then the task force needs to recommend that the organization consider closing. However, it's more often the case that an organization is doing a decent job, but without any passion, creativity, and enthusiasm. It is difficult to recommend that such an organization close, but it must be recognized that such an organization does the community a disservice to continue existing as is.

In the rare cases in which an organization does decide to fold, it is the job of the task force to decide how that will happen. Should another organization be given the office furniture and the mailing list? What termination package can be given to staff? Are there debts to be paid, and if so, who will take responsibility for paying them? What will the organization tell the public? Deciding to close is both a hard decision and surprisingly complicated, not unlike ending a marriage. If that is the decision, the task force will probably want to consult a consultant with experience in this arena.

2. What happened to bring the organization to this point?

Take the time in your first meeting to lay out what happened. This information will also inform your message, covered in Chapter Sixteen. Put up sheets of butcher paper and label one of them "Just the facts, ma'am" (if you are not old enough to remember the radio and television show *Dragnet,* then leave off the "Ma'am"). On that sheet you will write only things that you know for a fact are true. "She had probably been drinking for some time" is not a fact. "The Community Foundation will not pay the third installment on our grant no matter what we do" is one fact (will not pay) and one conclusion (no matter what we do). "We have $1,000 in our checking account as of this morning" is a fact.

People are free to say whatever they want, but whoever is recording for the group will write down only factual statements. Take the example, "The Community Foundation will not pay the third installment on our grant no matter what we do." You want to learn who said "no matter what we do." If it came from a program officer, then it would be good to find out the circumstances of the statement: Was the person angry about your situation? Might they reconsider when they are not as angry? Did they put this statement in writing? People say a lot of things when they are angry and hurt. Although these things may be true at the time, they don't necessarily *stay* true. If, on the other hand, "no matter what we do" is an interpretation put on the Community Foundation's news that they're not paying the third installment, then that interpretation should be left off of the list of facts.

Label another sheet of paper, "How did we get into this mess?" and make notes about what led up to the crisis and, in hindsight, what could have been done to prevent it. This discussion will not only give you information for your future plans but also ensure that everyone understands the full complexity of the crisis.

Make sure the meeting is run fairly strictly, or the tendency of the group will be to discuss the personalities around the crisis and try to point fingers. "Why didn't he see what was happening?" "I always knew she wasn't managing too well." "I heard that the board didn't even act on this until May." Statements like these are inevitable and shouldn't be censored, but in capturing what happened in order to prevent it from happening again, try to move people into an organizational analysis. For example, "The board chair will do anything to avoid a confrontation" becomes helpful when expressed like this: "The board chair had no training in conflict resolution, nor did anyone else in leadership, so the conflict wasn't resolved."

On a third sheet, write, "What else we need to know." In addition to needing to know the answers to the rest of the questions in the list you've just compiled, there may be other things you need to know—such as whether other organizations you work with might be willing to help you, or whether you are carrying debt, or what shape your fundraising infrastructure is in. Finding out what those things are will be among the first tasks of the task force after this meeting.

3. What is the cash flow projection for the next six months?

When I was first in fundraising, grassroots organizations that had money in the bank to pay all their bills for the next month were considered well off. To have three months' reserve was the ideal. Today, a reserve of three months is often considered minimal, and many organizations don't feel safe without knowing that they have money either in the bank or promised to them to cover expenses for the next year. In crisis times, this need for security must be reconsidered. Can you stay open for a month and use that month to raise money for the next month? This is a far easier task in the short term than thinking, "We must raise enough money for the next six months."

Think About Raising Money, Not About Cutting Costs

A cash flow projection for the next six months will show how imminent a financial crisis is. At least in the beginning, approach the crisis thinking, "How can we raise the money we need?" rather than "How can we cut expenses?" If there are obvious cuts or ways to save money, by all means, do them. You should be making any cost savings you can, whether the group is in a crisis or not. But most small organizations spend so little money that looking for places to save money without making cuts in basic programs is often not a good use of time.

You will find that the instinct of many people is to cut expenses rather than raise money. The task force should resist this reflex as much as possible and instead use this crisis to create new income streams. Cutting expenses will not provide any permanent solution to your crisis, nor will it move you in a new direction as an organization.

For example, an all-volunteer organization applied for a grant to fund their first full-time staff position. An activist who had helped found the organization and who already volunteered about twenty hours a week—when she wasn't at her paid job as a waiter—was to be the staff. Their proposal, which they had been told probably would be funded, was ultimately turned down. The organization concluded that they couldn't hire this person. She decided to keep her job as a waiter and continue to do the work as a volunteer. When I met with them, I suggested another option.

"Are waiter jobs easy to get in this town?" Answer: Yes.

"Does the organization have enough money to pay you the same amount you make as a waiter, including tips, for one month?" Answer: Yes.

"Then, are you willing to quit your job, work full time here, and raise the money for your salary for the next month? Are you willing to try that for three or four months while you and rest of the organization raise the money it needs to offer you permanent work, knowing that at any time you could fairly easily get another waiter job?"

Neither she nor the other members of the collective that ran this project had ever thought in these terms. They decided to try it for one month. During that month, the new staff person solicited six-month pledges and received positive responses from twenty people, which promised enough money to pay her a salary and cover her health insurance for the next six months. Six of the twenty donors offered to continue their pledge past the six-month point, and two others promised to replace themselves with other donors. The staff person and her group now have six months to work out a fundraising plan and to see what can be accomplished with a full-time paid staff person.

Your cash flow projection will also help you figure out your immediate financial need. Figure 15.1 presents an example.

4. What fundraising plans are already in place?

The cash flow chart will show the projected income for the next six months, but the task force needs to review what fundraising plans already exist so they can decide what new plans to add to the mix. They also need to make sure the plan is realistic and that the planning process isn't part of the problem. Many organizations set goals that they never meet, and over time, this laxness gets them into financial difficulty.

5. What, if any, financial reserves are there, and what are the terms of using them?

Sometimes organizations in financial crisis have endowments or reserve funds. (This is different from designated funding that has been granted to you for a specific program. Generally, you want to dip into that funding only with permission of the funder.)

One ten-year-old organization with a budget of $750,000 had $100,000 in a reserve fund in the bank. They received a string of bad news all in the same week: over the next three months, they would lose their lease and have to move; they were losing a government contract that provided 50 percent of their income; and two of their nine board members were having to relocate because of job loss. In that week, all of this would have constituted a serious problem, but instead of figuring out how to use the three months' lead time they had to start raising money, the board and staff panicked. Where should they move to? How much rent could they afford? Should they cut the program the grant was for or try to get other funding? Who was going to want to be on the board of an organization with all these problems? These questions were legitimate, but their panic made it hard for them to proceed systematically to find out what they needed to know.

Fundraising Cash-Flow Projections (Sample)

	Jan	Feb	Mar	Apr	May	June	July	Aug	Sept	Oct	Nov	Dec	TOTALS
General Expense													
Staff Salaries and Overhead	(2,200)	(2,200)	(2,200)	(2,200)	(2,200)	(2,200)	(2,200)	(2,200)	(2,200)	(2,200)	(2,200)	(2,200)	(26,400)
Fundraising Strategy													
1. Direct Mail													
Income		1,500	1,000		500								3,000
Expense		(3,750)											(3,750)
2. Major Donor Campaign													
Income					4,000	6,000					8,000	5,000	23,000
Expense				(500)									(500)
3. House Parties													
Income		1,000	1,000		1,000			2,000				1,000	6,000
Expense	(250)												(250)
4. Annual Dinner													
Income						5,000	4,000		12,000	1,200			22,200
Expense (including consultant)				(500)	(1,000)	(1,000)	(2,500)	(3,500)	(1,000)				(9,500)
5. Renewal Mailing													
Income			3,000	2,000							2,500	2,000	9,500
Expense		(250)								(250)			(500)
TOTALS	(5,200)	3,300	(200)		2,300	7,800	(700)	(3,700)	8,800	(1,250)	8,300	5,800	**25,250**

They wasted weeks dithering; after six months, they were in a financial crunch. They were using general operating funds to pay for the program whose grant had been cut, so these funds were soon exhausted; they still had no place to move to; and the smaller board was feeling overwhelmed. At that point, they started making decisions about cutting costs. Some staff were laid off and all but two others quit.

They moved to a large converted garage that belonged to a friend of a board member. Six months later, they had very little going on in terms of programs, they still were not fundraising, and they were slowly strangling to death. They refused to use any of their reserve to continue their work while they figured out what to do. "The reserve fund is for a rainy day," they explained to me. "Once we spend it, it is gone." All they could think of was to hang on and hunker down, as though the crisis were a tornado and they could only come out after it was all over and survey the damage. Their commitment to keeping their reserve was admirable but misplaced. They needed to use some of that same commitment to keeping their organization functioning.

Going into financial reserves, especially an endowment, is not a decision to take lightly; it should be done only to help with fundraising or to buy time. It is not a solution to a funding crisis. In the case of an endowments, an organization needs to review what access they have. For an endowment, the terms of the donor's will may make access difficult, but most of the time the board has the option to spend out of an endowment under certain circumstances. Reserve funds and saving accounts can be spent much more easily. On the other hand, knowing you have that money and that you could use it if you had to is so reassuring that most people will go to great lengths *not* to use it. This is healthy if it makes people raise money and do the work needed to keep the group out of a crisis or to get them out of a crisis. It is not healthy if protecting the endowment becomes more important than the mission of the organization, as in our example.

If you enter an aggressive fundraising program with a "the sky is falling" message, and then donors find out that you had adequate money in savings all along, they may feel angry. Similarly, laying off staff or cutting programs because you won't touch your reserve is a difficult position to justify.

Think of the reserve fund as a line of credit. You may borrow from it for cash flow if you can show how, in a few months (or next year), you will pay it back. Don't be afraid to spend it wisely, but again, see raising money as the key to getting out of this crisis. The reserve can then be used as front money for developing fundraising strategies that you may not have been using up to now.

Getting a Line of Credit

Many groups don't have financial reserves. In that case, you may want to approach your bank and set up a line of credit. A line of credit lets you borrow up to a certain amount and pay it back over a period of years. You don't access the money until you need it, and you take out—and pay interest on—only what you need. A line of credit allows you to pay for a mailing, to hire a consultant temporarily, or to spend money in some other way that is necessary in the short term for the long-term health of the group. If you find a line of credit hard to get, which may be the case, then you may want to get a company credit card with strict rules about who can use it and for what.

Using reserves, borrowing money—these are tactics we learn from businesspeople, who often recognize the problem in a nonprofit as being one of chronic undercapitalization. In our personal lives, we recognize the importance of being able to use savings or borrow money in order to send someone to college or buy a house or a car. Though we are going into debt, we have a plan for meeting that debt, and the goal is worth it. We need to use the same reasoning in our nonprofit.

Using Reserves to Get Out of a Crisis

A children's museum loses its third executive director in as many years. In her exit interview, she says what the previous two directors said: she has worked sixty hours a week, and she is tired of it, and she can't get the board to recognize that they need to hire more staff. Although they are not in a crisis yet, they form a transition team that functions pretty much the same way a crisis team would.

The transition team discovers that the museum's gift shop is a potential source of revenue, but it has not been run in such a way as to make it profitable. The board created a rule years earlier that inventory must be funded by the profits from sales, not credit. This rule has worked to the museum's disadvantage, as there is never enough profit to purchase inventory at the volume required for deep discounts, which would give the organization more profit. If the gift shop were to purchase one hundred kids' microscopes at a time, for example, they could get each one for $10; they sell them for $32. However, they never seem to have enough money to buy more than five microscopes at a time for $20 each, despite the fact that they often run out of microscopes on busy weekends. Given the slim profit margin of the gift shop, some board members question whether it is worth the effort.

The museum also has $50,000 in a savings account. The transition team recommends they invest $25,000 of that in the gift shop—purchasing inventory, advertising more widely, and jazzing up their website to create an online version of the gift store. Almost immediately, both the onsite store and the virtual store begin to show a much better profit and increased customer base. A year later the museum opens another gift shop at a mall across town. Between that and the online store, there is enough profit to pay for a full-time communications coordinator. The success of the stores and the work of the communications coordinator all increase interest in the museum, generating more admission fees. Visitors to the museum are invited to become donors, and the donor base doubles. The group is able to pay back the $25,000 "loan" from their reserves in six months, and they have hired a new executive director and an assistant to the director.

6. What is the immediate financial need?

In many cases, there is no immediate financial need, although the group can project that there will be one in a few months if a fundraising plan is not implemented successfully. However, sometimes there is an immediate problem—the organization needs money to cover debts already incurred or to pay staff. Figure out what the current expenses are and how soon they must be paid. Many times landlords and vendors are willing to work out a payment plan if they feel that you are making an honest effort to pay them in full. In a soft rental market, a landlord may even lower rent for a month or two rather than risk losing a good tenant.

7. What are the organization's other immediate needs?

One immediate need for most groups is to keep the staff in the loop. Often, in a larger organization, management staff may know what is being done to address the crisis, but a secretary, receptionist, or part-time person—and sometimes even program staff—may not have a clue. Should they look for another job? Will they be paid? These are scary questions, and when people feel they are being shut out of a process, they become suspicious; as each of them confides their fears to other workers, friends, and family, this adds to the rumors about what is happening and erodes morale.

In the same way that the instinct of many groups is to cut costs, it's also instinctive to want to maintain a veil of secrecy over everything. But it is very important to fight that shrinking, hiding, hunkering-down mentality—it doesn't raise money, and it doesn't build a team that wants to fight for the organization.

Making sure that people feel that decisions affecting them are not being made behind their backs or without proper consultation is very important to resolving a crisis. Often when a group finds itself in a crisis, in the course of resolving that crisis the members manage to create several more because of their process. Oral reports to staff are preferable to written ones. Phone calls are preferable to e-mail. It will take time to create an atmosphere in which people can ask questions, offer to help, and offer their own opinions, but will take less time than handling the fallout and the bad feelings that come of not doing so.

A weekly or biweekly meeting of all staff is very important. If you foresee layoffs, tell people as soon as you know for sure. In an economy with high unemployment, losing a job is hard enough, but losing it with little notice is devastating. Try to raise or keep enough money in reserve to give people at least two weeks' notice and a small severance package.

Another immediate need may be to deal with an executive transition. In that case, consider hiring an interim person while you figure out what the new director's role should be. Sometimes an interim executive director can take care of a lot of unpleasant things to make the job more attractive to a more permanent director. An interim director can change the way staff has been working, institute new systems, and generally do things that might not make the person popular but will make the organization run more efficiently.

For example, a small suicide prevention hotline had two long-time employees: a financial manager and an executive director. Over the years, the financial manager had never switched the accounting systems to a computer, but had continued to keep all records in a ledger, by hand. The executive director spent too much time buying office supplies on sale or attending conferences on volunteerism. Consequently, the organization had far too many office supplies and the executive director was less available to the volunteers than she should have been. Because their salaries were minimal and the hotline managed to stay in business, the board was willing to overlook the inefficiencies. For the past several years, however, the organization had been raising less and less money. Then the executive director quit.

Recognizing that the organization would gradually fade into nonexistence if its whole way of doing business was not addressed, the board decided to hire an interim executive director while they created a strategic plan for the agency. The interim executive director immediately asked that the financial manager learn to use a computer and get rid of the excess office supplies. The financial manager took this request badly and started calling in sick most days. The interim executive director then suggested to the board that both jobs could easily be done by one person (the new executive director) and that the financial manager be offered a three-month severance package. Although there were hurt feelings, the interim executive director was able to get the organization to a point where it was attractive to a new person seeking a challenge.

8. What do the funders and donors know about what has happened, and what do they think about it? Equally important, which funders and donors should be told and how much?

Ideally, a crisis is handled internally in such a way that as few people as possible outside the organization know about it. This approach is not meant to be secretive, but rather to keep attention focused on the work. However, funders, major donors, key volunteers—anyone with close ties to the organization—need to find out from the organization first what has happened. That way you can control rumors and get out a consistent message about the health of your organization, as discussed in the next chapter. Knowing what the donors know and what they think about the crisis may give you a sense of who may be willing to make a one-time-only extra donation to pay for the immediate need, so that the organization can create a plan to move forward without carrying debt.

9. How, how often, and to whom should the task force communicate what it is doing?

If you have regular verbal reports, and if everyone in the organization feels that their questions or concerns are welcomed and they have someone they can go to with them, then you can augment all that with written reports to the board, staff, and volunteers.

Above all, reports from the task force and from the board and executive director to staff should focus on the present and the future. There should be ways for people to be involved. Don't be afraid to ask people to help—they will be pleased and flattered that you have included them.

Chapter Sixteen

Mission, Message, and Damage Control

Whenever the economy goes into a tailspin, I hear donors say things like, "I have always given to the Film Festival, but this year we need to be marching in the streets, not going to the movies," or, "In an ideal world, we would have a ballet here in town, but right now the money needs to be used for homeless people," or "Of course preserving species is important, but with children going to bed hungry, I just can't see giving money to save birds."

These remarks are indicative of how, in hard times, people begin to pose false choices: we cannot go to the movies until there is world peace, we cannot have a ballet until there is no homelessness, we cannot save birds until all children are well fed. They see redistributing their own gift-giving as the only way to respond to the economic downturn.

I say these are false choices because there is enough money for all our nonprofits—to feed the hungry and to continue the arts; to make sure people are housed and to house the ballet. To get them all funded, however, will require all of us—and particularly the government—to rethink national priorities and redistribute wealth, so that funding goes where it is truly needed and our taxes are used appropriately. A shortage of money is not the problem.

Once you have reminded yourself of that fact, you see why all nonprofits have to work together to advocate for fairer taxes and a more fair distribution of wealth. Then you can ask the most vital question for your organization: How can our organization raise the money we need? The answer is complex, but it starts with clarifying your message, which is the topic of this chapter. In the examples just given, the film festival, ballet, and endangered species groups may have failed to articulate a compelling message to their donors, so some donors felt all right about leaving them for what they perceived to be more pressing social issues. If you work with hungry children or homeless people, you may not care if people make that kind of choice until you remind yourself that these same people will stop supporting *your* organization for something more compelling—say, nuclear disarmament, elimination of land mines, or an end to malaria. Consider this comment from a (former) major donor to a low-income housing fund: "I am not giving any money to programs for poor people in the United States any more. The poorest person here is not nearly as poor as people in Africa." If a donor operates out of a hierarchy of needs, there will always be someone more needy and some concern more pressing than your organization's.

In creating a message for your organization, you find what is important—in fact, what is undeniably persuasive—about what you do. You do not pose it as being more or less important than anything else. Your work is important in itself. If your organization should exist during economic boom times, why shouldn't its mission be important during more lean years?

Return to Your Case Statement

In Chapter Fifteen, I said that an organization facing or trying to avert a crisis needs to affirm, in no uncertain terms, its commitment to its existence—or it should close. It will be helped a great deal in this effort if it has a current and complete case statement. If you are in a crisis, the case statement is imperative for doing any damage control that may be required and for making sure that everyone close to the organization is using the same message in describing what has happened. Perhaps most important, the case statement is the cornerstone for raising money effectively—crisis or no.

Organizations that operate without a clear case statement are at a disadvantage in raising money before they even begin. They can't state why they need the money or what they have done with the money that has been given to them before. This lack of definition makes them unattractive to donors. The sidebar shows what a case statement contains in "normal" times. It is a living document that board members and staff work with to create programs and policies, and it is the foundation of a strategic plan. It should be used to orient new board members, and its language should be the basis of brochures, annual reports, direct mail appeals, and foundation proposals. Too often, however, board and staff spend a long time creating the case statement and then file it away. You should make it part of everything your organization does.

The Case Statement

A case statement should inform your work every day. Copies of the case statement should be present at every board and staff meeting, and it should be the basis on which decisions are made. It should be kept up-to-date and fully reviewed at least annually for relevance and clarity. Every person closely associated with the organization should be able to repeat from memory the organization's mission

---

THE CASE STATEMENT

The case statement includes the following elements:

- A statement of mission that tells the world why the group exists

- A description of goals that tells what the organization hopes to accomplish over the long term—that is, what the organization intends to do about why it exists

- A list of specific, measurable, and time-limited objectives that tells how the goals will be met

- A summary of the organization's history that shows that the organization is competent and can accomplish its goals

- A description of the structure of the organization discussing board and staff roles and the types of people involved in the group (such as clients, organizers, teachers)

- A fundraising plan

- A financial statement for the previous fiscal year and a budget for the current fiscal year

statement and goals and at least some of the objectives and history of the organization contained in the case statement. The fact that most people in most organizations cannot do so is what leads to some of the crises we are exploring in this book. During a crisis, a case statement becomes a combination of an oath of allegiance, a blueprint for action, and a source of inspiration for the work ahead.

So when you first find yourself in a crisis or trying to head one off, pull out your case statement. If you can't do that because you don't know where it is or you know it is inadequate, then you will have to create a new one or fix the problems with your existing one.

Creating a Message

Assuming you have an adequate case statement, when facing or trying to avert a crisis you need to add an element called *message*. The message is specific to your current situation. The crisis task force or the board poses the question: "What does this organization bring to the current reality that is so critical that the organization should exist right now?" To put it more baldly, many organizations are going to go out of business in the next few years. Why shouldn't yours be one of them? The crisis task force should answer the question themselves and also get answers from the board and staff. Look for consistency in the message—people may have variations on a theme, but what is the theme?

A clear message doesn't mean that your fundamental mission changes or that you even change your work at all. It simply shows that you understand your work in the context of the larger world.

Here's an example. An affordable housing group believes people should be able to live in the community in which they work, if they so desire. When they started their organization, their community had low unemployment, but a lot of people commuted from nearby towns because housing near their workplace was so expensive. Two years later, the community has high unemployment and people are losing their homes because they can't pay their rent or mortgage. The affordable housing organization maintains the same mission—"People should be able to live where they work"—but now they institute other actions to fulfill their mission. For example, to help people stay in their homes, they create an emergency loan fund so people can borrow money easily for housing costs, and they work with local banks to stop foreclosures. Their message is, "We make sure that losing your job does not mean losing your home."

Their mission is the same, but the message reflects what is happening with housing in their community. It also reflects some very hard work on the part of the board and staff to create these new programs.

Here's another example of a distinction between mission and message that an organization uses to avoid a crisis. A well-regarded youth symphony orchestra serving a large geographic area has as its mission, "We believe children should be able to develop their musical talent as fully as possible and the community should benefit from the talents of its younger members." Over the course of a few months, two sources of funding are threatened: a state arts endowment grant is cut, and a foundation whose funding they had counted on tells them they have more pressing needs to fill. At the same time, more kids are signing up for the group's summer music camps and trying out for their various programs. They realize that many kids are eager for a musical education that the public schools no longer offer. Although their mission remains the same, their message becomes more compelling for these times: "Children should be musically educated. We augment the work of the schools in providing musical education for our community's children." This message puts forth their belief that the public schools should provide music and art education while reaffirming their need to exist to augment meager public resources.

They form an advocacy task force of parents and board members to pressure the school district to find money for music education in the public schools. In the meantime, they are continuing to meet an immediate need. When they present this point of view to their foundation funder, the funder reconsiders and restores most of their grant. With its new message, the group is also able to attract donors who may not be that interested in hearing young people play music but who agree that music should be part of children's education.

Mission is forever, but message is more urgent and immediate.

When Message Is Damage Control

When an organization is in an internal crisis, the message is more along the lines of damage control—explaining what happened and making sure everyone who should have the necessary information does have it. Here's an example:

An organization has a history of sloppily kept or nonexistent donor records. Often, gifts are not recorded properly, people are not thanked or they are thanked for the wrong thing, donors are reminded of pledges they have not made, and some donors who have made pledges are not reminded of them. A new development director has been hired to improve the situation, and the message has gone out to board members that these problems are now over. However, early in the new development director's tenure, a number of events cause the board to question whether recordkeeping has actually improved. First, a major donor tells a board member that the pledge form he received commits him to a ten-thousand-dollar gift, but he had pledged only five thousand dollars. The executive director speaks to all parties; though the development director insists the pledge was for ten thousand dollars, the donor is equally sure it was for five thousand. The executive director changes the pledge form, reassures the development director that this donor has been inconsistent in the past, and lets the board member know this was probably not a recordkeeping issue. Next, the development director seriously overstates the percentage of return on a direct-mail appeal. When the discrepancy surfaces, he claims that he was so busy entering respondents into the database that he made a math error in figuring the percentage of response. The third month, the development director announces an impending grant for twenty-five thousand dollars. When the executive director calls to thank the foundation funder, she learns that no such grant has been proposed nor is one forthcoming.

Now the executive director realizes that the previous truth of bad systems has been supplanted by a bigger current truth: the development director is a liar. She fires the development director immediately and calls the board chair, who informs the board members of what has happened. The executive director talks to the other two staff. They and the board chair agree on the message to go out: "We were unable to get accurate information from the development office. Because the development director was still on probation, we have terminated his contract." The board members and the staff will know more specifics, but no one else needs to.

The executive director lets the foundation funder know that the development director has been terminated because he sometimes gave misleading information, and she asks the funder to pass along the information to anyone who needs to know. This funder is a reliable and trusted member of the funding community and likes this group. Her word among funders and major donors that things are being handled properly is important.

This organization averted a more serious crisis by handling the situation immediately once they understood it. In this crisis, only a few people really needed to be involved, but they were kept informed throughout. By enlisting a trusted messenger to the larger funding community (the foundation funder), the organization was able to control any fallout from what the development director had done.

Getting the Board on Board

In crises, we often focus on the opinions of people outside the group—the donors, the clients, even the general public. Yet our greatest difficulty in forming a message and relaying it is often at the board or staff level. It is critical that board and staff know that their opinions and feelings are welcome; further, they must not feel that they are being asked to lie or be evasive with others, but they must also understand the importance of good judgment and tact in handling difficult matters. Board and staff must be involved in the process of exploring options and discussing all the points of view, or they can quickly feel stifled. In one such situation, the board chair explained to a major donor, "I'll tell you what I am supposed to say and leave you to read between the lines." As one funder later reported to a small group, "Even the board chair just says, 'read between the lines.'" Needless to say, this is not good message development or message control.

Your message should not be evasive or vague. If there are legal issues involved, ask your lawyer what you can say and what would be legally dangerous or off limits. But if there are no legal issues, then figure out how you can tell the whole truth but keep returning to the mission of the group. Underscoring these recommendations about developing your message is my firm conviction that you are always better off telling the truth and only the truth. However, you may not be telling the whole truth right away in a crisis until you are sure that you *know* the whole truth. In big crises, the truth has a way of changing with time and with whoever is doing the telling.

Message development may take some time and may surface some important discussions as the crisis develops and is worked through. The process of developing the message can also be part of the message, particularly when board members have divergent opinions, as in the following example.

An after-school program for teenagers provides a basketball court, a bank of computers for doing homework, an art room, and volunteer adult counselors. Half the funding for the program comes from the local Department of Parks and Recreation and the other half from the business community and a cross section of parents. The program has one paid staff person and fifty volunteers; its annual budget is $150,000.

Because of the economic downturn, the parks and rec department is forced to make serious budget cuts in their programs, resulting in their canceling two-thirds of their funding of the after-school program. The downturn also causes some businesses to cut back on their donations to the program. In a matter of a few months, the organization experiences a 40-percent decrease in funding.

The board calculates that they can run the program at its current level for six months while they figure out how to raise more money. They announce to the parents and students, "Everything is fine right now. We are seeking other sources of funding, and we encourage each of you to give money and help raise money."

As the board works with the executive director to create a fundraising plan, philosophical differences develop. Many board members have worked hard to advocate for government funding for the program. The mission of the organization, "Teenagers are a community asset and need to be nurtured," implies that the government has a role. These board members feel that even if the program could be sustained with private donations, it shouldn't be, and that it would be more principled to close it. "That's not fair to the kids," says the other faction. "We have to try to run the program on less money or raise money elsewhere." The board is further split when one member suggests raising money by renting part of the space to armed services recruiters, supporting the view that the armed services represent good jobs and scholarships for kids along with the option of income for the program. Long-time peace activists in the group are appalled at the potential sellout. Amid these discussions, fundraising planning is stalled. The public message, "We are exploring options," is wearing thin, particularly as the various arguments begin to be put forward to the parents, students, and business community. Everyone has an opinion.

The board decides on a bold course: get concerted community input on the various options. The board writes a short letter to parents, teachers, business people, and the community at large, presenting the dilemma: "How do we best show how much our teenagers mean to us? We believe our program deserves government funding, but in these times, that kind of funding is not available. If we are to replace our lost government grant, we must have the help of the entire community. We need to know your opinions. Please come to a town meeting on March 23 at the Center. The meeting will start at 6 P.M. sharp, and a light dinner will be served. Bring your opinions and an open heart for listening and hearing others."

About fifty people come and engage in an intensive discussion. With skillful facilitation, they reach a consensus: the program will seek private funding, but the city council will be asked to pass a resolution declaring the program a city treasure. Seeking government funding will be a top priority. The center will not be available to armed services or any other recruiters. As has always been true, employers can post job announcements there, and anyone can post announcements of scholarships, internships, and volunteer or job opportunities.

The message created at the meeting is simple: "We have chosen to put the teenagers ahead of all other concerns. We believe teenagers are a community asset, and we as a community pledge to keep this program open." By going public with their differences, this organization ensured that differences of opinion about the future of the center could be reviewed in one place at one time so that they could be resolved.

Let's look at another example in which the board had to overcome differing points of view. This situation turned out differently, but in its own way, just as well.

The founding executive director of an organization advocating for the civil rights of lesbians, gays, bisexuals, and transgendered (LGBT) people dies suddenly of a heart attack. A small inheritance had allowed her to work without salary, and she had devoted her life to the cause. A dedicated and articulate advocate, she had spoken about the rights of LGBT people to every church, synagogue, service club, chamber of commerce, women's group, conference, or gathering in her state that would allow her to, and she taught a course at the local community college on counseling in the LGBT community. Her death has devastated the organization.

The group has two paid staff. One is the executive director's personal assistant, who has handled correspondence, phone calls, and speaking arrangements; the other has handled the finances, both helping to raise money and to record how money was spent. The staff and board have mainly been in place to support this vibrant and activist executive director. Her vision was their vision. Without her there is, at least temporarily, no viable organization. Now the board has to figure out what the organization is without her. The board chair calls together the board, staff, and some other volunteers, all of whom were long-time friends of this woman. Calls are still coming in, asking to book her as a speaker; letters and e-mails need to be answered; and there is an upsurge in donations to honor the executive director's memory.

The board chair hires an organizational development consultant to help figure out what to do. After listening to them for a while, she outlines their choices:

1. Close down. Admit that the organization was really all the wonderful work of one person and now that person is gone. You still will have made an extraordinary difference in thousands of peoples' lives. Ending does not mean failure.
2. Find another organization with similar goals and let your program become a program of theirs. Give that group the list of your donors and what money remains in the bank account, then refer all calls and letters to them.

3. Hire a new director and reinvent the organization. Raise the money to pay an executive director, keep the two staff people, and keep the program going or create new programs.

The consultant says that first the people left in the organization must recommit themselves to their mission, which reads: "We believe all things created by God are good, including all sexual identities. We imagine a world free of prejudice and stereotype, and we work for full inclusion of the LGBT community in all daily life."

Everyone agrees this is important work, but one by one each board member explains her or his position. Says one, "I mostly did this work for her." Another says, "When she was here, there wasn't much work to do—we just supported her." Still others use words to the effect of, "I don't have the energy, or time, patience, or knowledge to recreate this group without her." One or two board members say that they think most of the work is done, as there are now more groups doing advocacy work and people have far different attitudes than they did fifteen years ago. It is quickly clear that no one has the energy to continue the organization. A board committee finds another organization to give the organization's money, donor list, and office furniture to, and the group closes up the office. A letter goes out over the signature of the board chair explaining that, with the death of the founder, the time has come to let another organization carry the work forward. He names the organization they have transferred their assets to and asks that donors give money there from now on. With little more fanfare than that, the organization closes.

There are some groups that really are the vision and the work of one person; without that person, there is no group. As the consultant pointed out, ending is not failure, and sometimes closing the group is the most mission-driven decision.

Delivering the Message

The process of creating a message cannot be separated from the larger process of creating a response to a crisis. However, groups usually cannot wait until a full response is put in place before putting forth some kind of message. Donors, staff, and the public will need information about what is going on with the organization. The message that you start with, then, is the least amount of truth you can say without appearing to be hiding something. In fact, part of the message can be that you will be sending out more information as it becomes available. Don't be nervous about admitting that you don't know everything yet. It is better that "not knowing" be part of the message than to say something that later turns out to be false and have to issue a correction. Further, the message cannot be separated from the messenger. Finding well-respected and trustworthy people to help you deliver your message is just as important as the message itself. They can deliver the message and then conclude (assuming they feel this way), "I think everything will be fine," or "I have a lot of confidence in the team of people who are working on this." Finally, fundraisers always have to take into account the order in which the message will be delivered. Make sure that you don't inadvertently alienate someone simply by not informing them of the situation early on. The process of delivering the message, like the response to the crisis itself, happens in several parts.

Make a list of the people who need to hear about the crisis first. In addition to board and staff, think about any who think of themselves as close to your organization—the organizational "family." This will include active volunteers, long-time funders, long-time major donors, and sometimes former staff and board. In choosing who to tell first, you don't want to create such a long list that time you should be spending on planning is spent calling people. At the same time, these close-in people often are also people you will be approaching for donations. Remember, you can always tell someone, but you cannot untell them. When in doubt about whether someone is appropriate to tell, wait.

Next, you have to figure out who should be delivering the message to these people and how they should get it. Generally, people should be told through a call or a visit. Avoid e-mail; this can be forwarded too easily and may take on a life of its own, and inaccurate meanings can be read into phrases that would be clear if the message were delivered more personally. Long-time donors, funders, and volunteers make great messengers. Board members, particularly the chair of the board, can deliver the message, but may be perceived to be too close to the situation, possibly involved in creating the problem, and too defensive. Major donors are usually best told by the people who have solicited gifts from them in the past. The people who are told first can be enlisted to tell others. As they will probably want to tell someone anyway, this provides some control over message delivery.

Institute a regular way to keep the people on the list updated about what is happening. If, as in many crises, the situation unfolds over time, create a phone tree to keep people up to date. You can, at this point, decide to do an e-mail newsletter, but again, remember anything you write on e-mail can wind up anywhere—at the office of the FBI, on the front page of the paper, at the e-mail address of the person you have fired. You must think of e-mail as public information—no amount of marking it *"Confidential"* will change that.

Talking with Major Donors About the Crisis

All donors are important for three reasons: they chose to give to your organization when they could have chosen any number of others; any amount they give is that much less left to raise; and no matter what size of gift they start with, they may be able to give bigger gifts over time. A twenty-five-dollar donor may bring in her good friend who gives you ten thousand dollars. Further, someone who makes minimum wage and gives your organization thirty-five dollars is giving almost a day's take-home pay, whereas someone who earns one hundred thousand dollars a year would need to give about four hundred dollars to make an equivalent gift. Thus we respect every donation.

However, major donors get more fundraising time because they are giving more money. They usually feel they have made a bigger investment in the organization than a donor who gives a smaller amount, and a few extra major gifts from them will be a big help in getting an organization through a crisis.

When an organization is in a crisis, major donors need attention and reassurance. The donors who agree to talk with you, even on the phone, mostly need reassurance that their gift is not going down the drain. Will you raise the money you need? Will you be back next year with yet another crisis? Do you really know what you are doing? And if you do, how did you get into this mess in the first place?

Most donors realize, even if they are not able to articulate it, that a crisis is not just a big problem in an otherwise smoothly functioning organization. Although what caused the crisis may not be your fault, a crisis has a longer history than the crisis event. Remember also that these donors are likely being approached by other organizations that are also in crisis; moreover, they are reading about scandals, funding cutbacks, closures, and the like every day. In general, in a time of crisis, donors become insecure. They may tend to hold back or cut back, and they need more handholding and reassurance than they normally would.

There are four elements that will reassure almost all major donors: an explanation, a plan, evidence of other donors, and an escape clause. Most of them need to hear about just one or two of these.

An explanation. Major donors, particularly long-time major donors, are like family. In a family, when someone has a heart attack, or a couple decide to separate, or someone loses a job, the relatives expect more information about the situation than a neighbor does. Major donors to your organization are also likely to be big donors to a few other groups, and part of their insecurity is that, if it could happen to you, can the others be far behind? Tell these donors whatever you have agreed can be told to anyone close to the organization. Major donors should usually be told about as much as any funder or board member. Don't feel you have to launch into a long explanation. Give a brief summary of what happened, then be open to fielding the donor's questions. Some people will be far more curious than others; we don't want to bore people with details they are not interested in, but neither do we want to appear secretive.

A fundraising plan. A fundraising plan is a great reassurance for everybody, because it shows that you have thought through what is going to be required in the next few months to move out of the crisis. Your plan should be as realistic as possible, but reality is also shaped by plans, so your plan must be hopeful and optimistic. Be prepared to show any active or potential donor your cash-flow chart and a strategy-by-strategy description, including gross and net incomes for each strategy. Show them your gift-range chart and talk about the number of other people you are recruiting to help with funding during the crisis.

Help from other donors. Evidence that other people have bought into this plan is important. As you get gifts, ask if you can share the donor's name and the size of the gift with other prospects. If a donor knows that Manuel has given $5,000 and Sydney has given $2,500, and he likes and respects those two people, he is more likely to make his gift. Some donors are reluctant to have their names used; some are reluctant to reveal the amount of their gift. That is their privilege. You can always tell a prospect, "We have two other people who have given ten thousand dollars" without using their names. Having a board that has bought into the plan is critical here. Even if the board members are not able to be major donors themselves, you need to be able to say, "One hundred percent of our board members have made a gift that is significant for them to demonstrate their faith in our future."

An escape plan. Some donors need to be offered a contingency— they will give only if certain things happen. Of course, such a way out should be offered only if the person clearly indicates that's what is needed. If an organization seems to be telling the truth about what happened, has a reasonable fundraising plan that shows that the crisis will not happen again, and has commitment from the board and some other donors, most people do not require this fourth element.

Nonetheless, some of your biggest donors may want an escape plan. What does an escape plan look like in fundraising? Let's say you approach someone for a lead gift of ten thousand dollars on a one-hundred-thousand-dollar goal. The person is committed to your organization but hesitates, asking a lot of questions about where the other ninety thousand dollars is going to come from. Ask the donor how much money you would have to have raised toward the goal of one hundred thousand dollars for the donor to feel that the campaign was going to succeed. Some people will say, "If you had half of it, I would feel better." Others will say, "If you are able to get one more big gift, I would feel better." Offer the person the option of pledging conditionally. "Would you give ten thousand dollars when we get to fifty thousand dollars? Can we tell people that we have a challenge of this sort?" Some people want to see the rest of the money in place before they give their money. Offer that person the option of giving the last ten thousand dollars. "I understand your worry that we may not be able to find the rest of the money we need. We have a plan, but plans don't always succeed. What if you committed ten thousand dollars to be given when we have raised ninety thousand dollars?"

A challenge gift is a great motivator for the major donor committee to get out there. Sometimes the challenge is not about the amount of money but about who is giving it. "I'd feel better if I knew Fred was in. He is so smart about these things." You would then say, "How about if we get back to you after we have talked with Fred?" Go even further and say, "Can we tell Fred you said this? I think he would be flattered." When you go to Fred, you can truthfully tell him that his leadership gift will lead to at least one more gift. Obviously, if Fred doesn't give, the prospect doesn't have to give.

Some people want to give some amount now and another amount later. They give an amount now because they know you need it, but it is less than they can afford to give; they want to wait to make sure you can raise more from other people. Consequently, one or two people may provide both your first gift and your last gifts.

When the Crisis Is Caused by a Financial Scandal

Simply getting more donors will not be that reassuring to someone who is wondering how your executive director managed to skim off seventy-five thousand dollars over three years without anyone noticing. That the treasurer of the board knew about it and tried to deal with it quietly will not be helpful news. Or, how can anyone ever trust an organization's veracity or judgment when it turns out that a program person filed a false report on progress with a foundation—a report that was signed by both the executive director and board chair? Their protestations that they didn't have time to read the report do not make anyone feel better. In both cases, an enterprising young reporter has scooped these stories for the local paper, and they are the talk of the town (or at least the talk of the part of town that cares about these organizations).

Scandals are difficult to deal with because they break trust. Now the question is not whether your plan will succeed but whether you really can fix an organization that has allowed such behavior. Going back to message, you will want to identify people who can say they think the organization can be trusted again and the problems are being dealt with responsibly. Talk with those people. What would they need to see in the organization to feel confident about saying good things about it or putting their own money into it?

In a scandal, finding out the context of the problem often goes a long way to reassuring people that the problem can be solved. For example, the executive director who skimmed off seventy-five thousand dollars over three years has worked in the organization for twelve years. Five years ago, he went to a casino for the first time and got hooked on gambling. He very quickly incurred gambling debts, which led him to steal from the organization. The treasurer of the board and one other staff person knew the director was stealing, but tried to deal with him quietly so as not to embarrass him. The director has now been fired and is in a recovery program. The organization has learned a lesson in how to deal with painful situations and has even allowed a consultant to write up their situation as a case study and cautionary tale for other organizations. Although context does not excuse anyone, knowing that context does allow for more compassion.

In the second scenario, context is even more important. The newspaper story rightly said that a staff person filed a false report. But what was the nature of the falsification? The staff person lied about the progress the organization was making on creating an earned-income venture. She claimed that a business plan was almost complete and they were ready to hire a staff person when those accomplishments were actually projected to happen at least six months in the future. The executive director signed the false report—and the board chair went along—because they thought the project delays might cause the funder not to pay the second half of the grant. The executive director should have simply gone to the funder and admitted that the project was behind schedule. It would not have been the first time they ever heard that! But instead, he tried to operate in secret, and the newspaper reported that the organization was lying when the error really stemmed more from bad judgment. When the program officer of the foundation found out what had really happened, she gave an extension on the grant and paid for the executive director to get executive coaching to help him make better decisions in the future.

In a scandal, donors need to know that the circumstances that allowed the scandal no longer exist and that the organization is thoroughly evaluating itself to ensure that nothing else is amiss. Most people know that families, businesses, and nonprofits can make terrible mistakes, but that doesn't mean everything they do or stand for is a mistake. The issue is how to put the mistake behind you without simply covering it up.

From a fundraising viewpoint, a scandal is very hard to deal with and will require even more reaching out than other kinds of crises. Tell the truth, and tell it to people whom other people look to and trust.

In the end, donors are your friends, and major donors are your family. They may not like what you do, but they will generally stand by you if they have enough history with you to know that this scandal is something you *did*—and not something you *are*.

Everything Comes Back to Mission

Creating a message during a crisis is actually relatively simple once the organization recommits itself to its mission. Program or fundraising direction may have to change because of the crisis, but that step is possible as long as there's a group of people who care deeply about the organization. If you see telling the truth as the only option, that limits what you can say (which can be a blessing). You are not going to make something up or pretend something is true that is not. You are simply going to figure out who needs to hear the truth from whom, and when they need to hear it.

Chapter Seventeen

Fundraising Strategies for the Next Six to Twelve Months

While you are raising enough money to get you through the most immediate crisis, you must begin planning as soon as you can for strategies to get you through the next six months to one year. Otherwise, you are simply a group in remission from a terminal condition, rather than an organization on the mend. For most organizations, the time right *after* the immediate crisis is over is the hardest. A colleague describes a situation that illustrates it well:

> After my car accident I was very banged up, with broken ribs and a broken leg. Friends were great. They came to the hospital in droves; one brought me home to a house full of people, and for about ten days people came with food and kept me company. Someone cleaned my house and someone else did my laundry. But after about two weeks, everyone was back in their own life. I was much better and could hobble around, but I still needed help. The crisis was over, but I wasn't recovered. At that point, my neighbor started helping me. He did my dishes, helped me get dressed, took me to physical therapy. My neighbor had not visited me in the hospital and did not come over very much at first. He is the kind of friend who may not be as helpful in an emergency, but who will help every day over many days. That's the kind you need when you are healing but not healed.

Organizations go through similar phases. After your organization gets through the immediate crisis, it needs friends of the longer-term, lower-key variety. There is, of course, some overlap between one group and another, and if you haven't burned out your volunteers completely during the emergency, many of them will convert to the long-term types that you need.

The Dissolution of the Crisis Team

It is at this point that your crisis team dissolves. They have done their job, and if they have been able to do it right, you are now on a path different from the one that led you into the crisis. You hope that most of these people will still be available for various fundraising tasks from time to time. They should also have surfaced some other people who want to help you for the longer term. These may be board members who are reinvigorated and have a better understanding of their role, donors who have been brought into the work of the group and want to keep helping, or staff who are not in the development department but who see the need for integrating fundraising into their work as much as possible.

The strategies that you will pursue to get you through the next year are simply mini versions of traditional fundraising strategies that you will use for the long term. However, there are several differences in scale between how you raise money for the next twelve months and what you will be doing when you are fully back on your feet.

- *Web, e-mail, and mail fundraising:* Jazz up your website and use your e-newsletter and e-list to raise money. If you use mail at all, use if only for appeals to small lists of people. For both e-fundraising and mail appeals, you are still figuring out a profile of your donors, and you don't want to spend a lot of time and money appealing to a cross section of donors who may not be your actual best donors.
- *Events and personal asking:* Do small-scale fundraising events to keep cash flowing in and continue personal solicitation for larger gifts.
- *Foundations:* You may even pursue some foundation funding, although if that is what got you into this mess in the first place, be cautious about how much time you put into that strategy.

- *Strategy documentation:* Continue the habit of documenting and evaluating your fundraising—every time you do something, write up a report, including the following information:
  - Purpose of strategy, besides raising money (acquire new donors, approach major donors, renew donors, raise money from people or places who wouldn't give otherwise)
  - Volunteer time and number of volunteers required
  - Staff time required
  - Budget—itemized expenses and income
  - Time line
  - Evaluation of strategy:
    - Did it meet its goals?
    - What would we do exactly the same next time?
    - How can we pursue this strategy again with less time spent?
    - What would we do differently next time?

By systematically evaluating everything you do, even if you make only brief comments about these questions, you will learn what works for your organization and how it can work better. You will still be working harder on your fundraising now than you will need to later, but you should be putting in fewer hours than when the crisis struck (see also Chapter Eight, Analysis and Evaluation).

Every fundraising strategy requires a series of tasks to accomplish it successfully. There are many how-to books and websites with that detailed information (see the Bibliography for some suggestions). Exhibit 17.1 shows some possible fundraising strategies I recommend, depending on your situation. You can mix and match elements of these fairly easily.

A Critical Time

The period of time between the end of the crisis and the end of the post-crisis healing is a critical one. It is a great time to begin to develop a culture of recruiting a lot of volunteers for intensive short assignments and for learning about your organizational capacities to attract donors using various strategies. The crisis is a time to really change organizational culture, and it is important

---

Exhibit 17.1: Sample Fundraising Plans

Plan One

Note: You can also use this plan to get out of your immediate crisis by shortening the time frame on each strategy.

Assumption: You have enough money for three months.

Goal: Raise enough money in those three months for the next three months.

Strategy: Saturday Yard/Tag/Garage Sale

Income: $500 to 5,000

WORKERS NEEDED:

Prior to the sale: Two people to find a space to have the sale, to store stuff, and to advertise the sale.

The day before and morning of the sale: Four people (can include the previous two or can be four new people) to price everything and set up the morning of the sale.

The sale itself: Two or three people for every two hours the sale is on. One stands by the money and the other circulates, bargaining with people. (You can add an extra income stream by selling baked goods, but this requires more workers.)

Keep in mind: Location is key. The ideal space is a parking lot for a business that's open only during the week, such as a doctor or dentist's office or a bank, or an empty storefront if you think the weather could be bad. Make sure it is on a busy street so that many people will see your sale.

Upside: Many people know how to do these kinds of sales, and it is not hard to get stuff donated. Basically, you can send an e-mail to everyone you know in the immediate area asking them to donate all their used but usable stuff. Price the stuff, set up the sale, and collect the money. This is a great training opportunity for new volunteers or people who don't like fundraising. Also, some people love these sales, and they are very good at spotting items that can be sold for more money. You don't have to explain your crisis or even anything about your group, as most people are there simply to get bargains.

You can do a good job with this strategy in one month; if you have two or three months, you can advertise more, or you can decide to sell some of the nicer items online or hold the sale over two days.

Downside: Storage before the sale and weather the day of the sale can both be real problems. You can get a lot of junk donated and then have to spend precious time disposing of it. Be sure to identify, in advance, a thrift store that accepts drop-offs, and take what is left from your sale to them while they're still open. The sale does not recruit new donors who are likely to be loyal.

Strategy: Phone-a-thon to current donors

Income: Varies depending on the number of current donors you have, but generally you should be able to get a donation from 10 to 20 percent of the people you reach, at an average of $35 to $75 per person.

Add-ons: People who have ever given money; people you would like to invite to be donors. The response from this list will be about 5 percent of all calls made. (You will need to make sure you haven't already approached these people as part of your immediate fundraising plan.)

WORKERS NEEDED:

Prior to the phone-a-thon, two or three people to compile lists, find phone numbers, and write up scripts and FAQs.

One or two people to find a bank of phones to use: A real estate office, a large social service agency, or a law firm will often be willing to loan their phones for an evening. You can also do this with the phones at your office, augmented with cell phones. (Find plans with free minutes in the evening or people willing to use their minutes this way.)

During the phone-a-thon: Calculate using a formula of one worker for every fifty to seventy-five names for each three-hour shift. Volunteers with a lot of experience will move through their names faster than new people who will need to debrief after each call or get something to drink after they encounter a rude person. Workers should take a five-minute break each hour and a ten-minute break in the middle of the shift.

After the phone-a-thon: One or two to send thank-you notes, process credit cards, and clean up the database as needed.

Keep in mind: Some people really dislike being phoned, or seize the opportunity to express their frustration with the whole rest of their sad life; callers need to be ready to encounter great rudeness. They should be taught to say, "I can make sure you are on our no-call list. Would you like that?" This usually mollifies people and allows the conversation to end on a civil note.

As a welcome counterbalance to such calls, you will reach some people who are very glad to have a chance to hear what has been happening and may offer to help in other ways besides money. Many studies indicate that younger people are more

➤

receptive to phone calls than older people, so this strategy may surface a number of donors you have not been reaching successfully with your other strategies.

Provide a training and practice session ahead of the actual calling, and make the calling as fun as possible. It's fun to give each person a little bell or clicker to use when they have gotten a pledge; so is providing little prizes for the person who gets through the most names, or the person who gets the biggest pledge of the evening, or the person who encounters the most rude people. Giving everyone who helps a coupon for a free pizza or movie is a cheap way to reward volunteers.

Upside: This is an easy strategy to complete in two weeks, and it attracts volunteers who want to help you and are willing to put in a lot of time in a concentrated period of time. Some people love phone-a-thons and are able to make it a game for themselves and their fellow callers. It is a good way to train people to ask for money, because it is somewhat anonymous—even though the callers say their names, the people called rarely remember—yet it requires talking to a live person. Finally, it is an easy and fast way to clean up your database: you'll learn which people have moved, divorced, or died, and you can then update your records.

Downside: Can be hard to find phone numbers, can be a lot of work with not too much payoff, and can be hard to find volunteers to do this work.

Strategy: Facebook or other Web 2.0

Your organization should have a Facebook page in any case, but in this strategy you take advantage of the fact that you can ask for money on your page, or on "Causes" on Facebook. You also can encourage board members, volunteers, and other staff to link to your organization from their Facebook page and to link your organization to their website.

Income: Varies widely, but there are many stories of Facebook requests raising hundreds and sometimes thousands of dollars.

Workers needed:
Two or three people who keep up with all the new and emerging ways to raise money online and find it fun to get your organization onto those.

Note: This can be a very large and ongoing strategy, and if you want that, you will need to take the time to make a much bigger plan than this.

Strategy: Mini-major donor campaign

Goal: Upgrading current donors or attracting donors who can give larger-than-average gifts.

Income: Varies widely and depends on how many prospects you have not already contacted. A small organization should be able to raise $2,500 in one month with this strategy. Subtract $1,000 if you are in a poor and rural community. Add $2,500 if you have a major donor program in place now and you have not already asked your major donors for an extra gift.

You are looking for one gift of $500, four of $250, and five of $100—a range of gifts that are within the reach of many working people. You will need about thirty prospects to ask. About fifteen will say no; some will give less, but if they say no to $250, they may give $100, so you should have ten gifts when you are done. If you cannot find any $500 donors, you will have to raise the number of potential $250 or $100 donors.

Plan One grand total for three months: At least $7,500 and as much as $30,000.

Process for the plan

You adopt this plan at the beginning of the quarter. First, determine how many and what kind of volunteers you are going to need. If you have a development director or other staff in charge of fundraising, that person's job is to recruit a chair for each of the strategies.

That chair, with help, will recruit an ad hoc committee for the strategy they are heading up, which includes all the workers needed. Try to have different volunteers for each strategy: people who love yard sales may not be willing to work the phones, and those on the phone may not be willing to ask for large amounts of money. Because you also are using these strategies to build your fundraising team, you should not have very many overlapping volunteers.

Think widely as you recruit: in one organization, teenagers were recruited from a high school sociology class that needed to do some community service as part of their course work to staff the phone-a-thon. They loved being together, they had little fear of being on the phone (a natural occupation for them), they learned quickly, and they raised a lot of money. In another organization, a board member said that her mother always goes to yard sales. She asked her mother to help, and her mother brought along three of her friends. They priced the items quickly because they knew the market well. One woman pulled out some very fine antique dinnerware and sold it to an antique dealer for much more money than it would have brought at the garage sale. They had a great time.

By building this plan around flexible ad hoc committees, you can bring in all kinds of people who are willing to help briefly, and you can play to people's interests and strengths.

➤

Plan Two

Assumption: You have enough money for the next six months, and you have some money you can use for front money.

Goal: Raise enough money for the three months after that.

See the Plan One strategies—any of those ideas can be used in a longer time frame. Consider adding or substituting the following:

Strategy: Mail Appeal

Send a mail appeal to all your donors at the $1 to $99 level describing the work you will be doing in the next quarter and asking for an extra gift to support it. Be specific. "We have fifteen more clients every day than we used to before the recession. It costs us $35 an hour to work with each one, and they pay what they can, but few can pay more than $5 or $10, as they are either out of work or in minimum wage jobs. Can you help with an extra gift for these extra clients? A gift of $25 is the difference between what we spend and what one client pays, so it really makes a difference." Your reply device might have these choices:

- $25 = one client
- $100 = four clients
- $375 = one day's worth of new clients
- $ _____ Whatever you want to give. Every gift is put right to work and is so appreciated.

Income: Varies widely with the size of the donor base; should yield a 10-percent response with the same median gift that you get on your annual appeals. You may want to use a similar letter to attract new donors. Count on a 1- to 2-percent response, which will not bring in very much money but will help you expand your donor base.

Strategy: Three-Part E-Ask to your E-List

Send out an e-mail to all the people on your e-mail list, telling people what you have been up to and what you need money to do and asking them to contribute. Include a link to your website's online donation portal. A week after this first e-mail goes out, suppress everyone who has given and send a second letter. This letter is a little different from the first one, usually saying, "We have already raised $XX toward our goal of $XX. Won't you help?" A week later, suppress all who have already given and send a third letter with slightly different content, perhaps talking more about a program you have only briefly mentioned before, and ask again.

Generally, you can count on raising $1 for every name on your e-list if those people who are on it have signed themselves up. If you have simply entered names you got from various places, you may not do as well.

Strategy: Organize an All-Volunteer Door-to-Door Canvass for One Saturday

Income: Varies widely; you generally can expect 12 percent of households in the catchment area to contribute something. You should be able to raise at least $150 per volunteer per three-hour time period. Twenty volunteers (ten in the morning and ten in the afternoon) will raise at least $3,000.

WORKERS NEEDED:

Prior to canvass: Two or three to map out an area, create a script, and recruit volunteers.

Day of canvass: A coordinator to keep track of where everyone is and to take care of money raised as volunteers end their shifts.

As many as possible are needed to walk the route. You will need to decide if you want the canvassers to go in pairs or by themselves. If they go alone, two people should be in the same block or able to easily check in with each other every few households.

Keep in mind: Make sure you research and obey any city laws concerning getting a permit to canvass.

If you are able to broadcast a PSA on the radio—for example, "Look for a volunteer from the Rape Crisis Center this Saturday; please be as generous as you can"—some people will be expecting you. If you can include other advertising—"If you are not home, please go to our website and give on-line"—you can pick up some extra money that way. Many groups will also leave a door-hanger with that message on households where no one is home.

Some organizations have been able to build this volunteer canvass into a large special event, which uses upward of two hundred people on one Saturday afternoon and raises $30,000 or more. Obviously, something of that scale takes longer than the time allotted here, but if a small-scale volunteer canvass works for your organization, you may want to explore building this into an annual event.

Plan Three

Assumption: You have enough money for the next three to six months.
Goal: You want to develop a year-long plan.

Any of the strategies already described can be used in this longer time frame as short elements, one after the other.

Strategy: House Parties

Income: $1,500 at each party

House parties are one of my favorite strategies because they are so malleable and require little staff work. Basically, a loyal fan of your organization invites his or her friends to their house. The invitation is clear from the beginning: "Come learn about the important work of It's About Time and what is happening in the world of juvenile justice. It's About Time is launching a new campaign to change the way prison sentences are determined. Bring your questions and your checkbook." The host of the party provides refreshments, and someone from the organization describes the campaign the group is embarked on, or simply what the organization does. Someone—ideally the host, but if necessary another volunteer or a staff person—gives a pitch for donations, the audience members write their checks, and the party concludes shortly after that. An added component, which is very effective, is for the person doing the pitch to ask both for money and for two people among the guests to sign up to give their own house party. Each party leads to two more parties. In the course of three months, an organization could have six to ten parties. Most house parties average twenty to twenty-five people and raise $40 to $50 per person or couple attending. A college student throwing a party might raise only $500 from fifty other students, and a person with a small apartment might invite only five or six people but could raise $1,000. As much as possible, aim for each party raising $1,000. That way, a house party program with ten parties can raise $10,000 or more, plus bring in a world of new donors. Sometimes wealthier donors invite a few people who each give $1,000 or more. In that case, the house party is more of a soiree, and the discussion might go on for several hours.

Upside: An easy and inexpensive way to attract new donors and to educate a cross section of people about your issue. It is also a relatively easy and short-term way for someone to help your organization.

Downside: People may promise to do house parties and then keep postponing them, so it is not a strategy that can be implemented quickly. Sometimes people expect too much of staff in terms of organizing and follow-up, and the host, if not trained and practiced, can give a really bad pitch so the party ends up not raising much money.

Strategy: Second-Collection Sunday

Income: $300 and up, depending on the number of congregations involved.

WORKERS NEEDED:

One or two regular members for each church that is approached. People in your organization who belong to a church approach their minister or church board about letting your organization be the recipient of a second collection.

After the church takes up its usual offering, either someone from the church or someone from your group gives a brief pitch and the baskets are passed a second time. You can do this with just one church or organize several churches to do it on the same Sunday.

Dinner Dance

Income: Net varies; generally from $3,000 to $10,000

This event requires front money for printing up invitations, tickets, and an ad book (if that strategy is included), rental of the venue, and deposit for the band or disc jockey and the caterer; it is more expensive all around than the other recommended strategies.

WORKERS NEEDED:

Three or four to plan the event, lay out the tasks, and find other volunteers to do most of the work. These three or four people might also take responsibility for deciding on a date and securing a venue.

Three or four more people are in charge of the ad book, if you decide to do one. They sell ads to vendors, larger nonprofits, lawyers, financial planners, and accountants who may want to advertise to a nonprofit audience.

Three or four more people are in charge of advertising, sending out invitations, and handling the details prior to the event.

A week before the event, three or four more people join the team to handle all the details of the evening, and most of the people already involved will work the night of the event to make sure it goes smoothly.

Upside: Volunteers love events, and it is easier to get them to work on something like this than on the major donor campaign. It is a good way to train new volunteers and to build community among the team members. You also attract people who might not give you money otherwise, as well as people who may be interested in your group and use this as the entry point.

Downside: Although dinner dances can raise quite a lot of money, they also can cost a lot of money. If you have little front money or don't want to take a big risk, do this on a smaller scale. See if people like it and let the event grow over time.

Here are some cost-reducing alterations to the dinner-dance event: rather than a hotel ballroom, hold the event in a community center or the school gymnasium, which should cost little or nothing to use. Use paper streamers and balloons to make it festive, but don't invest a lot in fancy centerpieces. You can do the food as a competition. People will pay a small fee to enter the food competition in different categories, such as main course, salad, or dessert. All who come to the event get a sample of each entry and vote on which is the best. A cash bar can provide extra income, but be sure to comply with the law if you are serving alcohol. Dance music can be provided by a local band or local disc jockey who wants to become better known, so you get a good rate. Instead of sending out invitations, advertise the event by word of mouth and posters hung in the neighborhood of the event. Ask ten board members to sell ten tickets each at $20 to $35 per ticket. If a hundred people attend, at an average of $25 per person, plus the entry fee of twenty food competitors who each pay $10, plus the $2,500 or more from the ad book, you are looking at a gross income approaching $7,000 or more.

Expenses will include the layout and printing of an ad book (unless you are able to work out a deal there), buying drinks to sell, printing up tickets and nice-looking certificates for the winners of the food contests, and possibly mailing thank-you notes to volunteers after the event. Expenses could be as high as half of the gross, but if you really work on doing this in a grassroots way, you should be able to keep expenses to one-third of the gross. This is the kind of event that can grow.

Here's an example: An event called Kiss My Sweet—a dessert competition put on by a small organization whose total annual budget was $250,000—was organized along the budget lines just described. By the fifth year the event had become a must-attend occasion and netted $50,000! It attracted top chefs from every restaurant in town, in addition to amateur cooks entering their favorite brownies or hot chocolate.

that in the post-crisis period you don't drift back into bad habits, like letting fundraising become a one-or-two-person activity, or gradually letting go of high-touch elements in your fundraising.

The strategies outlined here are a sampling of possibilities, which may lead you to other ideas. For example, a PTA trying to raise money to keep the art and music program going in the face of draconian cuts in public school spending will not do a second collection Sunday (but that is a perfect strategy for a homeless shelter). However, the idea of one thing happening in several places at the same time leads the PTA to go to every art gallery, music store, or nightclub in town to ask if, for one day, each of them would donate 5 percent of profits for the school art and music programs. This idea gets into the paper, and those places experience an uptick in business on that day, which means the 5 percent for the PTA is a nice amount of money, and the businesses want to help again.

A group working primarily with low-income people may not have good prospects, at least in the short term, for a $50,000 major donor program. However, they start a pledge program instead, recognizing that although their constituents cannot give $250 at once, a goodly cross section of them can give $20 a month. In one organization, five board members committed themselves to finding thirty people among their constituents to give $25 a month and raised $9,000 in a year—the exact amount that had been cut from their budget by the county. Their work is almost entirely with minimum-wage and out-of-work people for whom $25 a month is a steep stretch. These are their major donors.

Setting Priorities

No group will be able to do every strategy I have suggested, and choosing which ones will work best is tricky. Of course you need money, and you don't have much money to spend to raise your money. But keep in mind that as you are coming out of your crisis, you need an able team of fundraising volunteers that is beginning to jell, and you need to attract donors. As much as possible, choose a selection of strategies that will do these two things. You might pick a garage sale primarily because it is a low-cost way to raise money, a phone-a-thon because it is a good way to give people practical experience in talking with donors, and a special event like the dinner dance because it builds a team of volunteers. With the skills that you learn from all three of these strategies, you might feel more ready to launch a major donor campaign. You will have the money for the materials needed, the volunteers trained to ask for money, and the knowledge of how to create a team. At the end of that experience you will have more money, more sophisticated and trained volunteers, and a lot of practice perfecting your message and learning what people who are making a big investment in your organization really want to know.

I hope you are also starting to realize that, ironically, coming at this problem with the idea that your *only* choice is to raise money gives you a *lot* of choices. Cutting back simply leads to more cutting back. When you really move into the paradigm of fundraising, you become much more creative, outgoing, and resourceful.

Part Four

Challenges and Opportunities

So far we have explored the endemic problems confronting the nonprofit sector and what might be done about them, the ways in which an organization has to function in order to be healthy and to have a productive fundraising program, and what to do if your organization is already in a crisis.

This final part of the book looks at the challenges we face going forward. I have already discussed many of these challenges, but I want to spend some time in this part on some particular challenges that I also think provide enormous opportunity for creativity, growth, and change.

Beginning with the board of directors, I propose some ideas about how to organize a board in a way that will enable it to do its job with regard to fundraising. However, the challenge of that chapter is bigger than that: I challenge nonprofits everywhere to experiment with new organizational forms altogether—structures and processes that play to people's strengths and that abandon ways of doing business that clearly don't work.

The next chapter looks at the four generations that make up our nonprofits and suggests ways to work with all of them while constantly moving with the tide of generational change. We have a confluence of people living longer than ever, able to be involved in organizations into their eighties and nineties; a huge generation of baby boomers who built the current nonprofit sector; and two more generations, whose worlds are very different from each other's and from those of the two older generations, and who bring ideas and concepts to the work that will revolutionize it yet again.

Next, we look at a problem that affects successful organizations that experience a lot of growth (those that have successfully incorporated the changes I have recommended up to now): that is, taking donors for granted.

Related to both that pitfall and the effort to get the job done in the time allowed is good time management. Time management starts with a philosophy of what our limited and short time on earth should be for and some very practical ways to use our time to make us happy.

Finally, I end where I started: with vision. What kind of world do we want to create? What is the role of nonprofits—and specifically, your nonprofit—in creating it? This is the most exciting time of my professional life, and the future holds the promise of real and lasting change for the better. Alice Walker said recently in an interview that this is the best time to be alive, because so much is at stake.

We have hoped for better days ahead over the past hundreds of years, yet too often, as the future became the present, we have experienced it as simply a repeat of the past. We don't have that luxury anymore because of climate change. Our planet must be rescued, or life as we know it will end. War, famine, and disease also take an unprecedented toll on billions of people. Alice Walker is right—in fact, everything is at stake.

Our nonprofit sector can be one of the leading causes of social justice in the world if we take this challenge seriously and get right to work.

Chapter Eighteen

The Truth About Boards and What to Do About It

I have been teaching fundraising, consulting with organizations, working as a development person, and serving on boards of directors for more than thirty years. In that time, I have taught thousands of organizations; I have consulted individually with upward of a thousand of them, been on the staff of a dozen, and served on about twenty boards. Out of all those experiences, I have seen only a handful of boards that really worked, including only two of the boards I have served on.

I have tried many methods of getting boards to work, and I have written widely on the subject. For years, it never occurred to me to question the premise of an all-volunteer board carrying fiduciary responsibility for a nonprofit organization. Then, about ten years ago, a young woman approached me after a training session I had conducted for board members and said, "I am sorry if this sounds impertinent, but do you really know any boards that work?" Being quick on my feet, I named a few, and she wandered off, seemingly satisfied.

I hope that woman questioned the authority of my answer, because I owe her a great debt for that question. I had never really thought about what it means that almost every board I see is not functioning properly and that the most common complaint about an organization—whether from board members, staff, or volunteers not on the board—is something about the board. People complain about its performance, its composition, its lack of involvement or over-involvement with program, and its relationship to staff. I had thought that, in the same way a doctor sees a disproportionate number of sick people, I was seeing boards that needed help and not seeing the thousands that were functioning well. However, I finally had to wonder whether there isn't something wrong with the idea of a board of directors, rather than a particular problem with each individual organization.

Consider this:

Board members are asked to take moral, legal, and fiscal responsibility for an organization: to hire, evaluate, and, if necessary, fire the executive director; to approve programs and budgets; and to monitor expenses and income. They are volunteers who, on their volunteer time, are to supervise paid professionals.

The board structure that we have today has evolved over the past several decades as a growing number of nonprofits have sought to meet a growing number of needs. No coalition of the finest minds ever sat down and said, "How shall nonprofits best govern themselves?" and then wrote a document that described a board of directors. So we are working with a structure that grew as the sector grew. However, the structure ceased to evolve significantly after the 1960s, which means that we are working with a structure that suited nonprofits of a very different era, and imperfectly even then. Although much about running a nonprofit has changed in the last twenty years, the structure used to govern them has not. Small wonder that many organizations have a hard time making this structure work.

Far from solving problems with boards, as I had thought I had been doing all these years, I was collaborating with the idea that a board of directors is an appropriate structure and thinking that each individual board just needed some coaching. I was fooled by the following facts:

- A few boards function very well.
- On most boards, some board members are very involved and carry the work of the board.
- Some staff people are pleased with their boards most of the time.
- I am generally a good board member.

I had tried over and over to help everyone be a "good" board member and to help every executive director work more easily with their board. In short, I had made a large part of my living helping to solve individual board problems, and my successes kept me from realizing that although boards can work better, with some conscious effort, the root problem is the structure itself.

I still get calls from exasperated executive directors who say, "Can you come and knock some sense into my board?" Or from board chairs or nominating committee people who say, "We can make this board work if we have some corporate types, or some investment people." Sometimes, when I am invited to sit on a board, I am told, "I think with your help we can whip this board into shape."

I'd like to give up the idea of knocking, whipping, or making a board do anything, and move on to two nonviolent suggestions: (1) let's put our collective heads together and see what variations on this structure we can create, and (2) until we have a better way of running nonprofits, let's help each board member and staff person understand the structure of the board and work with it.

The Role of Nonprofit Boards in the United States

I am assuming that your group is incorporated as a nonprofit, tax-exempt entity designated under the IRS code of 501(c)3 or under the umbrella of another organization's 501(c)3 status. If your organization is a 501(c)4, a PAC (political action committee), or a service club, some of what is said here will apply to you and some will not. If you have chosen not to apply for tax-exempt status (which is the case for millions of all-volunteer organizations, including more informal block clubs and associations), or you are from a country other than the United States, then the laws I describe here will not apply to you. However, if your organization works for the public good (even if the public is as small your neighborhood) and is not set up to make a profit, the moral implications of what I say here apply to you, so you may wish to skim the legal parts and move to the end of this section.

When an organization receives nonprofit, tax-exempt status from their state and from the federal government under the IRS category 501(c)3, it takes on a large fiscal responsibility in return for a large government subsidy. A 501(c)3 tax status entitles an organization to the following benefits:

- It can receive donations for which the donor can take a tax deduction.
- It is exempt from most taxes, including taxes on property used for a tax-exempt purpose, income in excess of expenses in a year, capital gains, and, in some states, sales tax. It does have to pay payroll tax and to collect sales tax on products it sells regularly.
- It has access that a business or individual doesn't have to money from private foundations (which cannot fund groups that don't have this status), public foundations (which can give a certain percentage of funds to groups without tax-exempt status, but tend not to), corporations (which also prefer to fund groups with nonprofit, tax-exempt status), and government programs.
- It receives substantially discounted bulk mail rates from the U.S. Postal Service.

All of these privileges have to do with money, specifically tax money. The government realizes that an organization working for the public good under nonprofit status cannot be expected to survive in a for-profit, free-market economy without significant help. Decreasing or eliminating taxes is the best way government can help. The government calls this tax relief foregone revenue. Some experts estimate that the government underwrites upward of $50 billion in such foregone revenue annually.

Most of us would argue that this is a good deal—in return for $50 billion, the nation gets nearly 1.5 million nonprofit groups engaged in everything from advocacy, protecting civil rights, community organizing, providing health care, conducting research, and providing social services to running museums, theaters, schools, and religious organizations, and much more.

In return for this subsidy, 501(c)3-designated organizations are required to be good stewards of the privilege, as well as of the money donated to them directly. Specifically, 501(c)3s are limited in what they can do or say about political campaigns or candidates, they cannot have paid shareholders, and they must follow all laws that apply to corporations: the workplace must be safe, they cannot discriminate in hiring and firing practices, and the like. In addition, they cannot pay "excessive" compensation to the staff, and board members serve as volunteers.

The dealings of a nonprofit are supposed to be fairly transparent: minutes of board meetings are public information, their tax-return form (Form 990) is available to the public, and in general the nonprofit operates so that there is nothing to hide.

Thus it is accurate to think of 501(c)3 tax status as a "contract" between the group and the Internal Revenue Service. The people who are charged with overseeing the nonprofit—for making sure that it lives up to the contract—are the board members.

The Fiduciary Responsibilities of Being a Board Member

The government asks each board member to act like a "prudent person." In other words, you are not required to know everything about running a nonprofit, but you are required to use common sense in making decisions and to plan ahead. The "prudent person" standard is most obvious in issues of how money is handled. A prudent person, for example, will realize that any person may be tempted to steal money if it is easy to do so, and so will ensure that embezzling funds is not easy by requiring that at least two people be involved in every large financial transaction: two signatures are required on checks, two people count cash after an event, one person opens the mail and codes the checks for a deposit and another person makes the deposit, and so on. A prudent person ensures that money is spent properly and accounted for through budgets, financial reports, and, in larger organizations, audits. Failure to be prudent can result in fines, suspension, or even revocation of tax status—and, in extreme cases, financial liabilities that individual board members have to pay.

Most people learn about their responsibilities as board members the hard way. Certainly that is how I learned. When I served on my first board, I was twenty-four years old and flattered to be asked. The group was pioneering a creative approach to alcohol and drug addiction—the counselors had to be recovering addicts, with less than six months' sobriety.

Their jobs would be temporary, and they would be replaced by people coming through the program. The idea was that the counselors were very close to the problems they were addressing and therefore of more help to the clients. The program was funded by a grant from the state health department.

The executive director was a charismatic recovering alcoholic. She said she had been sober off and on for twenty years, having never stayed sober for more than three years at a time. She said she understood failure and had deep empathy for people coming to the program. She understood recovery, and she was determined to stay sober. She was warm, funny, and hardworking. We board members (none of us knew anything about alcoholism) thought she was perfect for the job. All five of us were serving on our first board; the oldest of us was twenty-five. We knew nothing about what to look for in a director or what the rest of our jobs as board members entailed.

The director did well for about six months, then started being absent from work a lot. Finally she left town altogether, leaving piles of unpaid bills, overdue reports, and general chaos in her wake.

The state pulled its funding immediately and demanded an accounting of the money that had been spent. They sent an auditor, and although it appeared that none of the money had been embezzled, it had been misspent on office furniture, travel expenses, food for meetings, and so on. The number of people helped by the program was very small.

The program was closed down, and the state demanded part of its grant back. We sold all the assets the organization had and still owed $15,000. Much to my surprise, because the grant was government money, the state held the board members personally liable for the debt. However, because of our age and lack of assets, they settled for $5,000 and waived the interest. Each of the board members paid $1,000. Because I was earning only $6,000 that year, I had to take two years to pay my share. Looking back, I think of it as a relatively inexpensive lesson in board responsibility.

Despite the extensive responsibilities and liabilities of board members, in the thousands of trainings I have done, the majority of board members I have met have not understood the seriousness or the scope of their responsibility. By and large, they have not been told anything about what is expected of them except attendance at meetings. Often staff people are not aware of the extent of board liability, and because it's rare that a nonprofit's board members are held liable for imprudent decisions resulting in debts to the government, people sail through one board experience after another without knowing even the basics of what they have signed on to. All the details of a board's fiduciary responsibility and the punishments that can be meted out for failure to be good stewards can be found in various board handbooks, which go largely unread. It is enough to note that most people don't know enough to be prudent board members.

Although a board's participation in fundraising is not required by law, the implications of taking responsibility for the financial health of an organization are that board members must test on themselves the proposition that the group is worth supporting and make their own gift first, and they must help raise money.

It is in the arena of fundraising that I have found the least clarity among board members about their roles. In newer organizations, board members may not be aware that they are expected to help with fundraising; in older groups, although this expectation may be known, it usually has no structure attached to it, so what board members should be doing remains mysterious to them. This puzzle gives rise to the following types of frustrations for board members:

- They sense that whatever fundraising they do is not enough and that their reward for doing their work is more work.
- Individual members work hard on a fundraising project and finish what they committed to do, only to find that few other board members did the same, yet there is no consequence for those who failed to keep their commitments.
- They suspect that all decisions are made by a cabal that they are not part of.
- They notice that the staff resents them if they ask too many questions, particularly about budgeting or finance, yet staff expects them to be enthusiastic about raising money.
- They feel the only job expected of them is to raise money, often without a plan or guidance.

Many people go from board to board, looking for a better experience, and finally give up altogether. There are thousands of these people: board dropouts who are bright, well-intentioned, and committed to some issue or other but who have had one too many demoralizing board experiences. When a friend of mine serving as a board member questioned the organization's salary structure, she was reprimanded by an executive director for not being loyal. She told me, "If I wanted to be talked to like that, I would visit my ex-husband."

Clarifying Expectations

There are extensive and excellent writings, videotapes, and training materials on how to help board members understand their role. Obviously, all board members should have orientation sessions, some kind of job description or statement of agreement, copies of bylaws, ways to evaluate themselves, and so on. (The Resources section of this book can guide you to sources for this information.) A key question for our purposes is, why don't groups tell prospective board members what is expected from them? This disclosure would allow people who really don't have the time or willingness to do the work required of a board member to decline the offer to be on the board. It would allow board members to hold each other accountable and possibly even to ask one of their number to leave, if warranted.

A board member is like an unpaid staff member. No one thinks that a healthy staff position is one in which the person just makes up the job as she goes along, with no guidance and no evaluation. The logic of telling people what is expected of them is clear. The reason that board members are often not told what is expected of them is, at the most innocent end of the spectrum, the fact that no one in the group understands what can be expected of a board. At the most dysfunctional end of the spectrum, it is the fact that the organization has no confidence that people would want to make the sacrifices it takes to do the work entailed.

I have heard dozens of staff and board members exclaim, "If we told the board what was expected of them, we would have only three board members left." A group with that attitude has to face the fact that they have only three genuine board members now, and the rest of the people in that role are taking up space to no purpose. They have been invited to serve on the board because of a perception that they "have money," or they "have contacts" or they "can open doors." They are probably not told that is why they have been invited, and they may not perceive themselves the way the organization does. In fact, board members are often doing exactly what they were asked to do by whoever asked them to join the board. The board may have other expectations it doesn't set forth or doesn't realize are not clear. Clarity of expectations is key to the healthy functioning of any person who is part of a group, whether that group be a board, staff, family, classroom, or sports team.

A person should be asked to join a board for one overriding reason: because the person cares deeply about the work of the group. The person should be passionately committed to the mission and goals of the organization. And the person should have demonstrated that passion in some way—by volunteering for the group, by working in some capacity for a similar group, by donating significant amounts of money relative to the person's resources, and so on. People who have passion can learn to be board members. Their background, their education, their profession, their economic standing, and their networks are utterly secondary to that commitment.

So in order to have a working, functional board, you need to be clear about what the board is required to do, and you need to find people who are so dedicated to the organization that they are willing to do whatever it takes to keep it going.

Making the Structure Work

Knowing what the job entails and being clear about it with a dedicated board will solve at least part of the problem of boards that don't work. The other half of the problem will be solved by acknowledging that the structure of a board is problematic.

As many organizational development and board consultants have commented, a big part of the problem with board structure is the "one size fits all" nature of it. Many organizations try to squeeze themselves into a model that might work well for another organization but does not suit them at all. For example, some organizations run very well using an executive committee that meets frequently and a full board that meets rarely. Others find that such a structure depresses involvement. Some run well with a chair, a vice chair, a secretary, and a treasurer with very specific roles and terms of office. Other organizations rotate these functions every two or three board meetings; still others refuse to use any of these titles and work much more collectively. Being willing to try variations on board structure and to experiment with different ways of decision making, task division, running meetings, or board selection will allow your organization to find a structure that works for it. That structure will work until it doesn't; then you will need to revisit it again. As many organizational development experts have pointed out, an organization is a living organism. Its needs to change as the members of the organization change. To have a workable structure for your organization may mean changing parts of it or all of it from time to time.

Variations on Board Structures

The following are some variations on board structures I hope organizations will use and perfect them more and add more ideas to the list. To get them to work for your organization may require cutting and pasting; adopting all, then abandoning parts; or using these suggestions as launching pads for something brand new. I believe we can think of something better if we focus on finding a process that helps us keep changing, rather than defining a set structure that will always work.

These suggestions focus primarily on what works best to get a board to participate in fundraising, but my experience is that boards that do their job with regard to fundraising generally do their other work very well.

Alternative One: The Small Board

This alternative takes a common problem—only a few people on the board actually work hard—and solves it by having that small group be the board. This type of board has only three to five people on it. Those people meet with the director regularly. Quorums are not difficult to come by, decisions are made by people familiar with the issues and not just dropping in occasionally for a meeting,

A WORD ABOUT THE ROLE OF STAFF IN BOARD DYSFUNCTION

Although this chapter is focused on boards and how they can function more effectively, I would be remiss not to mention how often boards are blamed for problems that actually can be laid at the door of the executive director or other staff. As we seek out more effective and humane structures for boards, we should be on the look-out for better staff structures also, particularly for an alternative to the traditional executive director (or, in more mainstream organizations, the chief executive officer) role. The problems with the executive director role are similar to those of boards: placing too much power and authority in one position with little clarity as to what that means and not much more training than is provided to board members. Many executive directors are promoted to that position because of their considerable talent in program work. They may not have any talent—or sometimes even any knowledge—about administering the organization. They know little about supervision and so either micromanage or neglect their staff, and they constantly feel they have too much to do.

Executive directors often resent board members asking questions, and they often do not welcome suggestions or new ideas from board members. Just in the past nine months, I have personally witnessed the following actions by a number of different EDs:

- Instructing program staff to tell the board, "No one will fund this," as a response to any new idea
- Instructing staff to offer to take the minutes of the board meeting, then slightly changing the meaning of decisions made so they were more in keeping with what the ED wanted than what the board decided
- Scheduling meetings when "difficult" board members could not be there

These executive directors are good people, and committed to their organization, but they basically believe that the board and ED are in an adversarial relationship. Board burnout can often be traced to the treatment they have received at the hand of the ED.

As we explore better and more humane ways to work together, staff structure also has to be deconstructed. That is beyond the scope of this book, but not beyond the scope of all of our collective imaginations.

and some work can be done by conference call or e-mail because so few people are involved. Many groups have this system in place in the form of an executive committee that does a huge amount of work and reports to the board, bringing only large decisions to board meetings. Although an executive committee can work really well, it can also get bogged down in having to repeat discussions and revisit decisions at the board level.

A small board can be involved in fundraising, but this works best if it is augmented by a number of ad hoc committees of people not on the board who come together for certain fundraising tasks, such as a special event, the major donor campaign, or the membership drive.

To avoid becoming an insular elite, the five people must represent different constituencies in the organization, and two of the five should rotate out every year. Each person will serve a three-year term but would not serve all three years with more than one other person.

Alternative Two: Staff on Board

Just as I used to be a fan of big boards, I used to be adamantly opposed to paid staff being on the board. Having seen it work a number of times, however, I have modified my position. There are obvious problems with having paid staff on the board: they have to oversee work that they also implement; they have none of the distance from the work that is part of the reason for having a board (being able to see the forest, not just the trees), and they have a lot of power, because they have the power of the staff combined with the power of a board member. However, this structure also has a number of advantages. It blurs, and sometimes even erases, tension between staff and board. Staff get to see the work of the organization from two critical viewpoints—their own and the board members'. Further, this structure recognizes that staff carry out most of the work that the organization does and it allows them an equal say in what that work is and how it is evaluated. In organizations where staff sit on the board, I have noticed that there is no hiding of mistakes or figuring out how to tell the board something they may not be pleased to hear.

For this to work best, there should be more volunteers than staff on the board. Moreover, the executive director should not be the only staff person on the board; in fact, I think a legitimate argument can be made that the executive director is the one staff person who should never be on the board, because it gives that person more power than anyone else in the organization. Each organization will have to decide what is best for them, and in organizations that have only one or two staff, the director doesn't have that much power to aggrandize or abuse.

Alternative Three: Ad Hoc Committees

In this alternative, the board can be small or very large, but the work of the organization is done by a number of committees made up of board and nonboard members, possibly including staff. Each committee has a lot of autonomy coupled with a clear sense of their boundaries and responsibilities. They come together to complete a task, then dissolve and reform into another committee. The full board meets no more often than quarterly to decide what committees will exist for the next period of time and who will be on them. Once a year, the board and staff, in a one- or two-day retreat, prepare an extensive work plan for the year. This structure generally calls for some kind of oversight committee, which would traditionally be the executive committee. Don't be limited by the traditional committee names and functions like nominating, personnel, finance, and so on. You can have the winter, spring, summer, and fall committees, with five to seven people taking full board responsibility for each quarter of the year. The rest of the board participates as needed. This works well for the very busy people we tend to attract to our boards—they will carve out a lot of time to devote for a short period but aren't able to sustain that level of commitment.

This structure is ideal for fundraising because board members agree to work on some aspect of fundraising, and their reward for doing their work is that their work is over. For maximum effectiveness, one paid staff person will need to devote about half of her or his time to staffing these committees so that they do their work and don't spin out of control.

The Basics for Any Workable Structure

To get any structure to work for fundraising will require implementing the very pedestrian suggestions that follow. Like vacuuming, showering, or driving, there are certain motions one has to go through, and they will be the same regardless of the make or model of your vacuum, shower, or car.

Here is what you can do to have a board that works:

1. *Choose board members with the same care you use in choosing staff.*
   Board members are simply unpaid staff. When you hire staff, unless the perfect person materializes, you advertise, you read resumes, you interview, and you choose from a pool. Do the same for your board members. Draw up a job description. Put an announcement in your newsletter and send it around to people who might know others who would be good board members. Develop a simple application form and ask people to apply to be on the board. If someone won't take the time to fill out an application, then how much time will they have for the board position?

   Just as staff are sometimes promoted to new positions, volunteers and committee members who have shown themselves to be reliable and thoughtful and who work well in a committee can be promoted to a board position.

2. *Institute an evaluation process.*
   The board should evaluate itself every year. What are they doing well? What could be improved? As with any evaluation, this should be done in the spirit of seeing problems as opportunities for change and growth. Every person and every board has problems. The problems don't have to be terminal, and generally they can be solved—or at least changed into less serious problems.

3. *Maintain flexibility, but don't confuse it with having double standards.*
   What often kills the teamwork of a board is considering one or two people so important to the group that they are excused from raising money or coming to meetings. If you have some people who are very important to your cause but who don't want to do all the work of a board member, put them on an advisory council of some kind.

4. *Agree on how the meetings are run.*

   If you have seventeen board members, you will have at least seventeen opinions about how meetings should be run. One person has learned Robert's Rules of Order and is a stickler for that system. Someone else prefers a more casual approach where everyone shouts out their opinion. Some people get up and move around or get coffee during discussions, which other people interpret as not paying attention. The chair of the board, or whoever is the facilitator, needs to learn how to facilitate meetings. Most people know that running a meeting is a skill. What is less obvious is that being in a meeting is also a skill. Both are skills that can be learned. A fun in-service for a board meeting is a thirty-minute presentation on how to make meetings work. Then the board members can choose what style they want to follow and establish the rules of their meetings.

   The more casual the meeting style, the less likely shy people are to speak. I recommend having a more formal style in which people raise their hands and wait to be called on. Big group discussions work best for people who feel confident talking in front of big groups, and a facilitator has to make sure that all the members are given a way to voice their opinions, particularly if among board members there are significant differences in education, age, language, or culture. The facilitator should occasionally ask that everyone speak on the subject under discussion, going around the room so that each person can have their say. After asking, "Does anyone else have something to say on this subject?" often the chair will need to pause while slowly counting to ten.

5. *Make sure everyone knows ahead of time what will be covered at the meeting and has the chance to come prepared to discuss each item.*

   It is helpful to have a blackboard or an easel with paper and marking pens, or even a set of presentation slides for help with discussion of complicated items. Then everyone is looking at and responding to the same information. Many people need to see something in writing before they can really understand it. Although having written materials is important, simply relying on people looking at their own copy of the fundraising plan or the budget will mean that people will shuffle through their papers, and if they can't find the item or they do find it but can't understand it, they may be tempted to act as though they know what is going on (when they really don't).

6. *Give board members a number of ways to be involved in fundraising.* Because fundraising is the main place that board work breaks down, even in otherwise high-functioning boards, it is important to pay special attention to this responsibility. People need a range of choices with regard to fundraising, but they also must understand that doing nothing to help raise money is not one of the choices.

7. *Use board members' time wisely.* Even for the most dedicated board member, service on the board is a lower priority than many other things in life. Their family or friends come first, followed by their job, and then by what it takes to maintain their life, such as laundry, grocery shopping, cleaning house, driving kids to activities, and so on. For many people, there is not enough time to fulfill even those priorities, let alone add the six or eight hours a month necessary to be a board member. If most of that time is spent in meetings, there is little time left to do the work they committed to during the meetings. Cutting down meeting time will free up board members' time to do other board work.

8. *Structure, in detail, the work you want from board members.* If you want them to send in the names of friends who should be invited to a special event, send them a form to fill out and a return envelope, or ask them to bring their address books to a board meeting and take some time to fill out forms there, or make it easy for them to email names from their address book. Every task should be clear and have a deadline that is not very long after the task is agreed to. Most people do a task right before it is due, so giving them a long time to accomplish it only postpones the results. The more specific you are, the more likely it is that the task will get done and get done right.

9. *Make being on the board interesting and occasionally fun.* Make sure board members are as involved in developing the program of the organization as they are in fundraising, managing personnel, and revising bylaws. Board meetings

are too often seen by the board as boring and by the staff as a burdensome requirement of the law. There is no reason for this. If the mission and programs of your organization are important and interesting, then any gathering of people committed to them should be important and interesting also. Meetings should be used as a time to go deeper into organizational issues, think bigger in terms of program and money, and get recharged for the job of being an ambassador of the organization to friends and colleagues.

In the end, for a board to function well it must view itself, and be seen by the staff, as a group of people who care deeply about the goals of the organization and are willing to give some of their most precious nonrenewable resource—their time—to furthering these goals. A board that works is a board always in process and always looking at what it is doing well and what needs improving.

TEN WAYS BOARD MEMBERS CAN HELP
RAISE MONEY WITHOUT ASKING FOR IT OUT LOUD

1. Write thank-you notes. Board members can thank not only donors, but also volunteers, vendors who reduce their prices for the group, foundation funders, and anyone who has gone out of their way for the group.

2. Work on special events, from planning and all the work that has to be done beforehand, through setup and cleanup.

3. Help enter data about donors into the computer database, or update the group's website and link it to those of other groups.

4. Conduct research about potential donors—individuals, foundations, or corporations.

5. Proofread fundraising letters, reports, newsletters, and so on.

6. Set up a profile for the organization on Facebook and other social networking sites.

7. Make a list of friends who might be interested in the organization. Add their names to the next appeal, or better, write them a personal solicitation e-mail.

8. Collect other lists of people who might be interested in the group and send them a direct mail appeal. These lists might be board members they go to religious services with, members of their block association, or members of other groups they belong to. They should be sure they have permission to use the list, and from time to time they should offer to share the organization's list.

9. Help with mail and e-mail. Read the e-newsletters, journals, blogs, reports, and other information that comes through every development office and throw away what isn't useful; compile what is and summarize long reports into short paragraphs.

10. Help evaluate how well the group is doing on its annual plan, including looking at budgets, cash flow, cost/benefit, and income projections over several years.

Chapter Nineteen

Dealing with Generational Change

Around the world, the years from 1945 to 1964 were incredibly productive in terms of ideas, inventions, literature, and...people. In the United States alone, the generation that has come to be called the baby boomers today numbers seventy-eight million people. It is the largest generation in U.S. history, and currently the largest living generation in the country. The generation that followed, born between about 1965 and 1979 and known as Gen X, is much smaller, numbering around forty-five million people. Younger yet are those known as the Millennials—less frequently called Gen Y—born roughly between 1980 and 2000, numbering about sixty million. The oldest living generation, sometimes called the "greatest generation," "the World War II generation," or "veterans of change," were born roughly between 1915 and 1944.

The designation of what a generation is does not represent just a period of time, although the birth period of a generation generally spans about twenty years. The term *generation* generally refers to a period marked by world events, cultural shifts, and life-changing inventions. There is no exact agreement on when one generation ends and another begins, and sometimes we really don't know when a generation has ended—in the cultural sense meant here—until well into the next generation. Those people born in between 1960 and 1964, for example, sometimes feel that they bridge two generations: they are technically baby boomers, but they did not participate in much of the cultural changes that shaped that generation; on the other hand, they did not grow up with all that shaped Gen Xers.

Baby boomers built the current nonprofit sector. In the 1950s there were around fifty thousand nonprofits in the United States. By 1993, which was probably the height of when baby boomers were in leadership positions, there were 750,000 nonprofits; today, with four generations of people working in nonprofits, there are 1.5 million nonprofit organizations employing 10 percent of the workforce. Most of the baby boomers who built the nonprofit sector were white, and in many larger or older organizations most were men. Women have worked hard since the 1970s to break the glass ceiling that was as present in nonprofits as in the corporate sector, and we have succeeded so well that the leadership of most midsize and smaller nonprofits is now largely made up of women. Unfortunately, the sector is still not as racially diverse as it needs to be, but the younger generation entering the nonprofit sector is much more racially diverse than the boomer generation. Sorting out the race, gender, class, and age dynamics that affect who leads the nonprofit world is very important and not easy. However, even though race and gender play roles that cannot be discounted, there is a lot to be learned by looking at the nonprofit sector through the lens of generations. In this chapter, I look through that lens as it affects just a few elements of fundraising: dealing with donors, new organizational forms, and founder's syndrome.

Dealing with Donors

If you have a broad base of individual donors (which is what you should be trying to build), you are probably working with donors from at least four generations of people, in which the lived experience of the oldest and the youngest donors could hardly be more different. Some have compared the changes of the last hundred years to the Industrial Revolution, but I heard a better comparison from someone in a workshop. He said he thought the difference between someone who was born in 1920 and someone who was born in 1990 was more like the difference between people who spent most of their lives thinking the world was flat and then had to adjust to the idea that the world was round, and those who grew up knowing the world is round and had to comprehend what it must have been like not to know that. Millennials—the generation born since 1980—are what we call "technology natives." They have never known a world without computers, e-mail, cell phones. Compare that with someone who is now eighty years old, for whom most or all of their work life and three-fourths of their whole life happened with none of that technology in place. Even people who are only in their sixties grew up with early, shared-line telephones and black-and-white TV. Although many older people enjoy the Internet and are computer savvy, and some young people don't have access to computers, the largest digital divide is by age.

As an organization, then, you have to use a variety of communication strategies to make sure you reach your entire population. But that is not all. You can't just send the same information in a paper newsletter that you would send in an e-newsletter, and even that is different from what you post on Facebook. Generally, a paper newsletter is longer and contains more text than an e-newsletter, which tends to have headlines and a brief explanation of each story with a link to the website for those wanting to read more. Facebook entries are much more personal and interactive, with less focus on analysis or in-depth reporting.

Some organizations have moved away from using any paper communication tools, but they often find out to their chagrin that they are leaving some of their most loyal donors in the dust. A food bank that provides a variety of services to families in need finds out how many donors they are missing by phoning all their donors who fall into the category we call LYBNTS—"last year but not this." They have a larger-than-usual number of people in this category and anticipate that many people they reach will say the economy is causing them to cut back. However, most of the people they reach say that they never hear from the organization. Soon it becomes clear that these people have lost contact since the organization went from publishing a paper newsletter to an e-newsletter only. One woman says, "I called to see if you were still in business, and the person answering the phone said, 'Go to our website and you can see all that we are doing.' I don't have a computer, and I am not going to get one."

Another organization's board chair calls to set up a meeting with a longtime older donor. They agree on a time and place, and then he says, "Give me your cell and I'll text you if I am held up in traffic." The donor replies, "I have no idea what you are talking about—just don't be late."

As these examples make clear, you have to take into account what different generations of people will know how to do, and what will seem cool and cutting-edge to some but unintelligible to others. For example, the executive director of an international human rights organization goes to a large conference of human rights activists in Brazil. She posts a daily blog of her experiences, to which many people post comments and questions. When she returns, the development director compiles some of her blog posts into an article in the (paper) newsletter, along with the blog address for those who want to read about the whole experience. The executive director thinks people are going to object to reading the same information in the paper newsletter as online. Instead, several donors write or call to say, "Thanks for this article—I finally understand what a blog is," or "I can't figure out how to get on the blog," or "I loved your article—I had no idea you were in Brazil." This story shows that it is smart to use one type of technology to reach some donors and then a lower-tech mechanism to reach others.

For the next ten years or so, organizations will have to use a wider variety of communication methods to reach all their donors than they would have ten years ago and, possibly, than they will ten years from now, when it's reasonable to expect that almost all our written communication will be virtual. At the same time, the sheer volume of social networking sites alone can paralyze an already overworked development director. My advice is to focus your efforts on communication methods that make sense for your donors and to maintain those methods. It is better to do a few things well than to be scattered all over. Also, keep in mind that you don't have to know all the different ways you can communicate with people; find volunteers who cross age lines who can help your organization connect with other people like themselves.

New Organizational Forms

Sally, a sixty-year-old social worker, has been a development director and an executive director in several organizations over her thirty-year work life; for the last six years she has been executive director in a mental health advocacy organization. The agency has three other staff, ranging in age from twenty-five to forty.

Sally plans to retire in two years and has spent the previous five years working with her staff to ensure a smooth transition. Her forty-year-old development director, Marta, is slated to take her place. Over the past year, though, Sally has watched her retirement savings shrink to the point that she feels she cannot retire in two years. In fact, she questions whether she will ever be able to retire. Yet Sally doesn't really want to stay in the executive director position, and she feels that she has promised that job to Marta. She and Marta discuss options and agree to explore some nontraditional structures to accommodate both their needs.

A committee from the board, a consultant, and the rest of the staff take time to look at options over the ensuing six months. They decide to try a more collective structure for a while. Marta will gradually take over all the more public elements of Sally's job, which include a lot of the advocacy program work, speaking at conferences, serving on mental health advisory boards, and working with major donors and funders. Sally will work with the board and volunteers to get more people involved in the advocacy, something she is good at and likes to do and that has been neglected in the past few years. She will also be the staff liaison to the board. A third staff person, Amir, who is twenty-five, will take over most of the back office development function—database management, reports, proposals, appeals, and so on. Amir is primarily an administrator now, and this will give him more authority and autonomy. The fourth staff person, Sydney, who is thirty-one, will continue organizing among mental health consumers and their families, but her job will now also include some fundraising. The idea is that gradually Marta will become more and more the executive director, but to prevent confusion her title will be program director. Sally will move away from directing to more organizing, and her title will be organizing director. Amir will be operations and fundraising coordinator, and Sydney will be the community liaison.

Many baby boomers face Sally's dilemma. They want to retire but can't afford to. Finding new organizational structures is an important way of dealing with this problem. With so many leadership positions filled by baby boomers who need (and often want) to continue working in some capacity, organizations must abandon the notion that a traditional, one-person-in-charge, hierarchical model is the best one, or even that it is workable at all anymore. Collectives have made a comeback from their 1970s and '80s heyday, but with several important differences from the old model. In the new model, each person in the collective has a specific area of responsibility for which he or she is accountable. In some collectives, the development director has authority over the other members of the collective with regard to fundraising decisions, and the program director is in charge when it comes to program decisions. This allows, and indeed actually forces, an organization to integrate program, fundraising, and administrative functions because everyone is involved in all these areas, and for the organization to run efficiently, all parties must look at each task from all angles and make sure they are performing each task with all organizational elements in mind.

Another model many organizations are moving toward is a codirector arrangement, with all executive director functions shared between two people. This setup works when the two people are able to be completely honest and open with each other and when they are careful not to undermine each other's authority with other staff. Some people think a codirector model can work only when the two people involved get along very well and complement each other, but I believe being codirectors is a skill and can be learned even by people who don't know each other. Boomer directors willing to move in this direction bring on a younger codirector, and with coaching, thoughtfulness, and planning, this setup works well. (Read between the lines: without honesty, a codirectorship is a disaster.)

A third model entails the organization's adopting revolving responsibilities, in which the executive director, development director, program coordinator, community organizer, and other staff regularly rotate roles—say, every two years. Everybody learns how to do each job. Redundancy in skills is actually very important—an organization in which only one person knows how to sort data or only one person can call on donors is an accident waiting to happen.

There are undoubtedly many other models, but the point here is not to try to find the ideal model, but rather to play to the strengths of the people in the organization. Look at the work that needs to be done and the talents and skills of the people who can do it, and match talent to task. If someone wants to learn something but does not yet have that skill, figure out a way the person can learn it. Baby boomers have a lot of experience that they need to share. However, experience is not just a component of age—a twenty-five-year-old bilingual immigrant certainly has as much experience in knowing what immigrant need as someone who has been doing immigrant rights work for twenty-five years but is not bilingual and not an immigrant.

I am hoping that discussions about organizational form will also lead to organizations banding together to create jobs that cross organizational lines. Some organizations already share a web designer or an accountant. Even development directors sometimes work half-time for one organization and half-time for another. A boomer executive director willing to share his or her skills over two or three organizations and be paid by all three makes room in the primary organization for a new person to take on more responsibility while the boomer continues to work.

Founder's Syndrome

The most common complaint that often presents as a generational conflict is something that does not intrinsically have anything to do with generational change: founder's syndrome. Sometimes we see young founders who are every bit as problematic as their older counterparts, but I include founder's syndrome in this chapter because more often than not it has generational elements, and it is about passing the torch from the founding generation to new leadership, regardless of the age of either the founders or the successors.

The process of starting an organization, nurturing it to success, and then relinquishing it to a new generation of leadership is one that eludes most founders. Many feel that, having worked so hard, they should now stay and reap the benefits of their work, as the organization follows a smooth trajectory to success built on their efforts. They fail to understand that for some personalities the greatest satisfaction comes from starting something; those people should then move on to start something else. They may feel that everything isn't in place just yet, and after _____ happens (the next hiring, getting through this downturn, building up the reserve fund) it will be time to quit. Certainly, many founders have a lot of anxiety about what they will do next and fear becoming a has-been as soon as they leave the organization.

Although founders can be any age, currently many founders are baby boomers, and many of the people who work for them are younger than they are. Many boomer founders suffer from an excessive identification with work and don't know where they end and the organization begins. The tension between older and younger staff will be compounded over the next ten years, as founders and other older staff who intended to retire find themselves financially unable to do so, and younger staff who hoped one day to become the executive director realize they may have to wait years for that job to open up.

People often blame founder's syndrome on the founder. However, blaming anyone here is counterproductive. The founder can have the power she has only because she surrounds herself with people who excuse her behavior on the basis that she is the founder.

We have an idea that because someone starts something and because that person works harder than anyone else during that start-up phase, she or he should have more power than anyone else—in essence, that because a person started the organization, that person owns it. In certain settings this is true. For example, if a person starts a small business, appoints herself the president of the company, and hires people to work for her, then that person should have the most say in how the business is run. However, when somebody starts a nonprofit, which is overseen by a board and operates as a public charity, that person has chosen a model in which there is no right of ownership.

There are many ways that founder's syndrome debilitates an organization, but three are most common:

1. *The founder is a visionary and is constantly moving the organization on to new ideas and programs.* The board often is hard-pressed to keep up with her but feels compelled to go along. If this process is not watched carefully, the group is in danger of moving away from its original mission or taking on projects that are simply too big and too ambitious.

2. *The founder builds a successful organization.* After a few years, thanks to his leadership and charisma, the group is big and

strong. In fact, it is bigger than the founder's ability to run it. The founder lacks the management skills needed in an organization of the size that his has reached. To make up for the lack of management skills, many founders become micromanagers. They resist suggestions for change from other staff, who are often younger, and there is often a high turnover in younger staff. Sometimes the founder takes the organization back down to a size he can manage, and he will do his best to keep the group from growing further.

3. *The founder works day and night for a few years.* No one comes close to working as hard as this person. She accepts low pay and dismal office conditions. She sacrifices personal relationships for her job. Work is everything. At some point, her passion becomes martyrdom. She consistently feels that no one appreciates her and that she "deserves better" from the organization. She demands an ever-higher salary, more benefits, sabbaticals, a nicer office, a secretary. She is no longer creative; she is simply demanding. The danger here is that the group will no longer do good work, but will still take up a space in the nonprofit community so that no other group will form to do that work. No one dares to challenge the founder, and everyone simply hopes that she will quit.

I have seen groups where all three factors were present at once, as well as other variations on the founder's syndrome theme. Interestingly, founder's syndrome can be present in people who were not, in fact, the founders. They may be staff or board members who have been in the organization from the beginning or close to it. Founder's syndrome can also exist in several people at once. This is often seen in small groups where a few volunteers or board members form a clique. Nothing can get done without the approval of this group.

The symptoms of founder's syndrome in any one person are varied, but they are usually easy to identify. Working long hours, being anxious about both the work and those doing it, obsession with control and with knowing everything that is going on at all times, refusal to take a vacation or calling and e-mailing in to work during vacations—these are the garden-variety manifestations of founder's syndrome, and if all the staff are good-humored, these symptoms can often be dealt with. More serious are angry reactions to organizational change: seeing disagreement as disloyalty; raging when outvoted, or refusing to be outvoted by bringing a topic up over and over again until it goes her way; not sharing information even with board members. At an organizational level, these behaviors beget other symptoms: high turnover of staff and board members; a few people with intense loyalty to the founder who defend her, no matter what; and staff who feel that they must always tread lightly when the founder is in the office, and who feel a sense of welcome relief and freedom whenever the founder is out of the office.

Founder's syndrome obviously has a negative impact on fundraising. In organizations that have a development director, that person's creativity will be stifled. The development director may have to defend decisions that she or he didn't agree with to donors and funders, and, more difficult, explain the founder's difficult or irrational behavior. When people have questions about the founder, they may turn to the development director as someone perceived to have the ear of the founder or be close to the founder.

Of all the trials to plague an organization, founder's syndrome is one of the worst, because it is so much about personality and so little about organizational structure. Nevertheless, there are a number of ways that founder's syndrome can be addressed organizationally. The following attitudes and actions can help prevent or turn around potentially damaging founder's syndrome behavior. In fact, these suggestions can prevent most of the problems an organization may face.

1. *Assume good intent.* This Quaker saying is important in all organizational work and is probably a decent motto for life. Underneath all the problems that anyone in an organization has or creates, there is generally a shared basic commitment to fairness. By believing that ultimately, when pushed, people do want what will best accomplish the mission and goals of the organization, you will not be tempted to add to the gossip, plotting, anger, and frustration that are so often present in any effort to address founder's syndrome. By each person assuming good intent—good will—on everyone's part, people may rise to that assumption.

2. *Examine what you are about to say.* Is it true? If true, is it kind? If kind, is it necessary? The Sufis call this the "three gates of speech." In a meeting or when you are with people who are not your closest friends, don't add to the gossip and innuendo, even though that can be temporarily satisfying. Vent your frustration and your need to say nasty things with people who aren't immersed in the organization and whom you can trust completely not to repeat what you say.

3. *Be proactive.* This is the most important aspect of dealing with founder's syndrome, especially as it crosses generations. From the day the organization starts, talk about bringing in new and younger leadership. If the idea of turning over leadership is built in from the beginning and has always been part of the plan, transferring leadership will be seen as a primary accomplishment rather than as something to be resisted as long as possible.

4. *Review the organization's case statement and keep in mind that everyone's first loyalty should be to the mission of the group.* Obviously, people will have personal loyalties and friendships, but these must be secondary to the goals of the organization. The organization itself is secondary to its mission, and sometimes the organization will have to be profoundly changed in order to accomplish the mission.

5. *Separate likes and dislikes from serious organizational issues.* Let's say you are a board member trying to deal with a founding executive director. The executive director constantly looks at his cell phone during meetings, even when other people are talking, and this seems rude to you. He appears to be bored and sometimes gives the impression he is not listening. He also keeps bringing up a decision he disagreed with, hoping to get it changed. Ask yourself which of these behaviors is the most important to try to change. (I would vote for trying to get the founder to stop bringing up decisions that have already been made.) Because you will have the most success changing yourself, and the least success changing someone else, concentrate on making sure changes you ask for from someone else are really critical ones. If you ask for too many changes, you will get none.

6. *Suggest that the founder expand her skills.* This can be done in the context of upgrading the skills of all the staff and board members. Talented founding staff should not be forced to leave an organization that has outgrown their ability to manage it; management skills are learnable. The ability to supervise, delegate, evaluate, and hire and fire staff—these are all skills and can be learned. Even the smallest organization should have a line item in its budget to pay for some of this training. In some cases, a training program may be too expensive for the organization to pay the tuition. Foundations, corporations, and major donors who have worked with an organization for a while are often amenable to picking up all or part of the tab for this kind of training. I know of cases in which founder's syndrome has been averted or corrected because the founder got the training she needed.

Dealing with founder's syndrome requires everyone, including the founder, to make some decisions about whether the group will exist beyond the involvement of the founder. If it will, how will that happen? These can be painful conversations, but if they are handled sensitively and evenhandedly among board members and staff, they can be freeing to both the founder and everyone else who is concerned about fulfilling the mission of the organization.

Some groups cannot be saved from founder's syndrome. Perhaps the founder's mark is too deep. Sometimes it seems that founders derive a certain satisfaction in seeing that the organization cannot run without them, and sometimes those left behind do not have the wherewithal to pull the organization together and go on. It is also true that not all founders suffer from founder's syndrome, but rarely do we find healthy groups where the founder is still the director after ten or more years.

The lesson here is that whenever people in an organization, whether they are board or staff, believe that the organization cannot run without a certain person, that person needs to plan to leave. Founder's syndrome is a leadership vacuum. A healthy organization is strong enough to operate regardless of who leaves. One of the many jobs of the founder, the board members, and the key people in the organization is to build leadership. This mandate is as important as building an endowment or building a donor base, and it has just as much impact on fundraising.

Five Short Lessons on Dealing with Generational Change

A great deal has already been written on generational change (see the Resources for my favorite book on this topic), and much more will be. Age is the most constantly changing identity, and what the world looks like now, with millions of middle-aged baby boomers, is very different from what it will look like when I am ninety-two and the Millennials are middle-aged, dealing with the generations that follow them—which don't yet exist or have names.

But we have learned from fundraising the following five lessons that can smooth the way for any change we want to see:

1. *Assumptions: don't make any.* We all make up stories in our heads about other people, and we all make up stories about whole groups of people: "They are so east coast," or "Typical corporate types." We do it about generations as well: "These young people have no work ethic"; "That guy is stuck in the sixties." But we need to stop ourselves from doing that. We really don't know a whole lot about a person just from her age, and although generations may have things in common, there is also a huge range of personality and experience inside any generation.
2. *Be interested in others.* See what you can learn from someone very different from you. Ask questions and listen to the answers. Share your experience, but don't dominate the conversation with yourself and what you know.
3. *For those of you who are older, remember what you were like when you were young.* For young people, think about what you will want to be like as you age, and look for models of behavior you like—and that you don't.
4. *Show appreciation and praise.* No one can be thanked too often, and none of us ever feels quite as appreciated as we may think we deserve to be. Praise others' work and efforts, and the people being praised will work harder.

5. *Be genuine and honest and do not seek out, create, or avoid conflict.* Take conflict resolution trainings—dealing with conflict is a skill that anyone can learn.

Our society is ageist to its core, but this does not work to the advantage of any particular age group. Although we are youth-obsessed in some ways, young people will not be given the best jobs or trusted with important assignments. Although we value the experience and wisdom that comes with age, older people often feel marginalized and mocked. Like all the changes that we need to make, rethinking age is one of our tasks. How would a just society treat people of any age? Its elders? Its very young people? Having that conversation across age lines is interesting and informative and takes us a long way toward understanding each other generationally.

Chapter Twenty

Staying Excited About Donors

A while ago, I temporarily took on the development function for an organization that was having some staff crises. The executive director had become too ill to work and had resigned; the development director's husband had been transferred out of state, and she had chosen to move with him. An office manager remained. The board was busy searching for a new ED and wanted that person to be able to hire his or her own development director. When I first got there, I thought that the donors might wonder what was going on with the organization, so I called the most longtime givers and the biggest donors and had nice talks with many of them. They were supportive and understanding of the organization's temporary inability to do much program work. I wrote, and the office manager sent, an e-newsletter with an appeal, and we had an excellent response. I wrote personal notes on all the thank-you's that went out.

After a couple of months, however, the thrill of seeing a lot of donations come in through the mail or getting reports about on-line giving wore off; it was replaced with a feeling of not being able to keep up with the response. We got behind in entering donor information. The next e-newsletter was thrown together in a hurry, but still people sent in money in response to the appeal it carried. Thank-you notes were going out later and later. To catch up, I stopped writing personal notes on them.

I was falling victim to something I warn everyone about: taking donors for granted. I was shaken out of my bad habit when I ran into a donor who had also attended a number of my fundraising workshops. Laughing, she said, "Hey—I thought I would get a personal note from you when I sent in my donation. That's what I thought you said to do in your workshop." She seemed to be kidding, but I felt busted. Feebly, I explained that I had gotten behind. "So it happens to the best of us," she said, and moved on.

The lesson here is that donors don't give us much feedback, and we often don't know what they notice and what they don't. If a name is spelled wrong or left out of an annual report, or a donor is sent duplicate copies of an appeal, we will probably hear about it with varying degrees of irritation. However, few people will call to say, "Thanks for the personal note" or "Thanks for the phone call reminding me about the event." Under the pressure of time, we abandon the smaller gestures of appreciation, and we don't really know what that costs our organizations.

This lack of attention to donors takes on bigger forms, however, and the costs can be measured. For example, as organizations grow, they often cease to pay attention to patterns in their donors' giving. This is often compounded by the limitations of the database they are using. Let's say a donor sends in $35 to renew his membership and is thanked with a form letter. That same donor sends in an additional $50 using the return envelope in the newsletter, and later gives $100 in response to an appeal. This donor has given three times in six months, but every time, he is thanked with the same form letter. No one is paying attention to the fact that his cumulative giving is becoming significant and that he clearly likes the organization. Ideally, after the second or third gift he would receive a personal thank-you note that said, "Thanks for helping us so often—it means a lot." Further, his giving pattern should come to the attention of the major donor committee—perhaps, if given a little consideration, he can make a much bigger gift or become a monthly donor.

As mailing lists get larger, less attention is paid to finding duplicates or making sure addresses are current. Donors may receive three or four copies of a mailing—one to Kate Hernandez, another to Francis Moreno and Kate Hernandez, a third to K. Hernandez, and a fourth to Francis and Kate Moreno. Each of these names will reflect a gift that Kate made and how she signed her response card at the time, or the checking account on which she wrote the check. Although some donors will call your attention to this, many more will mean to but will not take the time, and others who don't understand the limits of "merge and purge" technology will cease to give altogether.

Sometimes the lack of attention presents an even greater missed opportunity for the organization. One version or another of the following story has happened several times to organizations I have consulted with. A donor sends in a gift of $1,000. The check is given to the finance person and the return card is given to the development director or data entry person. Here's an example: A return card with the name of the donor written on it (Joe Burgos) and the amount he has chosen from the donation string ($1,000) is passed to the data entry person. This information is entered into the database, along with the date of the gift and the fact that the gift was in response to the spring appeal.

However, the check that accompanied this gift was printed with "Howard Family Foundation" and signed by Joe H. Burgos. The development office never saw the check and did not connect Howard Family Foundation with Joe Burgos. A quick search of grant information on the Foundation Center's website would show that the Howard Family Foundation gives away $2 million a year and that Joe H. Burgos is on the board. Perhaps his middle initial stands for Howard, making him a blood relative of the Howard family, and possibly a prospect for a much bigger gift or a grant. Most organizations are missing important information because they don't use the checks as a source of information, but simply go from what is written on their reply devices. Sometimes this can be embarrassing. Suppose you haven't made the connection between Joe Burgos and the Howard Family Foundation, and your foundation research independently shows the Howard Family Foundation to be a good prospect. You write a proposal and are asked to make a presentation. Joe is at the presentation and seems surprised that you don't know that he is already a donor to your organization.

E-mail compounds these problems. An organization asks their donors to sign up to get the newsletter by e-mail instead of mail: "Save trees and get the information faster." Longtime donor Sarah Jones wants to save trees (who doesn't?) and so agrees to switch to the e-newsletter. She gets a lot of e-mail, though, so she often deletes their newsletter when she feels she doesn't have time to read it. She accidentally deletes their renewal appeal, which also comes by e-mail, and when she changes her e-mail address she neglects to tell the organization. They, in turn, do not keep track of the fact that she hasn't given in two years, even though she used to give every year. Sarah has ceased to be a donor simply because the organization lost track of her.

Finally, as an organization gets bigger, even larger donors begin to be neglected. I gave $500 a year to a group for about four years. The first year, someone had visited me and asked for the gift. The second year, someone called and asked me to renew. The third year, I got a personalized form letter. That year I didn't give for several months because I misplaced the letter. As a result, in the fourth year, my personalized renewal form letter came just three months after I had given my third-year gift. I had sent in $250 with a note that I would send the other $250 in a few months. I was never reminded of that pledge, and I forgot about it until the fifth year, when I got a form letter (not personalized) asking me to renew my gift in the range of $100 to $200. Obviously, for that organization, people giving $250 or less are in a different system than those giving $500 or more. At that point, I elected to be in the group that gives nothing and have never been asked again.

Organizations cannot avoid all the problems that come with having a large number of donors, but by making appreciation of donors a high priority, as well as training everyone who deals with the database in what to record, we can avoid many of the pitfalls I have described. Overall, of course, making sure donors know that your organization does good work will maintain the loyalty of most of them, so doing the work and letting donors know about it must be of paramount concern.

The Great Balancing Act

How can we balance all the work that needs to be done—which is, after all, what donors are paying us to do—with the need to cultivate the positive response that most humans have to gestures of appreciation? And how can we notice further fundraising opportunities in the clues our donors give us?

There are several solutions, which all begin with the fact that gratitude and appreciation have to be values in the organizational culture. Let me explain what I mean. It is true that the people who give us money year after year are grateful that we do the work we do. That's why they support us. But we, as organizations, need to understand our gratitude to them. They chose us when they had thousands of other choices; they chose to give away some of their money, when they could have used it in other ways; and they chose to do it year after year. I appreciate that because I value generosity in myself and in others. And, like most people, I value a bit of personal attention. In most cities, a person can go to the bank, the gas station, and even the grocery store without interacting with another person. Simply stick in your card and push the right buttons. Shopping on-line means that people can buy almost anything without leaving home. Although these services may be making life more convenient, they are also making people much more isolated.

People like to be noticed for their positive actions, and they are more likely to repeat such actions if they feel they have made a difference. Personal attention—in the form of notes, phone calls, or even visits—is the only way donors have of knowing that we have noticed their individual gift. Of course they know that as a group they make a difference. But each donor sometimes wants to know, "Does my gift help? Did my individual gift mean anything to you?" What we need are logistically feasible ways to keep in touch with donors and to keep ourselves excited about fundraising.

How to Take Care of Yourself and Your Donors

Here are a number of ways you can handle how your work gets done, which will help ensure that you don't slip into taking donors for granted.

1. *Let different people in the organization take the lead on fundraising strategies.* For example, no one person should write all the appeals. Ask board members or volunteers to write a first draft. Get someone who has benefited from your work to write a testimonial. You can then work with these drafts, but they will have a new tone and a different approach from what you would have come up with. Sometimes people will come up with entirely different approaches than you might have thought of. For example, an organization in Montreal received a donation from a music band and created a two-minute YouTube video singing their thank-you note to the tune of one of the band's

songs. Needless to say, the band was thrilled, and the staff had a lot of fun doing this.

Ditto for editing the newsletter. It is deadly for one person always to be in charge of the content, of tracking down stories, of nagging the writers to get their pieces in on time. Form an editorial committee, or rotate editing the newsletter. If you have a template and a word count, it is not difficult, even for someone with little experience, to put together a good newsletter. In the same way that some customers love the "staff picks" at the video or book store, donors get to know a little about staff and volunteers in a way they cannot if the same person is in charge of all communication. Certainly, the development director will want to look over the final draft to make sure you have maintained the "brand" of your organization, but you do not need to do the whole thing.

2. *Make sure your database program is adequate.* You should not be hampered in your ability to keep track of donor information, including patterns of giving, because your database is too limited, too old, can't sort quickly, can't hold much information, or whatever. You don't need to spend thousands of dollars on a database program, but you do need to take the time to find one that works for your group and then take the time to learn all that it can do. Many database programs can do a lot more than we are aware of, but we learn only enough to fulfill our basic needs. (See the sidebar in Chapter Ten: What Your Database Should Be Able to Store and Retrieve Easily.)

3. *Write, or have volunteers write, personal thank-you notes.* The body of the thank-you can be the same for all donors, but at the bottom there should be a note from someone saying, "Thanks again," or "Hope to meet you one of these days." With a good database program, you can enter the donor's gift and then generate a personalized thank-you note. Then add a handwritten personal note to that one.

4. *Train whoever does the data entry to look for key information.* The staffer should take note of the following things, then code them in some way or bring them to someone's attention:
   - *An unusually large gift after a series of smaller ones.* If a donor suddenly gives $200 or $500 when previous gifts were $35 or

$50, call to thank the donor. Show that you notice. Pay attention to what the donor tells you about the gift; find out what the organization has done that the donor liked so much. You may want to visit this person for an even bigger gift.

- *Notes that come with a check.* People who take the time to tell you something—even if it is a sticky note with "Keep up the good work!"—need to be noted. Your thank-you can refer to their note. Also, accommodate their requests. If they say, "Only ask me once a year" or "Please don't phone me," then do what they wish.

- *Any interesting information on the check.* In our example, Joe Burgos's check was drawn off of a family foundation. Others may be drawn off of a trust, a small business, or a corporation. Note the name of the institution behind the check and the need to research whether there is more money there. People sometimes tell you their professions on their checks: "Mary Esposito, Esq.," or "Vin Hang, M.D.," or "Phyllis Browne, LCSW." Sometimes their checks will show something that the person believes in: "Pro-choice" or "Save the cougars." Again, these things may indicate interests, beliefs, or ability to make a bigger gift. The check may tell you something about the household of the donor, such as the spouse or partner's name.

All of this information should be entered into the database, but it also has to be used. Data entry must be seen as a key fundraising function. If you have a person who does data entry, teach that person about prospect research and emphasize the need to make your organization a welcoming environment for donors. If you do the data entry yourself, don't do it when you are tired or rushed. This comes back to gratitude and appreciation. As you sit down to enter data about donors, take a deep breath and thank them in your heart for all they do.

5. *Don't promise anything on the front end that you cannot fulfill on the back end.* Many times organizations raise donors' expectations by how they cultivate and solicit the gift but do not follow through with the same level of attention after the gift is received. Probably nowhere is this problem more obvious than with foundations. Someone from the organization will

write an excellent letter of inquiry, visit the foundation staff, send a thank-you letter with more materials as needed, write a good proposal, call to see if anything else is needed, and generally be attentive and polite. As soon as the grant comes through, they send nothing to the foundation besides the six-month report until the next year, when their attention starts again with an eye to additional funding.

A similar sequence may be played out with donors. Your attentiveness in order to get the funding makes the donor think you will be attentive in other respects. If you promise that you will keep in touch, do so. Make a note in your calendar to send a newspaper clipping or something relevant to your work every few months. Put the person on your mailing list and send invitations to your open house or other special events. If you do whatever it takes to get the money but then do nothing to express appreciation for having gotten it, you risk appearing obsequious, groveling, and fake.

6. *Spread the work out over more people.* If you are a paid staff person in charge of fundraising, every time you find yourself doing a task that any reasonably intelligent person could also do with a little training, find that person and give that person the training. Thank-you notes, foundation research, phone calls to invite people to events or thank them for donations, and so on can be done by volunteers, interns, and board members. Although this may not save you a lot of time, because you will have to train and then supervise those workers, your helper may notice things that you don't, and you have involved more people in the work of the organization.

7. *Keep your list clean.* Once a year, print out your whole mailing list (if it is huge, you may have to do it in sections). With the help of people who have been around the organization for a long time, go through the list name by name. Look for typos, duplicate entries, people who are now deceased or divorced. The data entry person should be instructed to look for this type of information as well.

8. *Make sure you and the organization understand that the purpose of fundraising is building relationships, not raising money, and evaluate your fundraising program accordingly.* Obviously, money raised has to be one of the ways the fundraising program

is evaluated, but it also must be evaluated in terms of other numbers: new donors, retention rate (which is a good indicator of donor loyalty), new and renewing major donors, people involved in fundraising. In addition, look at the general attitude toward fundraising on the part of everyone in the organization. Donors get neglected and relationships are sacrificed when fundraisers are under inordinate and inappropriate pressure to produce cash rather than to build a community of donors.

9. *Develop people you can talk with about your work.* Just as we need close friends who are willing to hear us rant and rave or are happy to help us think through sticky emotional situations, we need close work friends. Sometimes these are other staff, but often it is better if you have one or two people who don't work and don't volunteer in your organization, who are discreet, and in whom you can confide. These people help you set priorities, talk you down from your anxiety, help you through writer's block, and go for a walk with you at the end of a long and frustrating week. I know people who form small cadres of three or four other people who are committed to doing that for each other. It keeps everybody happier in their work, and happiness is closely related to productivity.

10. *Redefine the jobs.* From time to time, all the staff of an organization should think through all the jobs they do and all the jobs that should be done and are not getting done. Then they should redefine the jobs to match the strengths of the workers and to make sure that what is important is what is getting accomplished.

So often we get into the habit of doing only what is urgent and in our face, and we forget to ask, "Is this urgent item also important? Will anyone even notice six months from now that I never did this?" Staff-wide discussion of what is important can help reprioritize our work. We are never going to get everything done, and in fact, many of us have given up on the idea that we will ever feel caught up. Knowing that some stuff is inevitably going to fall through the cracks, make sure it is the stuff that is not that important.

When we come into a new job, we often do the work in the way the person who had the job before us did it. Particularly if you haven't had a lot of experience, your tendency will be to copy your predecessor. However, your skill set and your personality may be different from those of the previous person, so you need to make sure you are doing the things you are good at and delegating the things you aren't as good at. For example, some development people are very good at detailed analysis, cash flow projections, and data collection. They may not be as good at picking up the phone and calling donors or board members. Some people are very skilled event planners, and some really are not. Know yourself, and do what you are good at. If you don't know how to do something (say, on-line fundraising or prospect research) and you want to learn how, then figure out a way to learn it. Go to a workshop, read a book, find a mentor. However, if you don't know how to do something and you *don't* want to learn how, find someone else who either knows how or wants to learn how, and delegate to them. By regularly reexamining all the jobs that need to get done and the skills and talents of the people available to do them, we can match people to tasks instead of stuffing people into rigid and outmoded job descriptions.

The coming years will see a lot of shakedown in the nonprofit sector. Venerable institutions will close, our sector will have unemployment rates as high as—or higher than—any other sector's, and it will be easy to be anxious a lot of the time. Anxiety is corrosive, though, and must be addressed. When you are excited by your job, when you are inspired by the work of your organization, and when you feel gratitude and appreciation for all the other people who feel as you do and who express their commitment financially or with time or other expressions of support, you will be able to ride the waves in this never-before-navigated economy.

Chapter Twenty-One

Time Management

When my sister, Candace, was about ten, she entered an art contest at school. She is an amazing artist, and her talent was evident even then. She worked hard on her piece and finished well ahead of the deadline. The night before it was due, our cat, who was not an art appreciator, threw up on the bottom corner of it. I think my parents advised asking for an extension so she could fix the piece, but Candace rightly pointed out that "the cat threw up on my entry" would go about as far as the classic "the dog ate my homework." Because my sister loved our cat and would not tolerate any criticism of him—and, more important for this book, because she had completed the work in plenty of time—she simply, calmly stayed up late that night, repaired the damage, and went on to win the show.

I learned a valuable lesson about time management from this incident: time management is not so much about getting the most out of our waking hours, being efficient, accurately predicting how long a task will take, or planning our work (although all of these are important) as it is about creating a way of working that allows you to stay calm and focused even when things go wrong.

Like fundraising, time management starts with a philosophy and then proceeds to the practical how-to's inside the boundaries of that philosophy. In many ways, time is both our most precious nonrenewable resource and our most democratic institution. We all have twenty-four hours in our day. When this day is over, it is over. We can't get it back. Thus, time is not money: we can earn more money, and people have vastly unequal amounts of money. To be sure, money helps people with their time, and people who must work two or three jobs to make ends meet rightly feel they have less time than someone who plays golf all day. Those of us in fundraising are at neither end of this spectrum. We have neither more nor less time than the other people in our organization or than most of our donors. We will not get everything done, so we have to choose among a number of important things. We will be late with some things, and we must choose what can be late and what really cannot. And then we have to be flexible enough to cope with events that are unforeseen, unplanned, and sometimes disastrous.

I believe that the chief goal of time management is to help us be happy. We must see being happy, and helping others to be happy, as social justice work. We must claim kindness, patience, forgiveness, and generosity of spirit as important and in fact as integrally related to integrity, commitment, and willingness to sacrifice for the common good. We have to love each other, and we have to love those who are difficult to love. Love is hard. That's why in every religious and spiritual tradition, love is a commandment. You don't have to command people to burp, or scratch, or gossip—people do that. We have to be commanded to love.

It is easy for me to see my biggest mistake over the course of my whole life: It was creating a hierarchy of my time and placing work at the top of it. For years, I worked all the time. Weekends and evenings were simply times to work uninterrupted. Airplane rides were times to read professional journals or political analysis. As I got older, I stopped devoting *all* my time to work. But work still took the bulk of my time.

People who work all the time, as I did, are actually kind of lazy. We never have to make any decisions about any other part of our life, because when we are not working, we are so tired that there is little else we can do but sleep. If I work all the time, I don't need to think, for example, *Should I bring my elderly, housebound neighbor some fruit or dinner? Or maybe just go visit with her? Or maybe she would like to be invited to my house for dinner—or would that be awkward for her, because she will feel she has to invite me back?* I don't think about any of that because I have to work, partly for the rights of seniors. Many of us in nonprofits love people, and we work very hard to secure their rights and to make their lives easier, but sometimes we don't take enough time to show our love to individual persons—in particular, our partners, our children, and our friends.

Our inability to care for each other extends to the planet. The crisis of environmental sustainability—summed up in the terms *global warming* or *climate change*—is related to and exacerbated by another crisis: the crisis of human sustainability, described by David Suzuki as "a scarcity of the conditions which nurture resilient, secure individuals, families, friendships and communities." Who has time to care for whom in this overworked culture, in which we social justice activists fully participate? The consequences of this crisis can be found in the rising incidence of clinical depression. By 2020, it is estimated that depression may be the world's most prevalent condition, and not just in first-world countries—it is documented also in the rapidly expanding urban areas of China, India, Bangladesh, and Mexico.

There is a lot of talk now about work-life balance, but the point of finding that balance is to be happy, to find a kind of freedom. (Even the phrase *work-life* implies that we are not living while we are at work.) Karl Marx said, "The politics of time is essential to freedom. The shortening of the working day is the basic prerequisite for that development of human energy which is an end in itself, the true realm of freedom." So the first step in good time management is to define for yourself how you want to use your time, and to think about what, at the end of your life, will make you feel good about the priorities that you set with the time that you had. With that framework in mind, there are some habits you can incorporate into your own life and into your organizational culture that will help you use your work time effectively.

First and foremost, in your organizational culture, and to the extent that you can influence nonprofits around you, define thirty-five to forty hours per week as the meaning of "full time," and although you may work more time in some weeks, you will balance this by working less time in others. In Scandinavia, where some of the world's most competitive economies are located, working overtime is seen as a sign of incompetence, either your own or that of your supervisor, who is judged to be unable to assign work properly. In the United States, particularly in the social justice arena, working all the time is a sign of commitment. We need to move to a much more Scandinavian understanding of work.

Time Tracking

For many of us, it is difficult to break the habit of working all the time. The way to begin to do that is to keep track of your time. Keep a log that creates a snapshot of how you spend your time. You can do this on paper or you can download time-tracking software that gives you an accurate accounting of the time various tasks take. Use your method to record what you have done for three days a week for one month, or every other week for two months to capture the most information. Vary the days you keep track of so that you capture most of the tasks you are engaged in. Put these tasks into categories and see what you learn.

At the end of each week, write down, too, what you didn't get done and how much time you think you would have needed to accomplish all you had hoped to do.

Exhibit 21.1 shows what Ravi, a thirty-four-year-old development director, found in his time tracking over the course of one month (160 hours).

Exhibit 21.1: Results of Ravi's Time Tracking

How Ravi used his time:

- ❏ 30 hours: writing, editing, and publishing e-newsletter, with most time spent figuring out how to send it to the e-mail list and get it on the website without losing the formatting

- ❏ 10 hours: setting up for the board meeting: e-mailing the agenda, budget, profit and loss statements, and fundraising report; buying food; photocopying the agenda budget and fundraising plan in case people forgot to bring theirs; making coffee; and so on

- ❏ 3 hours: board meeting

- ❏ 10 hours: putting together report for Demando Foundation

- ❏ 4 hours: going with ED to see three donors

- ❏ 2 hours: working with mail house to clear up problems with our list

- ❏ 2 hours: searching for, finding, then counting the # of return envelopes, stationery, etc., to see how much to order

- 1 hour: dealing with designer about stationery, etc., because each of us thinks the other has the originals
- 2 hours: personalizing thank-you notes
- 8 hours: staff meetings
- 4 hours: calls with board members regarding their major donor tasks
- 1 hour: attempted to reach three major donors; will try again
- 2 hours: starting to write spring appeal; still not done
- 30 hours: reading on-line fundraising stuff and answering e-mail not related to any of the above

What Ravi didn't get done:

- Personalizing thank-you notes: I am running out of ideas and doing these too fast.
- Ten more major donors to call, plus the three I didn't reach. Also, I need to keep ahead of the board members, who are actually on top of their major donor work right now.
- Meeting with ED to go over revised fundraising plan.
- Spring appeal: I keep getting interrupted and losing my train of thought.
- Working with chair of auction committee to create master task list.
- Changing content on website and adding information about our monthly donor club.
- Setting up New York fundraising trip.

Total time needed for tasks not done: about 40 hours

At the end of one month, Ravi has a week's worth of work not done that he had hoped to accomplish during that month. In looking at what he does, he observes that much of what he has spent time doing could have been done by a volunteer: most of the setup for the board meeting, figuring out inventory, and even checking with board members about their major donor calls. In both what he did and what he left undone, there is also room for volunteers: personalizing thank-you notes, for example, can be a shared task with other staff, board members, or reliable volunteers.

Some of what he did could be done in a fraction of the time by someone who knows what they are doing: posting the e-newsletter and the information on the website. The entire newsletter could be divided into tasks: writer, editor, and publisher. Ravi can supervise and even carry one of these tasks, but it is not good for him to carry all three. Of course, his organization, like most, is reluctant to pay anyone else to do anything, but the cost of Ravi's ten hours has to be equal to or less than the cost of an expert's two hours.

Ravi also has a huge time commitment for answering e-mails; he decides to do another time tracking, analyzing exactly what those are and how important it is that he respond to as many e-mails as he does.

Focus on What Is Important, Not on What Is Urgent

Many development people learn that they are doing a lot of work that is not actually in their job description. As a colleague says, "The development department can quickly devolve into the random department," to which all tasks that aren't anyone else's job—but that need to get done—are assigned. You have to get on top of this in order to have the time to do what only you can do or oversee.

After you do some time tracking, it is important to divide both the work getting done and the work not getting done into four categories, which can be displayed as four boxes as in the diagram.

Important	Urgent
Not Important	Not Urgent

Most tasks cross two of the boxes—that is, they are both important and urgent or not important and not urgent. However, some are important but not urgent—and it is dangerously easy for these to be neglected until they suddenly become urgent. What we want to do is not spend so much time on things that are not important, no matter how urgent.

Sorting through all this in real life is not as easy as the diagram makes it seem. For example, an intern comes into the office one day, clearly upset. She goes to her desk without saying anything, but she is dabbing her eyes and seems to be in distress. This seems urgent. But you are the only staff in the office at this time, and you have an important proposal to finish, which is due at the end of the day, so it is also urgent. Do you put your work aside and ask the intern if she is OK? Although there is probably no *one right answer* to this dilemma, the principles we have outlined here would suggest that the priority has to be the person and not the project. In this case, checking in with the intern's feelings is higher on the to-do list than finishing the proposal, although ideally you will be able to do both.

People sometimes imagine that good time management manifests as acting like an emotionless robot who will never chat about the weather or show colleagues pictures of a new kitten. This is not true, because all the quadrants allow for a commitment to being happy yourself and to contributing to other people's happiness.

Now, returning to our example, you will be happier if you get your proposal done, so you might say to the intern, "Are you OK?" If you determine that she wants to talk, talk briefly with her now, and ask whether you can have a longer conversation toward the end of the day. You may have to help her set priorities—leave work now and go take care of whatever is making her upset—or you may affirm that coming to work was the right thing for her to do and talking later will be fine.

As much as possible, stay with tasks that are important, and do these in order of urgency. You will be amazed at how much of what you do is not important but is in your face and appears to be urgent. This is particularly true of e-mail. You need to discipline yourself not to check your e-mail more than three or four times a day, and not to feel that you must respond immediately to everyone's e-mail. If there are e-mails you know you will want to respond to quickly, take care of those; don't open the ones that you know can wait. The same is true for postal mail: don't open each letter only to put it in a pile to be dealt with later. For those envelopes you know you won't be dealing with right away, put them aside and deal with them all at once. This is not a game show, where if you open an ordinary looking e-mail or letter you may suddenly win a prize!

The process of time tracking and using the quadrant system to analyze tasks leads many people to realize that they lose time in very small ways that add up to many hours each day. This is similar to keeping track of patterns of spending money or of eating. We are unlikely to conclude, "Oh, my, I shouldn't have bought that house," but rather, "Oh, my, look how much I spend eating lunch out every day." We probably won't end up saying, "I wish I hadn't eaten that entire cheesecake," but rather, "Having half a donut every day is adding up to a lot of calories."

Finding those small time leaks really adds up. If you can save fifteen minutes in a day, you will have an extra two weeks in your year!

Make Your Work Fit in the Time You Have

It may surprise you to learn that many of us are actually excellent planners, but we miss a key element of planning: you should plan for only half of the time in your work day. Here's what I mean: I have a task that I think will take eight hours to complete, so I set aside a day to complete the task. I do not make other appointments, and I don't return any phone calls. However, I don't get the task done in that day—in fact, it takes two days. I may think I am a poor planner, but this is not so. It probably did take me exactly eight hours to complete the task, but I cannot expect to work, uninterrupted and undistracted, for an entire eight hours. In fact, on most days there are several unavoidable distractions. For example, I am interrupted by another staff member with a serious problem, which uses up thirty minutes. I decide to take a break for lunch, which takes fifteen minutes longer than I had planned, and then I eat too much, so I am sleepy and not as productive after lunch as I was before it; that uses up an hour. My computer freezes and I have to reboot three times, which uses up twenty minutes. I can't remember where I filed the statistics I need for what I'm writing. As I scroll through my files, I see something I was supposed to take care of weeks ago, and I decide to take fifteen minutes to handle it. This, and looking for the missing file, uses up most of another hour. You get the idea. To compensate for these mostly unavoidable and all too human delays, plan work that will take only half the time you plan to be at work, and you will not get behind.

Don't Multitask

One of the big breakthroughs of this century is dispelling the myth of multitasking. For many years, time managers advised people to try to do two things at once: one that required a lot of concentration and one that did not. For example, if you used a headset on your phone, you could talk to board members or donors while stuffing envelopes for a mailing. Or you could write thank-you notes while attending a staff meeting. Even now, on a conference call you hear the unmistakable clicking that indicates people are checking their e-mail, and many people sit in meetings surreptitiously sending text messages or scrolling through e-mail on their BlackBerry.

What we have learned, however, is that when you are doing two things at once, you are doing neither thing very well, and you are making yourself more tired than if you just did one thing at a time. Moreover, you're shortchanging the people you are talking to or meeting with because they don't have your full attention. Focus on the task at hand, finish it, and move on to the next task. When you are at a meeting, be *in* the meeting. If the meeting is not that important to you and you don't have to concentrate on what is happening, then question why you are there at all. Ditto for conference calls, or any other effort in which you are tempted to do more than one thing at a time.

You Have Enough Time

Penelope is the sole staff of a tiny organization that provides information and referrals to parents seeking affordable childcare, particularly for young children with special needs. Volunteers answer phones, keep up with research, post new information on the website, and send out an e-newsletter once a month. Penelope oversees the volunteers, takes care of all financial functions, and coordinates fundraising with a small team of board members. Everyone works very hard, but Penelope works all the time, and both she and everyone around her are aware of this. Over time, the organization is able to hire an assistant for Penelope, and later another staff person. Yet Penelope still has no time, and she still says over and over, like a mantra, "I am so busy. I am so stressed out. I don't know how I can get everything done." The truth is, Penelope has pledged allegiance to the idea of being busy, and no amount of change in her work environment will make a difference.

We all have statements we say to ourselves over and over: "I am too fat," "I am socially inept," "I can't sing"—and these statements become true because of repetition. In practicing good time management, discipline yourself to always say, "I have time." If someone calls who you want or need to talk with and asks, "Do you have a few minutes?" say, "Yes, I do," and mean it. Then talk with this person and don't do something else at the same time. If you don't have time to talk with the person, make a time later that is better. (Consider the option of not answering the phone at all when you don't have a few minutes.)

You will be amazed at how much time you have when you tell yourself over and over, "I have time. I am not too busy. I have a lot of work and I'm getting it done." This approach to fundraising allows you to focus on relationships with donors, with board members, and with volunteers and other staff, which in turn will cause them to want to help more. A person who takes the time to be interested in others is far more appealing and fun to work with than someone who is always harried and frazzled.

Keep Your Eyes on the Prize

Futurist and organizational development expert Meg Wheatley says, "If we want our world to be different, our first act needs to be reclaiming time to think. No one will give time to you, because thinking is always dangerous to the status quo. Those benefiting from the present system have no interest in new ideas. In fact, thinking is a threat to them. We can't expect those few who are well-served by the current reality to give us time to think. If we want anything to change, we are the ones who have to reclaim time."

Time management techniques are simply ways to open up the time we need to think and to be happy. Raising money for our organizations as we face a very uncertain present and future requires deep thought, and leading an organization that will continue to inspire donors requires that the leadership be (at least relatively) happy and well-balanced. We must build sustainable organizations that people can work in for years at a time, and to do that requires using our time properly and well.

Chapter Twenty-Two

Our Main Job Now and into the Future

This book has been written for people concerned with raising enough money to keep their organizations alive and well during the current economic situation and all its permutations. The economic turmoil we find ourselves living in must be seen as the "new normal." This is how it is—in fact, at whatever point you read this chapter, sit back and think to yourself, "What if this is as good as it gets? How would I raise money with this as my framework?" From the president of the United States to the prime minister of Iceland, from all the professors of economics and all the deans of business schools around the world to the grassroots activists of the Landless Peasant Movement in Latin America—as far and wide as we can go, everyone is in uncharted territory. But as Paul says to the Apostles in the Christian testament, "Faith is the evidence of things not seen, the substance of things hoped for." Unlike uncharted territory in an actual forest or desert, this is not territory we are *exploring*, but rather territory we are *creating*. The discoveries we make will be based on the work we do and the values we adopt.

So even though fundraising for our organization is our primary task, it cannot be separated from the larger challenge to our organization and to the nonprofit sector itself. This challenge is neatly summarized by two people, stating intertwining philosophies. One is Spock in the movie *Star Trek II: The Wrath of Khan*. As he dies to save the spaceship, Spock says, "The needs of the many outweigh the needs of the few. Or the one." The other is Peter Maurin, a less famous person, but a real one, who cofounded the Catholic Worker Movement with Dorothy Day in 1933. Maurin believed that our job is to create a society "in which it would be easier for people to be good." To me, these short statements provide the marching orders for all of us going forward, as well as an excellent description of the common good.

All fundraisers know that fundraising is not an end in itself but a means to help an organization fulfill its mission. Of course, that is not the end in itself, either: organizations' missions, collectively, have as their goal to create the society we wish to live in, a society in which it is not that hard to be good because what is good for everyone is the primary criterion by which anything is decided. Imagine designing your work around those principles. What would fundraising look like, and how would that kind of fundraising meet the very real (and anxiety-producing) challenges of this present moment? Here are some ways we would change how we work.

Rethinking Branding and Identity

We need to stop some of the positioning of our organizations that became stylish during the 1990s obsession with what nonprofits could learn from business. We learned, and now must unlearn, the idea that we must "brand" ourselves, protect our brand, and thus position ourselves as uniquely qualified to do the work we do. Some organizations even went so far as to trademark their slogans, as though a description of a vision could belong to only one organization. Thousands of dollars were spent by hundreds of organizations searching for catchier names than the ones they had, and focus groups and marketing professionals helped organizations "define their niche." A marketing executive who was consulting with a number of small nonprofits advised me to stop saying that I work with "grassroots" groups and think of my clients more as "boutique."

I don't want to throw the baby out with the bathwater, so I hasten to add that there are valuable insights in rethinking how we talk about our work. Some organizations really did need a name change and have thrived under a new name that is also a more accurate reflection of their work. Finding a meaningful logo; maintaining a consistent look throughout your stationery, e-mail signature, website, newsletter, and so on; these are important for helping donors recognize your work in all its forms. (Certainly the brand identities of the Red Cross and Red Crescent societies are important not just for fundraising but also for providing a very real image understood the world over by people in need.)

However, we lost sight of the fact that we are not businesses—we are not trying to be the best pizza parlor or the favorite shoe store. Especially, we are not trying to drive each other out of business or acquire each other so that each of our organizations actually belongs to one giant holding company. In the new normal, we brand ourselves as working together: food banks feed hungry people, and the hungry people who are also homeless are referred to the homeless shelter. In many communities, these organizations work very closely together and work as well with housing advocates, rent control activists, and the like. The food security movement combines community gardens in a neighborhood with advocacy at the federal level for sensible food policy. Activists and academics in this movement have long pointed out that there is enough food grown on this planet to feed everyone, and that distributing it properly, stopping monocropping, restoring soil, and the like, are the ways to solve world hunger. In this example, the brand—the main message—is ending hunger not only by feeding hungry people, but also by addressing the root causes of hunger.

No organization is unique, one-of-a-kind, never before seen in human history. Nor do we want to be unique—we want to position ourselves as working with many other organizations toward a common goal. This position attracts donors who don't want to feel torn between saving seals and saving rivers, or between addressing sex discrimination in the workplace and ending domestic violence.

Neither do we want to follow the now stylish advice to merge, merge, merge and Wal-Martize ourselves. Many donors and funders erroneously feel that no organization should do work in the community that's similar to another organization's work. "There are too many groups doing the same thing," they criticize. "They should join together and become one organization." Again, there is insight here, and some organizations have successfully merged, but we know from economics, marketing, and environmental studies that there is health in having more than one version of something. A city that has one large downtown library will have fewer library users overall than a city that has several smaller neighborhood branches that can share books, do joint buying, and advertise each other's programs. Each neighborhood librarian can then make sure that their library meets the needs of the neighborhood: one has a large selection of books in Spanish, another focuses more on materials in Vietnamese, and another library uses its resources to build a large bank of computers for job seekers, students, and seniors.

By asking what is good for all, nonprofits can decide whether they need to (1) merge to better serve their communities, (2) position themselves differently, or (3) simply invite more people to give money and participate in their work. Gavin Perryman, an organizational development consultant in Vancouver, points out that at the end of the day the work is what is essential. The organization is not essential, and this insight has to drive our planning.

Share Resources and Information

Our fundraising planning must include a component of sharing resources and information. The building where I have my office in Oakland, California, houses a large number of nonprofits. Once a month, the development directors from these organizations, plus friends from other buildings, meet for a brown-bag lunch to share stories, questions, and tips. Generally there is a theme: renewals, on-line giving, upgrading. We are also exploring sharing equipment: many of us don't have fancy photocopiers or scanners, and there is no need for everyone to have one if we own or lease such equipment together or pay a small fee to use one already owned or leased by someone else.

Another group of nonprofits has formed a paper purchasing program; by combining all their paper needs (stationery, newsletters, annual reports), they are able to negotiate a much better price from an environmental mill that produces tree-free paper in a sustainable and water-friendly way. Prior to their combined program, none of these organizations could afford this kind of paper.

All Organizations Have Problems

If you don't have a problem, you are not an organization. But many of us are reluctant to share our problems; we talk and write as if our efforts to diversify racially or to increase the involvement of constituents in decision making or to move to a new organizational structure are all going smoothly and easily. It is far more helpful to look at what has really happened: What do you know now that you wish you had known before you embarked on this effort? What would you advise others? What was your greatest accomplishment and your biggest mistake? In this uncharted territory, we will make plenty of brand-new, never-before-seen mistakes. Let's commit to helping each other save time by not watching each other make predictable mistakes.

Expand Our Definition of *Qualified*

We need to rethink what makes a person qualified to be a development director. Speaking a language other than English will be important; in states like California or Texas, it will be imperative. Being bicultural and knowing how to raise money among a wide variety of cultures and communities is now even more important than the more traditional skills of knowing how to write a grant proposal. Many organizations, even in very racially diverse communities and even with racially diverse staff and board, still have a primarily white donor base. The very practical problem with this situation is that those donors are aging. A 2008 study by the database marketing company Merkle, called "Examining the Impact of Political Fundraising on Nonprofit Direct Mail Performance," showed that one-third of all direct mail donations came from people aged seventy-six and older. We need to attract younger donors just to stay in business, and many of those younger donors will be people of color and immigrants. We need to make our donor base as diverse as our community, and many organizations are finding a sense of direction for their fundraising by comparing the demographics of their community (age, race, gender, income, and so on) with the demographics of their donors and working to bring these into harmony. The people we need to attract into development need to welcome this challenge as their own.

Make It Fun to Be a Board Member

We have to create a board environment in which being a board member is fun. Board members should be able to look forward to the meetings the way they look forward to any discussion with interesting, informed people. Board members need to willingly take on work outside the meetings, particularly fundraising, but they also need to know that while they are doing their share, all the other members are also doing what they said they'd do. Board structure needs to be entirely rethought, but first we want people on boards who are able to do that creative and visionary thinking.

Be Scrupulously Honest and Transparent

Demands for accountability in the nonprofit sector will continue to rise. Scandals in both the corporate and nonprofit sector will continue to sap public confidence in all institutions. To regain public trust, we must be squeaky clean and show that we do steward money effectively. Publish your audit, your salary philosophy, and your budget on your website. Post an e-mail address of a staff person who will answer any questions about fiscal functioning that readers have. Very few people will write, but everyone will be reassured that you must have nothing to hide.

Nonprofits, working together, must educate the public on what makes an effective organization. Simply spending money wisely is not a guarantee of effective programs, and mismanagement of funds does not always mean the organization didn't do a good job at all. Talk about your work in every media outlet you can, and be sure to mention how much more your work would cost without volunteers. Help people understand the legitimate costs of administration. Work with other nonprofits to sponsor donor briefings and public forums on the topic of nonprofits, honesty, and effectiveness.

Work for Fair and Just Tax Policies

I have mentioned the need for enlightened taxes and tax policy throughout this book, but this is certainly a seventh area we must all work on. Congress, City Hall, and the White House must experience nonprofits as a strong and powerful lobby for the common good, and we must help them understand our power as an economic driver. The total income and expenses of the nonprofit sector in the past few years has been more than $1 trillion! In any economy, a sector that employs 7 to 10 percent of workers would be valuable, but with high unemployment, the nonprofit sector is even more valuable. We are also a skills-building and training ground for volunteers, who often learn skills in nonprofits that they then transfer to paid jobs; accounting, fundraising, financial forecasting, program planning, evaluation, design and layout, database management, and facilitation are just a handful of the skills that volunteers pick up from each other and from staff in the 1.5 million nonprofits in the United States today.

Invite People to Make a Difference

Finally, we must remember that the world over, most people give away money, and many of those same people volunteer their time and expertise. The forms that giving and volunteering take vary a great deal from community to community and country to country. But humans, by and large, want to be engaged and want to make a difference. This basic enthusiasm for life can carry people through extraordinary hardship.

In closing, here is a story that is not about fundraising, but those of us who love what fundraising helps us to do in the world will understand why I am ending with this vignette.

Meg Wheatley, in her book, *Turning to One Another*, talks about visiting Robben Island, the South African prison where Nelson Mandela and many others were imprisoned for more than twenty-five years during their struggle to end apartheid. She writes, "We were standing in a long narrow room that had been used as a prison cell for dozens of freedom fighters. They lived in close quarters in this barren room—no cots or furniture, just cement walls and floors, with narrow windows near the ceiling. We stood there listening to our guide's narration. He had been a prisoner in this very room.... He described the constant threat and capricious brutality they had suffered. Then quietly he said, 'Sometimes, to pass the time here, we taught each other ballroom dancing.'"

Resources

The following list of materials and information is not exhaustive. Every day new resources are being developed, published, made available online, and so on. This list contains the books, magazines, and websites I have found most helpful or important for effective fundraising, as well as books and materials I have developed.

One of the most valuable ways to find out more about fundraising is to visit the Foundation Center Collection nearest you. The Foundation Center (headquartered in New York City, with satellite centers throughout the country) is a nonprofit library service supported by foundations, fees for service, products for sale, and other fundraising strategies. The Foundation Center collects and disseminates information about foundations, corporations, government, and all other types of fundraising and grantseeking. A list of Foundation Centers and their cooperating collections (that is, public libraries or other locations that have materials from the Foundation Center) appears at the end of this bibliography. You can also find them online at http://foundationcenter.org.

Other Titles by Kim Klein

Getting Major Gifts (rev. ed.). Oakland, Calif.: *Grassroots Fundraising Journal,* 1999.

Collection of twelve articles on developing major gifts, reprinted from the *Grassroots Fundraising Journal.*

Fundraising for the Long Haul. San Francisco: Jossey-Bass, 2000.

For older social change organizations exploring their particular challenges. Case studies, personal experience, and how-to information.

Ask and You Shall Receive: A Fundraising Training Program for Religious Organizations and Projects. San Francisco: Jossey-Bass, 2000.

Easy-to-learn core competencies of fundraising presented in Leader and Participant Manuals.

Fundraising in Times of Crisis. San Francisco: Jossey-Bass, 2004.

How to identify, analyze, and solve problems in your organization and how to plan for both the short term and the long term and evaluate success.

Fundraising for Social Change. (5th ed.) San Francisco: Jossey-Bass, 2007.

The definitive book on how to raise funds from the individuals and communities you serve.

The following titles are coauthored with Stephanie Roth:

The Board of Directors. (3rd ed.) Oakland, Calif.: *Grassroots Fundraising Journal,* 1999.

A collection of ten articles, on creating and building an effective board of directors, reprinted from the *Grassroots Fundraising Journal.*

Como Recaudar Fondos en su Communidad. Oakland, Calif.: *Grassroots Fundraising Journal,* 2002.

Una introducción acerca de las estrategias de recaudación de fondos más comunes y exitosas, en 14 de los mejores artículos del *Grassroots Fundraising Journal.*

Raise More Money: The Best of the Grassroots Fundraising Journal. Oakland, Calif.: GFJ Publications, 2001.

Other useful materials include the following.

Video

"Ready, Set, Rai$e" (with Russell Roybal). Oakland, Calif.: Grassroots Institute for Fundraising Training (GIFT). (Available at www.grassrootsfundraising.org.)

A "crash course" in how to build a broad base of donors and achieve financial stability.

Periodicals

Grassroots Fundraising Journal, Oakland, Calif. http://www.grassrootsfundraising.org.

Bimonthly how-to periodical. The website contains more than a dozen free articles and an archive of the *Journal* and *Grassroots Fundraising* e-newsletter column "Dear Kim."

Chronicle of Philanthropy. http://philanthropy.com.

Biweekly publication.

The NonProfit Times. http://www.nptimes.com.

National business publication focusing on nonprofit management. Free subscriptions to full-time nonprofit executives.

Non Profit Quarterly. http://www.nonprofitquarterly.org.
Nonprofit management and practice information.

Books

Roth, S., and Ho, M. *The Accidental Fundraiser.* San Francisco: Jossey-Bass, 2005.
A detailed, easy-to-use guide to eleven fundraising strategies for people who have to raise money but do not intend to make fundraising a career (or even a habit).

Allison, M., and Kaye, J. *Strategic Planning for Nonprofit Organizations: A Practical Guide and Workbook.* (2nd ed.) New York: Wiley, 2003.
A definitive resource on how to create a strategic plan for your nonprofit organization.

Andresen, K. *Robin Hood Marketing: Stealing Corporate Savvy to Sell Just Causes.* San Francisco: Jossey Bass, 2006.
Ten rules for effective and ethical marketing.

Bollier, David. *Silent Theft: The Private Plunder of Our Common Wealth.* Routledge, N.Y.: 2002.
What the "commons" consists of and why we must concern ourselves with protecting it.

Burk, P. *Donor-Centered Fundraising.* Chicago: Cygnus Applied Research, 2003.
What does and does not influence donor retention, increase donors' desire to give more generous gifts, and influence the pace at which donors maximize their generosity.

Burnett, K. *Relationship Fundraising.* (2nd ed.) San Francisco: Jossey-Bass, 1992.
The techniques of effective communication with donors.

Carlson, M., and Clarke, C. *Team-Based Fundraising Step by Step: A Practical Guide to Improving Results Through Teamwork.* San Francisco: Jossey-Bass, 2000.
How to create—and use—a fundraising team that involves board members, executive staff, line staff, and volunteers.

Chait, R., Ryan, W., and Taylor, B. *Governance as Leadership: Reframing the Work of Nonprofit Boards.* New York: Wiley, 2004.
How to reframe and strengthen the structure of nonprofit board governance.

Colvin, G. *Fiscal Sponsorship: 6 Ways to Do It Right.* (2nd ed.) San Francisco: Study Center Press, 2005.

Models of fiscal sponsorship that pass IRS muster and the expectations and responsibilities of funder, fiscal sponsor, and project.

Drucker, P. *Managing the Non-Profit Organization: Principles and Practices.* New York: HarperCollins, 1990.

The tasks, responsibilities, and practices necessary to manage nonprofit organizations.

Flanagan, J. *Successful Fundraising: A Complete Handbook for Volunteers and Professionals.* (2nd ed.) New York: McGraw-Hill, 2002.

How to do large-scale fundraising events and campaigns.

Gary, T., and Adess, N. *Inspired Philanthropy: Your Step-by-Step Guide to Creating a Giving Plan and Leaving a Legacy.* (3rd. ed.) San Francisco: Jossey-Bass, 2008.

A step-by-step guide on how to match your giving with your values.

Giving USA Foundation. *Giving USA: Annual Report on Philanthropy.* http://www.givinginstitute.org/gusa/gusa_foundation.cfm.

Annual analysis of giving and trends in philanthropy from the Giving Institute, formerly American Association of Fund Raising Counsel.

Grace, K. S. *Beyond Fund Raising: New Strategies for Nonprofit Innovation and Investment.* (2nd ed.) New York: Wiley, 2005.

Strategies for developing long-term relationships with "donor-investors" and volunteers.

Graetz, M. J., and Shapiro, I. *Death by a Thousand Cuts: The Fight Over Taxing Inherited Wealth.* Princeton, N.J.: Princeton University Press, 2005.

Discusses why taxes must play a part in public policy and what a fair tax system would look like.

Hitchcock, S. *Open Immediately! Straight Talk on Direct Mail Fundraising: What Works, What Doesn't, and Why.* Medfield, Mass.: Emerson & Church, 2004.

The basics about raising money by mail.

Hogan, C. *Prospect Research: A Primer for Growing Nonprofits.* Sudbury, Mass.: Jones and Bartlett, 2004.

The terminology, tools, and procedures for prospect research of individuals, corporations, foundations, and government agencies.

Hopkins, B. *650 Essential Nonprofit Law Questions Answered.* New York: Wiley, 2005.

Authoritative answers to important questions on business, tax, legal, and fundraising practices.

Hopkins, K., and Friedman, C. *Successful Fundraising for Arts and Cultural Organizations.* (2nd ed.) Phoenix: Oryx Press, 1996.

Fundraising strategies for arts and cultural organizations of all sizes.

Kunreuther, F., Kim, H., and Rodriguez, R. *Working Across Generations: Defining the Future of Nonprofit Leadership.* San Francisco: Jossey-Bass, 2009. How to approach generational shifts in leadership.

Lakey, G., and others (eds.). *Grassroots and Nonprofit Leadership: A Guide for Organizations in Changing Times.* Philadelphia: New Society Publishers, 1995.
The nature of power and leadership, stages of social movements, and the social environment in which change organizations exist.

Minieri, J., and Getsos, P. *Tools for Radical Democracy: How to Organize for Power in Your Community.* San Francisco: Jossey-Bass, 2008.
How to build a community-led organization, train community leaders, and conduct campaigns that change public policy.

Nickerson, M. *Life, Money and Illusion: Living on Earth as if We Want to Stay.* Lanark, Ontario: Seven Generations Publishing, 2006.
What activists can do to influence the global economic system.

Quattman, V. *You Can Do It! A Volunteer's Guide to Raising Money for Your Group in Words and Pictures.* Maryville, Tenn.: Southern Empowerment Project, 2002.
Down-to-earth, picture-driven guide to the basics of fundraising. Available in both English and Spanish from Appalachian Community Fund (http://www.appalachiancommunityfund.org/html/pubs.html).

Robinson, A. *Selling Social Change (Without Selling Out): Earned Income Strategies for Nonprofits.* San Francisco: Jossey-Bass, 2002.
How to initiate and sustain successful earned-income ventures that provide financial security and advance an organization's mission.

Robinson, A. *Grassroots Grants: An Activist's Guide to Grantseeking.* (2nd ed.) San Francisco: Jossey-Bass, 2004.
Hands-on guide to researching and writing grant proposals.

Robinson, E. *The Nonprofit Membership Toolkit.* San Francisco: Jossey-Bass, 2003.
Step-by-step guide to building a membership organization.

Sargeant, A., and Jay, E. *Building Donor Loyalty: The Fundraiser's Guide to Increasing Lifetime Value.* San Francisco: Jossey-Bass, 2004.
The factors that drive donor retention, how to keep donors committed to an organization, and suggestions for developing donor value over time.

Sen, R. *Stir It Up: Lessons in Community Organizing and Advocacy.* San Francisco: Jossey-Bass, 2003.

The steps of building and mobilizing a constituency and implementing key strategies for social change.

Stallings, B., and McMillion, D. *How to Produce Fabulous Fundraising Events: Reap Remarkable Returns with Minimal Effort.* Pleasanton, Calif.: Building Better Skills, 1996.
Step-by-step guide to a successful fundraising dinner.

Stanionis, M. *Mercifully Brief Real World Guide to Raising Thousands (If Not Tens of Thousands) of Dollars with Email.* Medfield, Mass.: Emerson & Church, 2006.
How to raise funds through e-mail.

Tempel, E. (ed.). *Hank Rosso's Achieving Excellence in Fundraising.* (2nd ed.) San Francisco: Jossey-Bass, 2003.
The late Henry Rosso was one of the most famous fundraising consultants in America. This introduction to the theory and practice of fundraising is an invaluable tool.

Warwick, M. *Revolution in the Mailbox: Your Guide to Successful Direct Mail Fundraising.* San Francisco: Jossey-Bass, 2004.
Step-by-step guide to writing a successful direct mail appeal.

Warwick, M. *The Mercifully Brief, Real-World Guide to Raising $1,000 Gifts by Mail.* Medfield, Mass.: Emerson and Church, 2005.
Step-by-step advice on how to raise major gifts using the mail.

Warwick, M. *Fundraising When Money Is Tight: A Strategic and Practical Guide to Surviving Tough Times and Thriving in the Future.* San Francisco: Jossey-Bass, 2009.
How the economy affects fundraising; practical steps you can take to survive and go on to thrive.

Wendroff, A. *Special Events: Proven Strategies for Nonprofit Fundraising.* (2nd ed.) New York: Wiley, 2003.
A guide to producing large special events.

Wheatley, M. J. *Leadership and the New Science: Learning about Organization from an Orderly Universe.* San Francisco: Berrett-Koehler, 1999.
Using breakthroughs in biology, chemistry, and especially quantum physics, Wheatley paints a new picture of business management.

Wheatley, M. J. *Turning to One Another: Simple Conversations to Restore Hope to the Future.* San Francisco: Berrett-Koehler, 2002.
Explores the art of having conversations and why that is so important. Although not specifically about fundraising, this book is very helpful to anyone wanting to build relationships with donors.

Zimmerman, R., and Lehman, A. *Boards That Love Fundraising: A How-To Guide for Your Board.* San Francisco: Jossey-Bass, 2003.

Shows how *all* board members can learn to raise funds and provides tips for the more experienced fundraisers.

Websites

The following websites are not specifically about fundraising or philanthropy, but they can help with the many other questions common to nonprofit organizations.

Association of Fundraising Professionals. www.afpnet.org.

A trade association working to advance philanthropy and fundraising through advocacy, research, and education.

Accountants for the Public Interest (API). http://www.geocities.com/ api_woods/api/apihome.html.

Questions and answers as well as materials on accounting for nonprofits.

Alliance for Nonprofit Management. http://www.allianceonline.org/.

Professional association of individuals and organizations devoted to improving the management and governance capacity of nonprofits—to assist nonprofits in fulfilling their mission.

BoardSource. www.boardsource.org.

A major resource for practical information, tools and best practices, training, and leadership development for board members of nonprofit organizations.

Building Movement Project. www.buildingmovement.org.

Helpful information on the nonprofit sector as a whole, particularly new laws and regulations and analysis for organizations working for social justice.

CompassPoint. www.compasspoint.org.

Training, consulting, and research on nonprofit management, concepts, and strategies. Also the site for nonprofit genie (http://www .compasspoint.org/askgenie/index.php), which provides answers to frequently asked management questions.

The Non-Profit FAQ from Idealist.org. http://www.idealist.org/if/idealist/ en/FAQ/Nonprofit/Home/default.

Information, advice, and articles on numerous nonprofit management topics, including information on how to calculate program costs or fundraising ratios and how to value donated goods.

Technical Assistance for Community Organizations (TACS). www.tacs.org.

Good place to shop for accounting software.

United for a Fair Economy. www.ufenet.org.

Works toward closing the gap between rich and poor with clear information about economics, taxes, and the relationship of the distribution of money to the quality of life of most Americans. The website and newsletter are accessible and useful.

Mal Warwick and Associates. www.malwarwick.com.

A wealth of information about fundraising using direct mail.

TechSoup. www.techsoup.org.

Great site for finding the latest information and great discounts on fundraising software.

Groundspring. www.groundspring.org.

Will handle giving for organizations; also has an excellent downloadable manual on online fundraising.

Acknowledgments

As always with a book like this, the number of people I would have to name, if I were to name all who have been helpful, would be as long as the book itself. There are all the thousands of people who have shared their experiences with me over the years, and the organizations that have allowed me into their innermost secrets so that I could offer them "advice" that they were probably smart enough to have thought of on their own, and my many colleagues with whom I could compare notes.

A few people really helped make this book into what it is. Leah Dolgoy, the development director at Head and Hands in Montreal, Quebec, read every chapter and gave me very valuable feedback. She did this on her own time and for fun!

The staff and team members of the Building Movement Project—Frances Kunreuther, Caroline McAndrews, Trish Tchume, Robby Rodriquez, Linda Campbell, and Helen Kim—have been instrumental in helping make the link between nonprofits, the common good, and the role of tax policy in all of that. They have also given me a place to test ideas about the relationship of fundraising to these larger issues.

Manish Vaidya, program and development coordinator at the Grassroots Institute for Fundraising Training, helped me understand the use of Facebook, Twitter, blogs, and the rest of Web 2.0 for fundraising, and I appreciate his knowledge and his patience.

Allison Brunner, Kristi Hein, Mark Karmendy, and the rest of the gang at Jossey-Bass deserve a special thanks for moving this book so quickly into production and publication. All were unfailingly cheerful and positive, as well as thorough and excellent in their jobs.

The book would not exist at all if it were not for Nancy Adess, my editor (and best friend) for thirty years. She set aside other work to edit this book, which she did thoroughly and at warp speed. My writing doesn't exist without her help.

And of course, my partner, Stephanie Roth, who held down our business while I wrote and provided insight and help with difficult concepts and chapters, and our animals—Brooklyn, Gracie, Ruby, and Jack Daniels (two dogs and two cats)—who both force and allow me to stop working, and who keep reminding me about the purpose of good time management: to be happy.

Thanks to all of you!

About the Author

Kim Klein is internationally known as a fundraising trainer and consultant. She is a member of the Building Movement Project and is the Chardon Press Series Editor at Jossey-Bass Publishers, which publishes and distributes materials that help to build a stronger nonprofit sector. She founded the bimonthly *Grassroots Fundraising Journal* and is the author of *Fundraising for Social Change* (now in its fifth edition, 2007), and a number of other books. She is the featured writer for the e-newsletter of the *Grassroots Fundraising Journal,* with her "Dear Kim" column of answers to questions posed by readers.

In addition to writing for her own publications, she has contributed many articles to the leading books, periodicals, and websites in the field of fundraising. Widely in demand as a speaker, Kim has provided training and consultation in all fifty of the United States and in twenty-one countries.

Her work with the Building Movement Project is focused on the role nonprofits need to play in creating fair and just tax policies, and why and how nonprofits can work to protect "the commons"—that which we own in common (parks, libraries, the Internet) and that which cannot be owned (clean air, wilderness, fresh water) but must be preserved and passed down to future generations. Kim believes that the nonprofit sector has a critical role to play in the creation and maintenance of a democratic society.

INDEX